Published by
The Junior League of Shreveport-Bossier, Inc.
520 Olive Street
Shreveport, Louisiana 71104

The purpose of the Junior League is exclusively educational and charitable and is:

To promote voluntarism;

To develop the potential of its members for voluntary participation in community affairs;

And to demonstrate the effectiveness of trained volunteers.

The Junior League of Shreveport-Bossier Inc.
Shreveport, Louisiana

First Printing	March 1980	21,530 copies
Second Printing	May 1980	20,000 copies
Third Printing		10,000 copies
Fourth Printing	July 2000	10,000 copies

If you wish to order additional copies of ***Revel***, use the order blanks provided in the back of the book or write to:

Junior League of Shreveport-Bossier Publications
520 Olive Street
Shreveport, Louisiana 71104

Make checks payable to Junior League of Shreveport-Bossier, Inc.

Library of Congress Catalog Card Number: 79-89035

International Standard Book Number: 0-9602246-1-0

Printed in the United States of America

670 South Cooper Street
Memphis, Tennessee 38104

Revel
Revel
Revel
Revel
Revel

TABLE OF

CONTENTS

Recipe Revel

INTRODUCTION

In October, 1976, the Junior League of Shreveport, Inc., presented to the citizens of the Ark-La-Tex area the Red River Revel, a seven-day celebration of the arts. This bicentennial gift to the city, free to the thousands who attended, covered every conceivable form of the arts that could be displayed, heard or taught. The festival was held in the civic buildings and grounds on the banks of the Red River.

So great was the success of the first Red River Revel that it has become an annual event, an integral part of autumn in Shreveport, with ballooning community, state and national participation.

During our three years' work on this cookbook, we have been constantly inspired by the Red River Revel as it became a self-perpetuating celebration. Therefore, we honor the festival *and* the art of good cooking with this book's title:

Revel

Celebrate the Celebration!

The first four sections of **Revel** are a collection of parties, menus and traditions presented in vivid color and superb graphics covering Spring, Summer, Autumn and Winter. The fifth section, Recipe Revel, contains 600 selections from the more than 5,000 submitted and tested at least three times.

The index is a work of art in itself and allows the reader to locate every recipe, party or menu with the greatest of ease.

From the beginning this book was a feeling—the feeling that lingers after a successful party with good friends or a holiday gathering that brings the family together. Our challenge has been to bring to fruition that feeling between two covers, remembering that the joy of planning and preparation is as considerable as the event itself.

From ideas that seemed to grow and multiply, we are presenting one year's broad range of festivities. We hope each will inspire rather than dictate a celebration.

Come **Revel** with us!

COOKBOOK DEVELOPMENT COMMITTEE

Editor	Vicki Hanna
Business Manager	Suzy Ball
Recipe Chairman	Margaret Crow
Assistants	Sissy Harper
	Marie Rosenfield
Testing Chairman	Judith Quinn
Assistants	Susan Hall
	Michele Petersen
Testers	Betty Cannon
	Kathi Hamel
	Pat Harlow
	Kaye Kleine
	Martha McLean
	Nancy Nix
	Melissa Simon
Creative Ideas Chairman	Mary Tullie Critcher
Assistant	Ann Olene Querbes
Traditions Chairman	Ellen Kirkland
Assistant	Rebecca Roberts
Art Editor	Wesley Richardson
Creative Writing Editor	Margaret Crow
Assistant	Carolyn Flournoy
Promotions Chairman	Edie Williams
Assistant	Bonnie Gleason
Typists	Susan Blaylock
	Sandra Boyd
	Nancy Ketner
	Holly Pippen
Proofreaders	Mary Tullie Critcher
	Margaret Evans
	Susan Evans
	Susan Hall
	Carolyn Hamilton
	Sissy Harper
	Ginny Hill
	Ellen Kirkland
	Michele Petersen
	Ann Olene Querbes
	Judith Quinn
	Marie Rosenfield
	Suzanne Wray
Index	Suzy Ball
Concept: Cover and Artwork	Wesley Richardson
Graphic Design: Cover and Artwork	Mitch Mitton
	Neil Johnson
Title Designation	Catherine Evans
Sustainer Advisors	Carolyn Flournoy
	Marilee Harter
	Leone Reeder

To the reader:

The goal of the Cookbook Committee was to publish a thoroughly *professional* book: professional in appearance with first-rate artwork, graphics and color; professional as to content with over 600 *best* recipes, including dishes created by chefs for their cooking demonstrations at the arts festival; professional in editing with proper spelling and style consistent throughout; professional in indexing with every recipe, party and menu double or triple indexed.

Our goal has been reached after endless hours of work by members of the Junior League of Shreveport, Inc., their families and many friends in the community. Through this labor of love and patience, **Revel** is a reality.

The following are examples of consistency in the book's style:

All oven temperatures mean preheated unless otherwise indicated.
All recipe ingredients are listed in the order of use.
The word "divided" following an ingredient shows it will be used more than once in the recipe.
A rib is one piece of a stalk of celery.
A clove is one piece of a pod of garlic.
Brand names of ingredients have been used only when necessary.
Instructions for preparation of recipe are as explicit as possible.

The composition of **Revel** allows you to choose a season, a party, a menu, a particular dish or a tradition. The tradition even provides you with dinner party conversation!

We have set the pace for your festivities. Now let's set the table and begin cooking.

Revel — Celebrate the Celebration!

Cookbook Committee

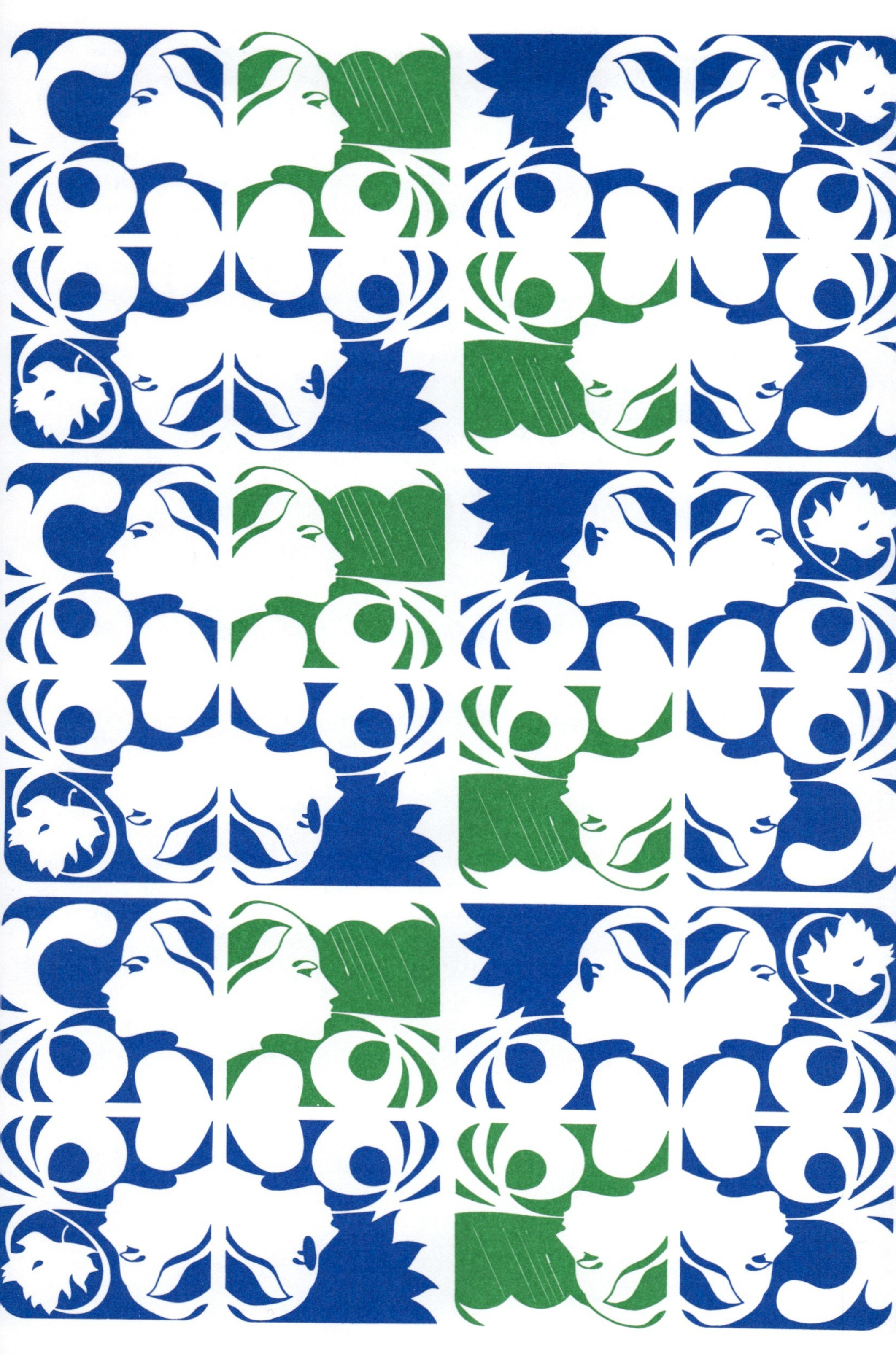

Spring Revel

EASTER EGG HUNT

Baskets are beribboned, and the pastel attire of the little guests matches the rainbow-hued eggs that are hidden on the lawn. A golden egg is somewhere out there with a special treasure for the lucky child with the sharpest eyes. Peter Rabbit has certainly been busy! These mid-afternoon treats are designed to please both the children and their parents.

MENU

Pink Lemonade **Cherry-Orange Fizz p. 44**

Cheese Straws **Liz's Shrimp Mold p. 78**

Super Shrimp Dip p. 55 **Pineapple Cheese Ball p. 61**

World's Greatest Fudge p. 381

or

Microwave Fudge p. 380

Popcorn Snack p. 384 **Pecan Divinity p. 383**

Chocolate Cheesecake p. 312

The ancestor of the Easter bunny, the Oriental hare, is associated with the new moon, which in turn determines the date of Easter. Eggs, symbolic of new life, have been colored and exchanged since ancient times in China. Egyptian and Hindu mythology credit the egg as the source of creation. In Europe and on the White House lawn, eggs are rolled down grassy slopes; but the sport in Greece is to roll them against each other until the strongest egg alone remains unbroken.

GREEK EASTER

In Greece, Easter is the most important religious holiday, observed with an outdoor midnight church service during which the priest holds three lighted candles and announces to the congregation, **"Christos Anesti"**—Christ is Risen!

Sunday is the feast day when families gather to enjoy lamb roasted in pits by the men of the village and traditional breads baked by the women. These classic Greek dishes feature food indigenous to Hellenic cuisine. Lemon, lamb, eggplant, Aegean olives, olive oil and herbs make this menu memorable any time of the year.

MENU

Salata **p. 118**

Dolmades with Avgolemono Sauce **p. 148**

Roast Lamb Athenian Style **p. 168**

or

Moussaka **p. 154**

Spanakopita **p. 300**

Holiday Cake **p. 318**

Koulouria **p. 346**

CHAMPAGNE BREAKFAST

The crowning touch for an elegant evening

After the curtain has fallen, after the orchestra has played its final note, after golden slippers have waltzed the last step...a buffet to enhance a night too beautiful to end. Champagne and delicacies sparkle in a candlelit setting, and guests departing at the break of dawn feel touched by enchantment.

MENU

Crabmeat Canapés p. 72

Chicken-Wild Rice Casserole p. 184 **Cheese-Oyster Bake** p. 226

Avocado Salad with Herb Dressing p. 107

Carrot Soufflé p. 289 **Sourdough Rolls** p. 260

Butter Nut Cookies p. 344 **Lemon Mousse** p. 370

Champagne

Champagne is the queen of all wines, named for a region in northeast France. For it, the world owes its thanks to a blind monk, Dom Pérignon, cellarmaster of the Benedictine Abbey at Hautvillers. It was he who, in the late seventeenth century, first fastened corks tightly in wine bottles, thus keeping the bubbles in "the bubbly." It is the carbon dioxide released by natural fermentation and aided by the addition of a "dose" of sugar that causes the wine to sparkle. When Dom Pérignon first tasted his new sparkling wine, he cried to his brother monks, "I am tasting stars!" Ironically, one of the three varieties of grapes used for true French champagne is the purple Pinot noir, whose skins are removed immediately after pressing to preserve the delicate golden color of the wine.

MOTHER-DAUGHTER TEA

Grandmother's legacy...teacups and silver services grace damask covered tables...a 4 o'clock formal tea for mothers and daughters to honor a special visitor, a new daughter-in-law, or simply a dear friend...platters of dainty food tempt "one-bite-at-a-time" appetites without interrupting feminine conversation...friends of the hostess take turns pouring tea...the ambience of Emily Post and white-glove parties, a rarity these days, prevails.

This traditional fête is a lovely answer to the generation gap.

MENU

Tea **Punch**

Crabmeat Patties **p. 208**

Cucumber Sandwiches **p. 241**

Toasted Asparagus Sandwiches **p. 241**

Apricot Bread-Sandwiches **p. 272**

or

Strawberry Bread-Sandwiches **p. 271**

Meringue Champignons **p. 381** **Coconut Bars** **p. 350**

Almond Wafers **p. 342**

Roasted Pecans **p. 71**

KENTUCKY DERBY PARTY

WIN: May 6
PLACE: 425 Elm Street
SHOW: 2:00 p.m.
ALSO RUNNING: Mary and Bob Jones

Really, your lawn should be Kentucky bluegrass and strains of "My Old Kentucky Home" should be in the background, but as long as there are plenty of racing fans and a large silver bowl of mint juleps, the afternoon will be a success.

Racing and riding paraphernalia are natural decorations and can be as elaborate as live horses, bales of hay and racing silks, or as simple as hobby-horses and horseshoes. Either way, during the Run for the Roses, American Beauties must be the flowers of the day.

The main activity is the 9th on the program of ten races held the first Saturday in May at Churchill Downs, Louisville, Kentucky. It can be enjoyed at your "downs" with televisions, a Calcutta, and perhaps a program of filmed races.

A continuous buffet of Kentucky's finest food is the winning ticket for your guests.

Continued...

MENU

Mint Juleps p. 47

Kentucky Pâté p. 70 Starting-Gate Shrimp p. 77

Bacon-Wrapped Water Chestnuts p. 81 Dill Dip p. 54

Southern Home-Fried Chicken p. 180

Baked Ham with Raisin Sauce p. 249

Homemade Mayonnaise p. 126 Sweet-Hot Mustard p. 257

Potato Salad p. 116

Eggplant Casserole p. 292 or Green Vegetable Casserole p. 306

Buttermilk Biscuits p. 262

Carrot Cake in Muffin Tins p. 312

Sugary Pralines p. 383 or Creamy Pralines p. 382

Irwin S. Cobb—"The first Kentucky Julep an alien drinks is a sensation, the second is a rhythmic benefaction, but the third is a grievous error."

40-LOVE LUNCHEON

A tennis-birthday party for a friend who is getting better, not older, at that magic age

After a morning on the courts proving that she is still as spry as she was yesterday at 39, (though we won't insist that she vault over the net!) the guest of honor and friends reassemble for a luscious luncheon alfresco. Tennis balls form the yellow centers of bold wooden daisies that sit atop the dining table, as fresh as a spring day at Forest Hills. With the queen of the courts at the head of the table, it's *your* serve with a menu that is at once festive, rejuvenating and easy on you, as all the work was done be-"forehand."

MENU

Wimbledon Strawberry Daiquiris p. 48

Senegalese Soup p. 93 or **Cool-as-a-Cucumber Soup** p. 82

Molded Chicken Mousse p. 101

Bacon-Cheese Fingers p. 58

Forty-Karat Gold Brick Pie p. 328

French Mint Iced Tea p. 44

To mix tennis players of all abilities, a bridge tally offers a formula.

BON VOYAGE PARTY

At this party, home-bound friends of the travelers share their anticipation of a trip to distant corners of the earth. Appropriately a progressive dinner, guests are routed to three homes for various courses of the meal, each a mélange of exotic food. Invitations and decorations are inspired by foreign ports of call. To brighten his spirit, each envious guest is asked to bring a gift which the travelers would least need on their journey. These will be opened at the third home, and might include a kitten, an American dictionary or an orchid corsage.

MENU

First home:

Wine Punch p. 50 Cocktails

Pirozhki p. 64

Stuffed Jalapeños p. 63 Mushrooms en Croustades p. 67

Second home:

White Wine

Veal Patrician p. 158

or

Chicken Crêpes p. 185

Chinese Asparagus p. 283

Whole Wheat Rolls p. 261

Third home:

Frozen Cappucino p. 371

Keflies p. 346 or Thirty-Dollar Cake p. 322

Coffee and Liqueurs

Summer Revel

FATHER'S DAY FEAST

Hail to Father, winner of bread and bringer of bacon, player of golf, watcher of baseball and eater of steak. A backyard lounge chair is thy throne, and thine only duty of the day is to appoint the hour of the feast and call forth the feasters. Thy glass shall be full, and thy newspaper unspoiled. If mowing the lawn be thy pleasure, do as thou wouldst, but woe unto the queen or knave who bids thee work. As feast time approaches, the grill will be lighted for thee, and a kingly repast spread for thine enjoyment.

MENU

Shrimp and Artichoke Appetizer p. 78

Chilled Avocado Soup p. 82

Fillets with Steak Sauce p. 248 or Marinated Shish Kabobs p. 127

Macaroni Salad p. 114

Boston Lettuce with Bacon p. 109

Miss Olivia's Bread p. 259

Fresh Dewberry Pie p. 338 Hollywood Black-Bottom Pie p. 330

This masculine meal is appropriate for either lunch or supper, as befits the schedule of dear old Dad. Each guest is responsible for cooking his own steak or kabob and serving his plate from the outdoor buffet.

BRIDESMAIDS' LUNCHEON

Something old: Inherited finery to set the most feminine of tables—lace and linens, cut crystal, silver and bone china

Something new: At each attendant's place, a gift from the bride, tied with a satin ribbon and adorned with tiny rosebuds and baby's breath to match the centerpiece

Something borrowed: The recipes from close friends happy to share their gourmet knowledge with the bride-to-be

Something blue: The azure ribbons that circle the flower arrangement and gifts, and the sky blue linen under the lace tablecloth

And...a lucky sixpence for her shoe

MENU

MIDSUMMER'S EVE

'Tis an evening that dreams are made of, when the enchanted presence of fairies and wood sprites is felt in the late darkness of the summer solstice. Guests dance in the twilight aglow with candles, torches and white twinkle lights in the trees. Garden blooms are complemented by cut flowers on each dining table, and pot plants at the base of every torch.

MENU

Strawberry Ice p. 47

Steak Tartare p. 79

Celestial Chicken Wings p. 62

Quiche Oberon p. 263

Ethereal Mushrooms p. 68

Crudités with Titania Dressing p. 124

Marinated Beef Tenderloin p. 127

Homemade Mayonnaise p. 126

Sweet-Hot Mustard p. 257

Oatmeal Carmelitas p. 349

Midsummer's eve, the summer solstice, the longest day of the year, coincides with the feast day of St. John the Baptist. It is celebrated in most northern European countries with lighting of bonfires. This was the night, in ancient belief, when fairies roamed the earth in search of mortal brides; hence, cautious fathers locked up their maiden daughters.

FIRECRACKER FESTIVAL

Celebrate that which makes the United States unique: no other nation can claim a day that *feels* quite like the Fourth of July.

Celebrate the way it once was: mile-long picnic tables covered with a true bounty of food...expanses of grass crisscrossed with the paths of barefooted children...rocking chairs placed on the porch for grandparents...lawn chairs arranged under shade trees for neighbors...late darkness scented with citronella, lighted by fireflies and orchestrated by crickets.

Finally the fireworks light the night sky, showing children's faces, as each burst explosively affirms our liberty!

MENU

Beer **Wine Cooler p. 51**

Pine Creek Cheese Spread p. 61

Artichoke and Shrimp Dip p. 52

Boiled Shrimp or Crayfish p. 216

Quick Rēmoulade p. 246 **Shrimp Sauce p. 247**

Easley's Slaw p. 120

Tiny New Potatoes, Tiny Onions and Corn on the Cob p. 216

French Bread

Homemade Vanilla Ice Cream p. 375

Toll House Pan Cookies p. 349

Pecan Crispies p. 345

BASTILLE DAY

Allons enfants de la patrie.
Le jour de gloire est arrivé!

The day of glory has arrived—an occasion to savor the finest French gifts to tables around the world: wines, cheeses and superb *haute cuisine*. It was July 14, 1789, when the reign of Louis XVI and Marie Antoinette was ended violently with the storming of the Bastille by revolutionaries. In modern Paris the 14th is a day of street parades and Gallic revelry, but *chez nous* it is an occasion for a glamorous dinner party combining the best of French *joie de vivre* and elegance.

MENU

Mushroom Petals **p. 69**

Crabmeat Rockefeller **p. 73**

Fruits en Saison with Poppy Seed Dressing

Dilled Veal en Crème **p. 157**

Flounder Rolls with Shrimp Newburg Sauce **p. 201**

Wild Rice Amandine **p. 280**

Carrots Vichy **p. 288**

Strawberries à la Marny **p. 358**

French Silk Pie **p. 329**

French *haute cuisine* actually evolved from the recipes and methods used by the Florentine chefs who accompanied Catherine de Medici to France when she married Henry II in 1553.

POSH PICNIC

The ultimate "pique-nique" is the one that takes place in a carefully groomed yard early on a summer evening, amidst the most lush blooms of the season: peonies, geraniums and daisies.

Awaiting each couple are baskets lined with floral chintz cloths containing splits of chilled wine or champagne, glasses, china, silver and linen napkins. After apéritifs a buffet table covered with the same floral cloth offers food seldom seen at picnics.

MENU

Stuffed Mushroom Caps p. 70

Guacamole p. 108

Gazpacho p. 85 or Gazpacho Seville p. 85

Regal Roasted Cornish Hens p. 192

or

Southern Fried Quail p. 198

Quiche Oberon p. 236

Iced Lemon Soufflé with Wine Sauce p. 264

Splits of Chilled Wine or Champagne

The term "posh," meaning elegant, was coined by seasoned English travelers to and from India during the colonial period of the 19th century. Those in the know requested the cooler and more desirable shipboard accommodations: **P**ort **O**ut, **S**tarboard **H**ome.

MASON-DIXON DINNER

Undeniably North is North and South is South, but when the twain meet at table, the result is a double buffet of regional food at its finest. Such a feast is equally at home in a stone and clapboard house surrounded by maple trees or a columned plantation manor in the midst of magnolias.

SOUTHERN FARE

Southern Home-Fried Chicken p. 180

Rice and Gravy

Green Tomato Pie p. 304

Emmie Lou's Creamed Turnips p. 306

Fresh Turnip and Mustard Greens p. 305

***Cushaw p. 291**

Crusty Biscuits p. 262

Chocolate Pecan Pie p. 327

*Cushaw is any of several of colossal squashes having long curved necks, green and white skin and yellow meat. It is rich in vitamin A and usually found growing in warm climates. This squash is traditionally prepared with sugar and served as a sweet accompaniment to the main course.

Continued...

Our Mason-Dixon dinner gives cause to rejoice that the great American melting pot has not mixed the cuisines of the Blue and the Gray. Maine blueberry salad and Boston brown bread play perfect counterpoint to fresh turnip greens and cushaw.

NORTHERN FARE

Spicy New England Corned Beef p. 134

Sour Cream Horsradish Sauce p. 245

Cabbage or Celery Sauté p. 290

Sweet and Sour Beets p. 287

Blueberry Salad p. 96

Boston Brown Bread p. 261

Fresh Apple Cake with Cream Cheese Icing p. 319

Pennsylvania Apple or Pear Pie p. 337

In 1767, Jeremiah Dixon and Charles Mason solved a boundary dispute between Pennsylvania and Maryland, thus creating the line that prior to the Civil War was believed to separate the slave states from the free states.

Autumn Revel

ITALIAN BUFFET

Swing into autumn with a Roman holiday.

For a gay Italian evening, tables covered with red, green and white cloths (Italy's national colors) are centered with rafia-covered Chianti bottles holding colorful candles. Recorded music from "O Solo Mio" to "Three Coins in the Fountain" plays in the background while posters of the Leaning Tower of Pisa, Venetian gondolas and the Colosseum decorate the walls.

Your menu features pasta* and co-stars a host of regional Italian dishes. The perfect Neopolitan touch: Soave (white) and Valpolicella (red) wines flow in abundance. *Ciao*!

MENU

Eggplant Spread p. 63 **Little Pizzas** p. 71

Minestrone p. 88 **or** **Maritata (Italian Wedding Soup)** p. 86

Italian Bread Sticks

Lasagne p. 152 **or** **Cannelloni Milanese** p. 160 **or** **Tufoli** p. 150

Green Salad with Mama Mia's Salad Mix p. 111

Garlic Bread

Biscuit Tortoni p. 371 **Zuppa Inglese** p. 361

*"The death of pasta," reads an old Italian saying, "is by boiling it: it can go to hell or to paradise in the process." Literally translated this means that overcooking pasta sends it to the devil's den. *Al dente* is perfect: each piece is bitable, not raw, and heaven to eat.

TAILGATE PICNIC

The all-American *fête champêtre* travels on four wheels with simulated wood paneling and locates in a football stadium parking lot on designated autumn Saturday afternoons. On arrival, lawn chairs are unfolded and a tablecloth is spread upon the tailgate, from which this festivity derives its name.

Ceremonial libations are dispensed from a styrofoam ice chest and consumed before the ritual feast is spread. It is probable that several convivial groups have gathered nearby, and these participants frequently mingle and even share elements from their hampers.

Abruptly the company divides, packs the remnants of its repast into the vehicle, and treks to a noisy stadium just as the warriors enter the arena.

MENU

Mexican Relish Dip p. 54 **Pickled Eggs** p. 252

Horseradish Cheese Spread p. 60

Marinated Vegetables p. 80

Artichoke Soup p. 81

Sunday Sandwiches p. 244

Bread and Butter Pickles p. 255

Black-Bottom Cupcakes p. 314 **Carrot Bars** p. 350

OKTOBERFEST

A late afternoon street party for revelers of all ages

The 1810 wedding of Bavarian Crown Prince Ludwig to his bride, Therese, is still celebrated annually in Munich with the sixteen-day festival known world-wide as Oktoberfest.

In early autumn, tourists join Germans in seemingly endless consumption of Teutonic food. Wine and beer are dispensed from tents while whole oxen are roasted over open pits.

The ebullient spirit of Oktoberfest can be shared at your neighborhood street party...recorded oom-pah-pah music guarantees a true *Biergarten* atmosphere. Each guest brings his own stein for beer. Rhine wine (as famous as the beer), or cider—for *der kinder,* Sauerbraten, Choucroute, sausage and strudel highlight this hearty Munchen feast.

MENU

Beer **Wine** **Cider**

Sausage **Cheeses** **Bread** **Pretzels**

Sweet-Hot Mustard p. 257 **Dill Pickles** p. 254

Sauerbraten p. 132 or **Choucroute Frankfurt Style** p. 167

German Potato Salad p. 115 **Sauerkraut Salad** p. 117

Bavarian Potato Dumplings p. 298

Crunchy Butterscotch Morsels p. 378

Bavarian Apple Tart p. 352 or **Easy Strudel** p. 356

Black Forest Cake p. 310

HALLOWEEN

Glowing eyes of jack-o'-lanterns and sheet-ghosts hanging from tree limbs appear in the front yard as soon as darkness falls.

All the ghosties and ghoulies and long-legged beasties (and probably a princess or two) may bring their normal-looking parents to a trick-or-treat party on this spookiest night of the year.

A marvelous witch-hostess answers the door and beckons youngsters to the breakfast room where some real nourishment will be their first course of the evening.

Meanwhile the parents enjoy cocktails and hors d'oeuvres and appoint chaperones for the trip out into the haunted night.

When the trick-or-treaters leave, the witch may clean up and refresh the buffet for the adults to enjoy while the children take stock of their loot.

MENU

Fog Cutter p. 47 **Orange Julius** p. 45

Marinated Mushrooms p. 68 **Creamy Shrimp Appetizer** p. 75

Green Salad with Anchovy Dressing p. 122

Hot Herb Bread p. 265

Black Beans and Rice El Carmelo Habana p. 287

Spicy Chili p. 145 or **Chili de Señor Pico** p. 145

Brownies p. 347 **Molasses Cookies** p. 344

ELECTION NIGHT BUFFET

Now that the polls are closed and the last campaign promise is only an echo, all that remains is the official count. There is no substitute for a houseful of politically compatible friends who can ultimately provide mutual congratulations or shoulders to cry on.

The hostess creates the proper atmosphere with patriotic flags and buntings, donkeys, elephants and election posters. Ample televisions offer all the networks' predictions, while a few calculators are great for those who like to figure for themselves. A collection of sage cartoons lends a little perspective and comic relief to an otherwise tense evening. This buffet is one that will be equally tempting for early arrivals, latecomers and nervous all-night nibblers.

MENU

Cocktails

Spicy Shrimp p. 76 **Somburo Special** p. 56

Cheese Ball p. 59 **Curry Dip** p. 54

Chicken Tortillas p. 177

or

Game Hens with Hot Tamale Stuffing p. 192

Zucchini Frittata p. 308

Asparagus Salad p. 105 **or** **Avocado Salad** p. 106

Viennese Bread p. 266

Coconut Sour Cream Cake p. 323 **Lemon Sponge** p. 355

Pots and pots of hot black coffee

TRADITIONAL THANKSGIVING DINNER

In this day of scattered families and jet-speed travel, very few horses still pull the sleigh "over the river and through the woods." Still, Grandmother's house is the most popular meeting place for Thanksgiving, when Americans' kith and kin make their greatest effort to reunite.

It is the day when Norman Rockwell paintings come to life, the day that not only sustains traditions but also creates them for the future. Family members of all ages gather at a table set with Grandmother's finest appointments, many of them probably her own grandmother's. No heirloom is too fragile to be used and enjoyed on this one day, even in the presence of the tiniest offspring.

The menu is flexible, as each family has a traditional dish with which they keep Thanksgiving.

MENU

Relish Tray **Oyster Bisque** p. 92

Baked Turkey with Giblet Gravy

Rice Dressing p. 275 or **Cornbread Dressing** p. 274

Baked Broccoli and Onions p. 284

Pennsylvania Dutch Green Beans p. 285

Scalloped Potatoes p. 297 **Baked Apricots** p. 309

Frozen Pumpkin Pie p. 336 or **Sweet Potato-Pecan Pie** p. 337

Rum Pudding with Raspberry Sauce p. 365

Cranberry Ice p. 376

A combination of the harvest festivals celebrated by both the Indians and the English produced the first Thanksgiving in 1621.

HUNT DINNER

When the hunter has provided wild ducks, the fruit after a mystical predawn communion with nature, an evening of elegant dining is in order. Set the scene for your black-tie dinner with hand-written invitations.

Honor the hunter by setting the table in a formal but masculine vein—gilded duck decoys and dried autumn flowers are flanked by candelabras with russet tapers. If possible, have the seven-course feast served professionally and accompany it with the finest wines; placecards and menus are *de rigueur*. Tonight's gourmet cuisine flatters the chosen guests and encourages the hunter to return to the wilds.

MENU

Crabmeat Mold p. 73

Escargots p. 62

Fresh Mushroom Soup p. 87

Garden Broccoli Salad p. 109

Shrimp Sauté p. 220 or **Scallops à la Meunière** p. 207

Grapefruit Sorbet p. 376

Fillets of Duck p. 196 or **Canards dans la Soupière** p. 194

Baked Zucchini p. 307 **Wild Rice Casserole** p. 281

Cranberry Apples p. 309

Soufflé Grand Marnier p. 366 or **Food-for-the-Gods Pie** p. 326

Café Brulôt p.46

Stilton Cheese and Fruit

Continued...

This gourmet dinner commands the serving of the proper wine for each course. Exceptions are the salad course—the vinegar dressing is not compatible with wine—and the Grapefruit Sorbet, a palate cleanser. The latter is always served preceding the main course of a dinner and is intended to do just what its name implies.

We have listed the proper kind of wine for each course (i.e. a white Burgundy with the fish course) and under each kind we have suggested some outstanding varieties. There are many other delicious wines, both foreign and domestic, that would serve you well for this dinner.

SUGGESTED WINES

Champagne: First Course	**Piper Heidsiech** **or** **Mumms**
White Burgundy: Fish Course	**Puligny Montrachet** **or** **Pinot Chardonnay**
Red Burgundy: Main Course	**Pinot Noir** **or** **Cabernet Sauvignon**
Sweet White Bordeaux: Dessert	**Barsac or Sauterne**
Vintage Port or Madeira Cheese and Fruit	

Winter Revel

CAJUN CHRISTMAS

From the bayous of South Louisiana comes food for a spicy buffet and raucous entertainment for adult friends.

Hang some Spanish moss over the holly and create the home of Cajuns, alligators and pirates where they say, **"Laissez les bon temps rouler!"**—Let the good times roll!, and they dance the *fais-do-do.* The generous Christmas spirit fades in the midst of a pirates' gift exchange* and Cajun pandemonium, while we scorch our palates with bayou food and "gimme" for the best present.

MENU

Hot Oysters Supreme p. 75 **Shrimp Patties** p. 218

Terrebonne Jambalaya p. 225 or **Red Beans and Rice** p. 286

Spinach and Orange Salad p. 120

or

Bayou Apple Salad p. 95

Choctaw Cornbread p. 264

Chocolate Pecan Pie p. 327

Cajuns (Acadians) are the descendants of the French Canadians, who immigrated to the bayou country of Louisiana after the French and Indian War. Creoles are the sophisticated descendants of French and Spanish colonists who settled in the city of New Orleans.

Continued...

*Directions for pirates' gift exchange

1. Each guest brings a wrapped gift (either a "white elephant" or under a certain dollar amount) which is placed in the "treasure chest."

2. Have pieces of paper numbered to equal the number of gifts brought.

3. Each pirate will draw one number.

4. Pirate Number 1 picks a gift and opens it in front of the rest.

5. Pirate Number 2 may choose to steal the gift from Pirate Number 1 or open one of the remaining gifts. If Pirate Number 1's gift is stolen, he then must open another gift.

6. Then Pirate Number 3 may choose Number 1's or Number 2's gift or open an unopened gift from the treasure chest.

7. So it goes...each greedy pirate taking what he wants...so that the last pirate has the option of taking any one of the opened presents or opening the remaining unopened present—his dilemma for being last.

8. Should the last pirate choose to take an opened present, the unopened gift then goes to the pirate without one.

LAISSEZ LES BON TEMPS ROULER!

CURRIER AND IVES CHRISTMAS

Nostalgia for a time we never knew

Invite families—babies to great-grandparents—for caroling and buffet supper. An old-fashioned sleigh ride is a rare and treasured experience in a modern world. Just once, we treat our senses to the sound of sleigh bells and hooves on packed snow, as we glide through dark, icy air. After caroling, mittens and scarves are abandoned to melt by the front door so the fire can warm us outside and hot wine ease the inner chill. In the air, the aromas of spice, fresh greenery and candles mingle while volunteer voices carol with piano or guitar. On the dining room table, the centerpiece of apples, fresh greens and candlelight accents a hearty and bounteous buffet.

MENU

Hot Mulled Cider p. 46

Shrimp Mousse p. 77 **Almond-Bacon-Cheese Spread** p. 58

Pork Loin Roast Vineyard Style p. 162

Fresh Broccoli with Cashew Butter Sauce p. 244

Wild Rice and Apples p. 281

Christmas Tree Salad p. 97

Refrigerator Rolls p. 260

Holiday Cake p. 318

English Toffee p. 360

When the evening is over, guests may be sent home with their Christmas gifts: goodies from your kitchen,* home-baked and preserved, wrapped country-store style in gingham and calico and tucked into a basket.

*See Index for gift ideas.

CHILDREN'S CHRISTMAS PARTY

An afternoon tea party for true believers, their grandmothers and Santa Claus...

For one day, mothers in charge of making Christmas will do without the "help" of little hands while the children accompany willing grandmothers to this Fete de Noël. Together they can make the Easy Graham Cracker House. When it is time to leave, each excited child may take home Magic Window Cookies which are the parting gift from the hostess, and his own Graham Cracker House.

Real tea parties are few and far between, and when Santa stops by, catch the moment with on-the-spot photos. The innocence and wonder that make this party special are short-lived.

MENU

Hot Chocolate **Hollywood Punch** p. 44

Gingerbread People p. 341

Chocolate Crunch p. 379

Sugar Cookies p. 345

Easy Graham Cracker House p. 341 **Magic Window Cookies** p. 340

Presents are delivered to good little children around the world by a variety of personages: Père Noël in France, das Kristkind in Germany, an elf in Scandinavia, Sintukla in Holland, the Three Wise Men in Mexico, Father Christmas in England and, of course, Santa Claus in the United States.

MEXICAN CHRISTMAS

The high school and college crowd give south-of-the-border food an A+.

For one night of the holiday season, the tempo switches from jingle bells to mariachis. Luminarias* glow along the front walk and lead to the gala fiesta. Authentic straw and tin ornaments add the flair of Old Mexico to the tree, while multihued serapes cover the candlelit buffet table. Overhead, piñatas are suspended for after-dinner entertainment, and the fireplace is banked with bright red poinsettia plants. Bid one and all, *"Feliz Navidad."*

MENU

Margaritas p. 48

Sombrero Hot Sauce p. 256 **Spicy Bean Hot Pot** p. 56

Chunky Avocado Dip p. 53

Tejas Fresh Vegetable Salad p. 121

Chicken Enchiladas p. 178 **Beef-Chili Relleños Casserole** p. 153

Calabasitas p. 282

Chocolate Torta p. 316 or **La Tapatia Lemon Pie** p. 335

In Mexico, Christmas Day is preceded by nine nights of posadas: torchlit processions through the streets. After each posada, the blindfolded children take turns trying to break a candy-filled piñata. The poinsettia is a native of Mexico, discovered in 1847 by Robert Pointset.

*To make luminarias, half fill lunch-size brown paper bags with sand. Illuminate with a candle, standing upright in the sand.

NEW YEAR'S DAY BRUNCH

A Red Cross brunch offers first aid for last night's party goers and is evident in all decorations.

The host and hostess dress the part of doctor and nurse, directing patients to the bar disguised as a rescue station. A centerpiece of red and white carnations on the buffet table is festooned with individual packets of aspirin, Alka-Seltzer, Tums, Pepto-Bismol and Band-Aids.

The menu is designed to tempt the appetite and please the palate. Good luck and good health are the doctor's orders for today.

MENU

Bloody Marys p. 45 **Milk Punch** p. 50

Spicy Cashews p. 71 **Stuffin' Muffin** p. 60

Cabbage Rolls p. 147 **Richard II Eggs** p. 229

Black-Eyed Peas and Sausage p. 295

Hearts of Palm Salad p. 96

Whole Wheat Biscuits p. 261

German Cream Cheese Brownies p. 348 **Orange Balls** p. 343

The Southern tradition of eating black-eyed peas and salt pork on New Year's Day for luck echos an international belief that pork and legumes are foods that bring good fortune. While fowl scratch for their food walking backwards and are then to be avoided on a New Year's menu, hogs hunt in a forward direction, symbolic of success and progress. The British custom of eating beans comes from a famine year when they were so scarce there were only enough for spring planting and eating on New Year's Day.

SUPER BOWL

Enjoy an afternoon of the ultimate in football and fix-your-own food.

A ticket to the real thing may be hard to come by, but the ones you send as invitations guarantee each guest a seat on the 50-yard line for the final clashing of the helmets. TV's in *every* room make sure that no one misses a play, and munching-food is well within every arm's reach.

Supper is in the kitchen, warm on the stove, so everyone can help himself while the hostess watches the game undisturbed.

MENU

Carrots Green Goddess p. 57 **Welcome Wafers** p. 60

Vegetables with Crabmeat p. 80

Horseradish Cheese Spread p. 60 **Jalapeño Spinach Dip** p. 50

Cheesy Zucchini Soup p. 95 **Five-Star Soup** p. 84

Corned Beef Brisket Kosher Style p. 134

with Rye and Pumpernickle Bread

Horseradish Sauce p. 246 **Sweet-Hot Mustard** p. 257

Homemade Mayonnaise p. 126

Dill Pickles p. 254 **Squash Relish** p. 255

Super Cream Cheesecake p. 320

Blueberry Cake p. 321

FEAST OF THE DRAGON

Conjure up dragons, and fire up the wok!

It may not be Hong Kong or even San Francisco, and firecrackers may be hard to come by, but the Chinese New Year is an excuse for a super party in February. Red, the traditional color of good luck, should dominate the decorations, and the animals of the Chinese horoscope can indicate the fortune of each guest. Chopsticks only, please!

MENU

Rice Wine

Chiao-Tzu (Kuo-T'ieh or Grilled Pot Stickers) p. 64

Special Egg Rolls p. 166

Sweet-Sour Pork p. 164 **Stir-Fried Chicken** p. 180

Stir-Fried Broccoli and Beef p. 140

Chinese Fried Rice p. 280 **Steamed White Rice**

Sautéed Snow Peas and Celery p. 296

Orange Dessert p. 355

Oriental Tea

The Chinese calendar is dictated by the moon rather than the sun, as it is in the occidental world. The New Year is celebrated for fourteen days, and each Chinese person considers it his birthday. It is a time to start life with a clean slate by cleaning, painting and paying all debts.

Good-luck signs decorate the home, and the paper image of T'sao Wang, the kitchen god, who has decorated the kitchen for a year, is burned in the stove and replaced with a new one. The day of the full moon, Yuan Shaw, or Festival of the Lanterns, is celebrated with feasting, firecrackers and the Pageant of the Dragon in the streets.

MARDI GRAS REVEL

By imperial order, bid guests join you for a *Mardi Gras* party ã la New Orleans—the city that care forgot.

Traditionally, this last of the Carnival* festivities is a masquerade ball and late-night supper—a perfect design for your gala.

The regal colors of Carnival—gold, green and royal purple—can be draped in satin around the entrance and over the supper tables. Give strings of glass beads and shiny doubloons (always tossed from parade floats) to the costumed guests. Glittered cardboard crowns and masks make effective centerpieces. Dance to the recorded music of a Crescent City jazz band.

The late-evening supper is fit for a king and his court—no matter that they pretend. Champagne in silver goblets and King's Cake are fitting finales for your majestic *Mardi Gras Revel.*

*In the Latin translation, *carnival* literally means "farewell to meat," while *Mardi Gras* is French for "Fat Tuesday," the day before the self-denial of Lent begins.

The first *Mardi Gras* was held in 1699, but not until 1857 did the festivities take on their current character. Costumed "Krewes" have parades and balls constantly from Twelfth Night (January 6) to Fat Tuesday, making the *Mardi Gras* season and New Orleans an inseparable match.

Continued...

MENU

Boursin Cheese p. 58

Crabmeat Remick p. 74

or

Crabmeat Peggy p. 72

Tenderloin with Beef Marinade Supreme p. 250

Fresh Broccoli with Hollandaise Sauce p. 245

Fettuccine p. 276

Spinach Salad p. 119

Refrigerator Rolls p. 260

Cream Cheese Pound Cake p. 316

or

King's Cake*

Flambé Bananas p. 353

Café Brulôt p. 46

*In Arthurian England a bean was baked in the traditional Twelfth Night King's Cake and designated the finder as "King of the Bean." In the modern New Orleans confection, the bean has been replaced by a plastic baby, and the finder must host the next *Mardi Gras* party.

Recipe Revel

Cherry-Orange Fizz

3 cups orange juice
½ cup red maraschino cherry juice
1 tablespoon lemon juice
½ tablespoon lime juice
1 12-ounce bottle ginger ale
1 tray frozen orange juice cubes
Maraschino cherries and orange slices for garnish
Fresh mint

Mix first 4 ingredients in large pitcher. Chill. Add orange cubes and ginger ale before serving. Float cherries and orange slices. Add fresh mint to each glass as garnish.

Serves 6

Flora Fogel Lebowitz

French Mint Iced Tea

2 family-size tea bags
1 6-ounce can orange juice concentrate
2 lemons, halved
1 cup sugar
8-10 mint leaves

Put tea bags in 2 pints boiling water. Steep. Twist and squeeze mint to extract flavor and drop in tea. Let stand a while. Add undiluted orange juice. Add juice, pulp and peel of lemons and sugar. Add enough water to make 2 quarts. Strain. Pour over ice and serve.

Yields 2 quarts

Wilma Whittington

Hollywood Punch

1 quart orange juice
1 quart orange sherbet
1 quart vanilla ice cream
1 quart chilled ginger ale

Beat orange juice, sherbet and ice cream until well mixed. Add ginger ale. Stir well.

Serves 25-30

Paula Wray Ewing

Orange Julius

1 6-ounce can frozen orange juice concentrate
1 cup milk
1 cup water
½ cup sugar, or less, to taste
1 teaspoon vanilla
12 ice cubes

Place all ingredients in blender. (Crack ice cubes before dropping them in blender, if your blender directions so state.) Blend thoroughly and serve immediately. *Children love this before or with breakfast and as an after-school treat.*

Serves 5-6

Phyllis Terry Bennett
New Orleans, Louisiana

Smoothie

1 banana
8 strawberries
1 tablespoon papaya juice
2 tablespoons unsweetened pineapple juice
1 cup crushed ice
Honey to taste

Put all ingredients in blender or food processor and blend for 20 seconds. *Can substitute any fruit for the strawberries.*

Serves 1-2

Judith Crow Quinn

Bloody Marys

46 ounces (5¾ cups) tomato juice
2 cups vodka
2 tablespoons lemon juice
1 tablespoon prepared horseradish
1 teaspoon Worcestershire sauce
¾ teaspoon salt
Tabasco to taste
Celery sticks

Mix all ingredients. Chill; pour over crushed ice and use celery sticks as stirrers.

Serves 6-8

Dorothy Davies Miller

Café Brulôt

45 sugar cubes
45 whole cloves
2 cinnamon sticks
1½ cups brandy
2 orange rinds
2 lemon rinds
8-10 cups strong hot coffee

Put all ingredients except coffee in a container overnight. In a double boiler, heat until mixture is almost to boiling point. Do not boil. Rinse brulôt bowl or large silver chafing dish with hot water and dry. Put mixture in bowl.

Ignite mixture by lighting a sugar cube soaked with brandy in a brulôt or silver ladle; transfer cube to the mixture in the bowl. Keep flame going by stirring with the ladle and lifting the lemon and orange rinds in the air with a fork. When flame is out, pour in strong hot coffee. Serve immediately in brulôt or demitasse cups.

Serves 18-20

Henry Bernis Alsobrook, Jr.
New Orleans, Louisiana

Hot Mulled Cider

2 quarts apple cider
1 teaspoon whole allspice
6 cloves (or more)
1 cinnamon stick
½ cup brown sugar
½ cup sugar
½ cup orange juice
½ cup lemon juice
22 ounces hearty Burgundy

Simmer cider, spices and sugars for 30 minutes. Add juices, wine and serve.

Yields 2½ quarts

Sally Jarrell McMichael

Fog Cutter

16 ounces lime juice
64 ounces orange juice
16 ounces orgeat syrup
16 ounces brandy
16 ounces gin
32 ounces white rum

Add 1 ingredient at a time and stir or shake very well. Serve over ice in 8-ounce glasses.

Serves 24 — Rebecca Strohmaier Roberts

Mint Juleps

3 cups sugar
1 cup water
Mint leaves
Kentucky bourbon

In a 2-quart saucepan combine the sugar and the water and fill to the top with mint leaves. Boil 5 minutes or until green. Strain into a pitcher and chill for 24 hours. For each julep, fill a 10-ounce glass with crushed ice and add 3 ounces of Kentucky bourbon and 1 ounce of syrup. Garnish with a mint leaf which has been moistened and dipped in powdered sugar.

Serves 32 — Cookbook Committee

Strawberry Ice

Ice
1 6-ounce can frozen orange juice, prepared according to directions
1 10-ounce package frozen strawberries
4 ounces bourbon

Fill blender with ice. Prepare orange juice and pour in blender until three-fourths full. Add strawberries and bourbon. Blend and serve.

Serves 4 — Edie Broyles Williams

Margaritas

½ cup fresh lime juice
Add ice to the top of blender (2 cups)
½ cup Triple Sec
1 cup tequila
Pinch salt

Prepare your glasses by dipping rims in lime juice and salt. Place in freezer to chill. Place ½ cup lime juice in blender and add ice cubes to the top of blender. Cover and mix until ice is crushed. Add Triple Sec, tequila and a pinch of salt. Blend for 5 seconds. Put mixture in freezer until slightly frozen. Pour into chilled glasses. Add a slice of lime to rim of glass for garnish.

Serves 10

Gregorio
Acapulco, Mexico

Wimbledon Strawberry Daiquiris

3 6-ounce cans frozen lemonade or limeade concentrate
3 cans water
1 6-ounce can frozen orange juice concentrate
1 pint frozen strawberries
½ fifth light rum

Place all ingredients in blender; blend well. Transfer to clean milk cartons and freeze. Will keep for weeks. Thaw *slightly* to serve. Spoon into glasses. *Peaches may be substituted for strawberries.*

Serves 10-12

Minnett Holley Thornton

Frozen Daiquiris

2 6-ounce cans limeade concentrate
1 6-ounce can pink lemonade concentrate
1 6-ounce can orange juice concentrate
1 10-ounce jar maraschino cherries, reserve juice
Reserved cherry juice plus water to make 6 cups
1 fifth Bacardi light rum

Mix all ingredients and put in freezer. Stir every 2 hours.

Serves 6

Debra Horn Landrem

Kahlua

2 vanilla beans
1 quart 100% proof vodka
4 cups sugar
2 cups water
2 ounces freeze-dried coffee

Soak vanilla beans in vodka for 30 days. After 30 day soaking period, make a syrup as follows: mix together sugar and half of the water; heat to dissolve sugar. Dissolve coffee in remaining water and add to syrup. Reheat, but do not boil. Cool and add vodka.

Yields 2 quarts

Leslie Szafir
Dallas, Texas

Milk Punch

1½ ounces bourbon or brandy
½ ounce white crème de cacao
4 ounces milk
Nutmeg

Combine first 3 ingredients in tall glass filled with ice and sprinkle with dash of nutmeg. *Good before brunch or luncheon.*

Serves 1

Jacqueline Labry Nesbitt

Wine Punch

2 pints fresh strawberries
1 cup sugar
1 pint Hennessey's cognac (no substitutes)
75 ounces German white wine
25 ounces good French champagne

Stem and slice strawberries; add sugar and cognac. (This must be done 24 hours before serving.) Chill wines. Day of serving, in large chilled punch bowl, put strawberry mixture; add wine and champagne.

Serves 8

Nan Smith Stewart

Wine Cooler

1 teaspoon lemonade concentrate
2 ounces Chablis
Crushed ice
Ginger ale
Lemon slice or mint

For each serving, mix lemonade and Chablis in large wine glass and fill with crushed ice. Add a little ginger ale and stir. Top with a lemon slice or a sprig of mint. This can be mixed in larger quantity and served as punch.

Serves 8 per
½ gallon Chablis

Anne Bigger Nixon
Dallas, Texas

White Sangría

4 cups dry white wine
¾ cup Cointreau
½ cup sugar
1 10-ounce bottle club soda, chilled, or 10 ounces champagne
1 orange, sliced
1 lemon, sliced
1 lime, sliced
1 small bunch green grapes
Green apple wedges
Lemon juice

Mix first 3 ingredients. Chill. Just before serving add chilled soda. Garnish with orange, lemon and lime slices and grapes. Put apple wedges dipped in lemon juice on each glass. *Excellent as spring and summer drink or served with Spanish and Mexican menus.*

Yields 1 quart

Mary Jane Ray Hall

Grind sugar in your food processor for super fine sugar. It dissolves instantly in iced tea.

Artichoke and Shrimp Dip

1 pint sour cream
1 0.6-ounce package Good Seasons Italian or Garlic Salad Dressing Mix
Worcestershire sauce
Tabasco
Garlic powder
Cayenne pepper
1 4½-ounce can shrimp, drained
1 8½-ounce can artichoke hearts, drained and chopped
2 tablespoons chopped chives
1 tablespoon chopped parsley
Paprika

Combine sour cream and salad dressing mix. Season to taste with Worcestershire sauce, Tabasco, garlic powder and cayenne pepper. Add shrimp and artichoke hearts. Mix and add parsley and chives. Mix well. Place in small casserole dish and sprinkle top with paprika. Refrigerate at least 2 hours. Better if made the day before. Serve with potato chips.

Serves 15

Nancy Talbot Sale

Artichoke Dip

1 8½-ounce can artichoke hearts, drained
Juice ½ lemon
⅓ cup mayonnaise
1 tablespoon chopped onion
3 or 4 slices bacon, cooked crisp and crumbled
Salt, pepper and cayenne to taste

Finely chop artichoke hearts. Add remaining ingredients. Stir well and check seasonings. Chill for several hours. Serve with corn chips.

Yields 1 cup

Karen Willis Burns

Chunky Avocado Dip

5 avocados, chopped
¾ onion, chopped
1 tomato, peeled and chopped
1-1½ teaspoons garlic salt
½ teaspoon pepper, or more to taste
4 tablespoons fresh lemon juice
7 heaping tablespoons mayonnaise
1 teaspoon Worcestershire sauce
1 teaspoon Tabasco, or to taste

In large bowl, chop peeled avocado in *chunks* by hand. *Do not mash.* Add onion, tomato, garlic salt, pepper and lemon juice. Add rest of ingredients and stir lightly. Put 3 avocado seeds in dip to keep it from turning brown and refrigerate at least 2 hours before serving. Serve with corn chips. Could be served as salad. *Delicious if you add shrimp.*

Serves 8-10

Marie Rountree Rosenfield

Hot Bean Dip

1 10¾-ounce can condensed black bean soup
1 11½-ounce can condensed bean with bacon soup
¼ cup water
1 teaspoon dry mustard
½ teaspoon red pepper
½ teaspoon chili powder
2 cloves garlic, pressed
4-5 drops Tabasco
1 tablespoon white vinegar
1 8-ounce carton sour cream

Heat all ingredients except sour cream in a medium-size boiler over moderate heat, stirring constantly. Add sour cream and simmer 10 minutes. Serve in chafing dish with corn chips. *Add 1 pound of ground meat for variation.*

Serves 8-10

Gail Bonneau Olmsted
Dallas, Texas

Curry Dip

¾ cup mayonnaise
2 tablespoons Durkee sauce
1 teaspoon celery seed
½ teaspoon Worcestershire sauce
Dash Tabasco
1 clove garlic, crushed, or 3-4 drops garlic juice
1 heaping teaspoon horseradish
1 teaspoon curry powder
1 teaspoon seasoned salt
Dash pepper

Mix all ingredients and chill. Serve with raw vegetables or use as a spread on ham sandwiches.

Yields 1 cup

Donna Banks Curtis

Dill Dip

1 pint mayonnaise
1 pint sour cream
3 tablespoons minced onion
2 tablespoons parsley
3 teaspoons dill weed
3 teaspoons Beau Monde

Combine ingredients. Let stand 1 hour. Chill.

Yields 1 quart

Nancy Hudson Ketner

Mexican Relish Dip

1 medium tomato, peeled and chopped
1 6-ounce can black olives, drained and chopped
5-6 green onions and tops, chopped
1 4-ounce can green chili peppers, chopped
1 tablespoon olive oil
2 tablespoons red wine vinegar
Salt and pepper to taste
Tabasco

Chop or process all vegetables. Add remaining ingredients. Mix well and refrigerate. Serve cold with corn chips. *May add 1 mashed avocado just before serving.*

Serves 6-8

Cynthia Johnson Nowery

Jalapeño Spinach Dip

3 ribs celery, chopped medium fine
½ large onion, chopped
1 6-ounce can mushroom pieces
5 tablespoons margarine or butter, divided
1 10-ounce package frozen chopped spinach, slightly thawed
Garlic salt to taste
8 ounces jalapeño processed cheese
1 10¾-ounce can cream of mushroom soup

Sauté celery, onion and mushrooms in 3 tablespoons margarine or butter. Drain and set aside. Cook spinach in remaining 2 tablespoons of margarine until no water is left in pan. Season with garlic salt. Melt cheese in double boiler and add mushroom soup. Combine all, and serve in chafing dish as a dip. This may be served as a vegetable in buttered ramekins, topped with crushed, canned French fried onion rings, and baked at 350° until hot.

Serves 6 — Corinne Garrett Clawson

Super Shrimp Dip

1½ pounds shrimp
1 pint mayonnaise
3-4 tablespoons dried parsley
3-4 tablespoons frozen chives
2-3 tablespoons horseradish mustard
Juice ½ lemon
½ tablespoon onion salt

Chop shrimp and mix with other ingredients. Chill. Serve with crackers or fresh homemade Melba toast. *If you use precooked frozen shrimp be sure to drain and dry the thawed shrimp before mixing it with other ingredients to keep it from being soupy.*

Serves 15-20 — Cynthia Johnson Nowery

Spicy Bean Hot Pot

1 pound ground round
1 onion, chopped
1 clove garlic, crushed
1 4-ounce can green chilies, chopped
1 16-ounce can refried beans
1 tablespoon chili powder
1 8-ounce can tomato sauce
¼ pound Cheddar cheese, grated

Brown ground meat in a heavy skillet. Add onion and garlic and cook until onion is clear. Add rest of ingredients and simmer 20 minutes, stirring occasionally. Serve in chafing dish with tostados or large corn chips. Can be frozen. *Could be used as filling for tacos or a side dish with a Mexican meal.*

Serves 8-10

Mary Graham Pate

Somburo Special

1 pound ground beef
1 cup chopped onion, divided
1 cup catsup
¼ teaspoon Tabasco
1 tablespoon chili powder
½ teaspoon salt
1 16-ounce can kidney beans with liquid
1 cup grated sharp cheese
½ cup chopped stuffed green olives
Taco chips

Brown meat and ½ cup onion in skillet. Stir in catsup, Tabasco, chili powder and salt. Mash in beans. Heat through and transfer to chafing dish. Garnish with olives in center, surrounded by cheese and remaining onions. Serve with taco chips.

Yields 3 cups

Rebecca Strohmaier Roberts

Carrots Green Goddess

4 cups (2 pounds) 1"-2" carrot sticks
1 tablespoon parsley flakes
½ cup finely grated onion or 2 tablespoons dried minced onion
½ cup green goddes dressing
½ cup Wish-Bone Italian Dressing (diet may be used)
1 teaspoon dill seed
½ teaspoon salt
½ teaspoon seasoned pepper

Barely cook carrots in boiling salted water, if desired. (You may prefer them raw.) Drain well. Put carrots in a medium-size plastic container that may be tightly covered. Mix all other ingredients thoroughly and pour over carrots. Cover and refrigerate for 24 hours, turning upside down occasionally. Serve chilled. These unusual carrot sticks will remain delicious under refrigeration for several days.

Serves 10-12

Frances Brock

Stuffed Dates

8 ounces grated Cheddar cheese
Red pepper to taste
1 6-ounce package whole dates
1 stick margarine
1½ cups sifted flour
½ cup pecan halves

Have cheese and margarine at room temperature. Grate cheese and mix with flour, margarine and pepper. Mix thoroughly. Work like pie dough. Stuff each date with a pecan half. Pinch small amount of dough and cover date stuffed with pecan. Bake at 400° for 15 minutes or until brown. *These dates are good for Christmas gifts and can be frozen.*

Yields 2 dozen

Gayle Strahan Gordon

Almond-Bacon-Cheese Spread

- ½ cup unblanched almonds, roasted
- 2 strips cooked bacon
- 1 cup grated American cheese, packed
- 1 tablespoon chopped green onion
- ½ cup mayonnaise
- ¼ teaspoon salt

Finely chop almonds and crumble bacon; blend all ingredients thoroughly. Blender or processor can be used. *Serve with sesame rounds, Melba toast or any favorite cracker.*

Serves 8-10 — Edie Broyles Williams

Bacon-Cheese Fingers

- 1 cup grated Swiss cheese
- 8 slices bacon, cooked and crumbled
- 3-4 tablespoons mayonnaise
- 1 tablespoon chopped onion
- ½ teaspoon celery salt (or celery seed)
- 30 rye bread rounds

Combine first 5 ingredients; blend well. Spread cheese mixture on each rye round. Broil until mixture is hot and bubbly. Serve hot or cold. This spread freezes well.

Yields 30 appetizers — Mary Groenewoud Hale

Boursin Cheese

- 1 8-ounce package cream cheese
- 1 stick butter
- ½ teaspoon fines herbes
- ½ teaspoon dill weed
- ¼ teaspoon garlic salt
- 1 tablespoon chopped fresh parsley
- Lemon pepper

Mix all ingredients except lemon pepper in food processor. Form into desired shape on wax paper. Chill. When firm, roll in lemon pepper. *Serve with thin wheat crackers.*

Serves 10-12 — Margaret Hunkin Crow

Cheese Ball

1 8-ounce package cream cheese
1½ cups grated mild Cheddar cheese
1 5-ounce jar smoke-flavored cheese spread
1 teaspoon Worcestershire sauce
½ teaspoon dry mustard
½ teaspoon salt
1 7½-ounce can chopped ripe olives
Chopped fresh parsley

Soften cream cheese. Blend with cheeses, Worcestershire sauce, mustard and salt. Beat until smooth or blend with your hands. Fold in olives and shape into ball. Sprinkle with chopped parsley. Chill. *If desired, make into logs and roll in chili powder and chopped pecans.*

Yields 2 large balls — Sissy Masters Harper

Chili con Queso

3 tablespoons butter
1 large onion, chopped
3 4-ounce cans green chilies, chopped
1 pound American cheese, grated
1 cup whipping cream

Melt butter in a heavy saucepan. Sauté onions and chilies. Stir in cheese and cook over low heat until cheese is melted, stirring constantly. Add cream and mix thoroughly. Keep warm, but do not boil after adding cheese. Serve in chafing dish with corn chips. *Can be made ahead and frozen.*

Serves 10-12 — Mary Graham Pate

Horseradish Cheese Spread

1 pound Velveeta cheese
1 5-ounce jar horseradish
1 cup Hellman's mayonnaise

Cut cheese into small cubes. Melt in heavy pot or double boiler. Stir occasionally to prevent cheese from sticking. Add horseradish, stir and remove from heat. Add mayonnaise and stir until smooth. Chill. *Serve warm or cool with crackers.*

Yields 1½ pounds

Martha Turner Schober

Stuffin' Muffin

1 cup grated Cheddar cheese
1 cup mayonnaise
1½ cups chopped ripe olives
1½ cups chopped green onions
1 teaspoon curry powder
1 teaspoon salt
1 teaspoon pepper
6 English muffins

Mix ingredients thoroughly. Spread on English muffin halves. Toast in hot oven until bubbly. Cut muffins into 6 wedges. Serve hot.

Serves 6-8

Virginia Hodges Jeter

Welcome Wafers

1½ sticks butter
½ cup grated Cheddar cheese
⅓ cup blue cheese
½ clove garlic, crushed
1 teaspoon parsley
1 teaspoon chives
2 cups sifted flour

Cream butter. Add remaining ingredients. Shape into 1½" rolls. Chill. Slice thinly. Bake at 375° for 8-10 minutes. *Cayenne pepper can be added for spicier wafers.*

Yields 3 dozen

Susan Sigler Updegraff

Pineapple Cheese Ball

- 2 8-ounce packages cream cheese, softened
- 1 8½-ounce can crushed pineapple, drained
- 2 cups chopped pecans
- ¼ cup finely chopped green pepper
- 2 tablespoons finely chopped onion
- 1 tablespoon seasoned salt

In medium bowl beat cream cheese with fork until smooth. Gradually stir in crushed pineapple, 1 cup nuts, green pepper, onion and seasoned salt. Shape in 2 balls; roll in other cup of pecans. Wrap in foil. Refrigerate until well chilled (overnight). *Serve with crackers.*

Serves 16

Alice Grace
Albany, Georgia

Pine Creek Cheese Spread

- 8 ounces cream cheese
- 1 stick melted butter
- ¼ cup sour cream
- ¼ cup chopped green onions
- 1 tablespoon paprika
- 1 teaspoon caraway seeds
- ¼ pound cottage cheese
- 1 tablespoon capers
- 1 tablespoon anchovy paste

Bring cream cheese to room temperature. Melt butter. Combine cheese and butter with remaining ingredients. Blend well in mixer, food processor or blender. *Serve with pumpernickel bread.*

Serves 10-12

Pine Creek Cookhouse
Ashcroft, Colorado

Celestial Chicken Wings

1 cup soy sauce
1 cup pineapple juice
1 clove garlic, pressed
2 tablespoons minced onion
1 teaspoon ground ginger
¼ cup brown sugar
1 7-ounce can beer
¼ cup butter or oil
2 packages drumettes (chicken wings, the part that looks like little drumsticks)

Combine first 8 ingredients and stir until dissolved. Pour over chicken and marinate overnight or at least 8 hours. Be sure sauce covers all pieces. Drain and save marinade. In a large skillet, heat a small amount of oil and brown chicken on all sides over medium heat. When brown, add ½ cup marinade; cover; reduce heat and simmer 15-20 minutes. Stir and add more marinade if necessary. This may be cooked a day ahead and then reheated in oven before serving. Add marinade to moisten before heating. Serve hot in a chafing dish.

Serves 8-10

Rebecca Strohmaier Roberts

Escargots

1 4½-ounce can snails
3 ounces unsalted butter
2 teaspoons parsley
1-2 cloves garlic, pressed
1 teaspoon green onion, minced
½ teaspoon salt
Pinch pepper and nutmeg
Juice ¼ lemon
24 snail shells

Rinse snails in cold water and drain. Melt butter and add remaining ingredients. Sauté for a few minutes until onions are limp. Add a small amount of butter mixture in bottom of each shell. Insert snails and fill rest of shell with more of the butter mixture. Heat in 400° oven 8-10 minutes or until butter sizzles. *Large stemmed fresh mushrooms may be substituted for shells, and prepared as above.*

Serves 4-6

Judith Crow Quinn

Eggplant Spread

- 1/3 cup olive oil
- 3 cups eggplant, peeled and cut in 1/2" cubes
- 1/3 cup chopped green pepper
- 1 medium onion, chopped
- 2 cloves garlic or garlic powder to taste
- 1 4-ounce can mushrooms, juice, stems and pieces
- 1 cup tomato paste
- 1/4 cup water
- 1 tablespoon red wine vinegar
- 1/2 cup sliced stuffed olives
- 1 1/2 teaspoons sugar
- 1/2 teaspoon oregano
- 1 teaspoon seasoned salt
- 1/8 teaspoon pepper

Heat the olive oil and cook eggplant, green pepper, onion and garlic gently for 10 minutes, covered. Stir occasionally. Add all other ingredients. Simmer until soft enough to spread on crackers. *Could be served on sandwiches. Will keep 1 week in refrigerator.*

Yields 1 quart

Eleanor Long Simmons

Stuffed Jalapeños

- 1 12-ounce can mild seeded jalapeño peppers, drained
- 1 4 1/2-ounce can small deveined shrimp, drained
- 1-2 eggs, beaten
- Cornflake crumbs

Stuff shrimp into peppers. Hold together with a toothpick. Dip stuffed pepper in egg; then roll in cornflake crumbs. Let dry. Repeat egg and crumbs. Let dry. Sauté in skillet or deep fry at medium-high heat until coating is brown.

Serves 6

Dianna Hughes Sentell

Pirozhki

¾ pound ground chuck
⅓ cup finely chopped onion
1 teaspoon butter
2 cups finely chopped mushrooms
1 tablespoon flour
1 teaspoon salt
½ cup sour cream
2 tablespoons chopped parsley
2 teaspoons dill weed
2 teaspoons Worcestershire sauce
2 9½-11 ounce packages pie crust mix

Cook beef and onion in butter until meat is crumbly. Add mushrooms and cook until tender, stirring often. Stir in flour and salt. Add sour cream, parsley, dill weed and Worcestershire sauce. Cook stirring constantly until thickened. Set aside and let cool. Prepare pie crust mix as directed on package label. Roll pastry ⅛″ thick on lightly floured board. Cut into 3½″-4″ circles with biscuit cutter. Center about 1 tablespoon filling on each pastry circle. Moisten pastry edges and bring up over filling. Press edges together and crimp. Make 2-3 small slits in tops. Place on ungreased cookie sheets. Bake at 425° until crust is done and slightly browned, about 12-15 minutes. Serve warm.

Yields 30-35 pieces

Anne Krison Mitchell

Chiao-Tzu (Kuo-T'ieh or Grilled Pot Stickers)

Hot Pepper Oil

1 cup vegetable oil
4 whole green onions
1 piece of whole ginger
¼ pound red chili peppers, chopped

Prepare 24 hours ahead. Heat oil to 375°. Add green onions and a piece of ginger. Remove from heat. After 5 minutes, discard onions and ginger. Cool oil for 5 minutes then pour over peppers in steel bowl. Let stand overnight. Strain the oil, and bottle to use as dip for pot stickers. Keep chilies in the refrigerator and use in cooking.

Continued...

Pot Stickers

- 1 pound ground lean pork
- ½ cup diced, soaked dry mushrooms (½ cup fresh mushrooms)
- ⅓ cup chopped green onions with tops
- ¼ cup finely chopped celery
- ¼ cup finely chopped water chestnuts
- ¼ cup finely chopped bamboo shoots
- 2 teaspoons finely chopped fresh Chinese parsley or ½ teaspoon ground coriander
- 1 teaspoon fresh ginger root or ¼ teaspoon ground ginger
- 3 tablespoons soy sauce
- 1½ tablespoons cornstarch
- 1 egg white
- 1 package won ton skins or egg roll skins, cut into 4 equal parts
- ½ pound peeled and finely chopped raw shrimp
- 3-4 tablespoons vegetable oil
- 1½ cups water
- White vinegar
- Soy sauce

Mix the pork with the mushrooms, onions, celery, water chestnuts, bamboo shoots, parsley and ginger. Gradually blend soy sauce with cornstarch and add to pork mixture. Add the egg white to the pork mixture. Blend thoroughly. Place approximately 1 teaspoon of the mixture in the center of 1 won ton skin. Brush the edges of the skin with a little water and fold opposite corners up and press together to make a stuffed dumpling, with the edges standing up and a flat bottom. Cover with a damp towel. Continue filling, using all of mixture. Brush finished dumplings with oil on all sides. If you plan to freeze, also brush the bottom of the pan in which you will freeze them with the oil.

To cook, heat 3 or 4 tablespoons of oil to high temperature in a large, heavy skillet, thoroughly coating the bottom. When hot, place the Chiao-Tzu flat side down in the hot oil, not touching until bottoms brown nicely. Be careful not to burn. Add water (1½ cups) to the skillet and cover. Steam for 6-8 minutes. The sides will be steamed and the filling cooked. Remove and serve with white vinegar, hot pepper oil and soy sauce as dips. Freezes well.

Yields 4-5 dozen

Lecie Roos Resneck

Rolled Meat Pies

Pastry

1¼ cups flour
1 teaspoon salt
½ stick butter
¼ cup shortening
½ cup cold water
(May use frozen phyllo leaves)

Sift flour with salt and finely cut in butter and shortening. Add water slowly to make soft dough. Roll out ¼ " thick and cut with small glass. Add filling and bring edges to center. Frozen phyllo or streudel leaves may also be used in place of dough. Cut in squares about 3" x 5"; put 4 leaves into each pie; brush butter between each leaf. Place teaspoon of filling at small end and roll over.

Filling

1½ cups ground lamb
Butter
½ cup chopped onion
¼ cup pine nuts
Vinegar to taste, slightly sour
Salt and pepper to taste

Fry meat in *butter* until done. Add onion and pine nuts and continue frying until onions are transparent. Add vinegar until slightly sour; add salt and pepper. Let *completely* cool. This is a must! Put about a teaspoon of filling in center of dough rounds and bring edges to center. Brush with melted butter. Bake at 400° until golden. Serve slightly warm. *Pine nuts can be found at the delicatessen.*

Yields 30-40

Joan Thomas Mack

Mushrooms en Croustades

Croustades

1 Loaf Pepperidge Farm White Sandwich Bread

Use small muffin pans or tart pans, well greased. Cut several circles (using a small biscuit cutter) from each slice of bread and press into muffin pans. Bake at 375° until lightly browned, about 10 minutes. These may be made ahead and stored in airtight containers or frozen.

Filling

6 tablespoons butter
4 tablespoons finely chopped shallots
1½ pounds fresh mushrooms
3 level tablespoons flour
1 cup whipping cream
1 teaspoon salt
⅛-¼ teaspoon cayenne
1½ tablespoons finely chopped fresh parsley
1½ tablespoons finely chopped chives
1 teaspoon lemon juice
1 cup grated Cheddar cheese
Butter

Use heavy frying pan. Melt butter and before foam subsides add shallots and stir constantly over moderate heat for about 4 minutes. Do not let them brown. Stir in mushrooms and mix well in butter. Cook 10-15 minutes, stirring occasionally, until moisture has evaporated. Sprinkle flour over mixture and stir until flour is not visible. Pour in cream and bring to a boil. Turn heat to simmer and cook a few minutes longer to remove flour taste. Remove from heat and stir in seasonings. Taste; transfer to bowl; let cool. Refrigerate or freeze until ready to use. Fill crusts slightly heaped, and sprinkle with grated cheese. Dot with butter. Cook at 350° for about 10 minutes. Serve immediately.

Yields 4 dozen — Linda McCutcheon Peavy

Ethereal Mushrooms

- 2 sticks butter or margarine
- 2 cups Burgundy
- 2 teaspoons Worcestershire sauce
- ½ teaspoon dill seed
- ½ teaspoon pepper
- 1½ teaspoons MSG
- ½ teaspoon garlic powder
- 1 cup boiling water
- 2 beef bouillon cubes
- 2 chicken bouillon cubes
- 2 pounds fresh mushrooms

Combine all ingredients except mushrooms in Dutch oven. Bring to slow boil over medium heat. Add mushrooms. Reduce to simmer. Cook 5-6 hours with pot covered. Then remove lid. Mushrooms will be very dark. Cook another 3-4 hours. Serve as appetizer in chafing dish with toothpicks, or warm in ramekins with meal. Freeze in small quantities (1½-2 cups) and thaw for company. *Good for Christmas gifts. Don't be alarmed by the long cooking time. It is well worth the effort.*

Serves 8-10

Julia Miles Blewer

Marinated Mushrooms

- 1½-2 pounds fresh mushrooms
- ⅔ cup white vinegar
- ⅔ cup salad oil
- ¼ cup minced dry onion
- 2½ teaspoons Italian seasoning
- 1 teaspoon each: salt, garlic salt, onion salt, Accent, sugar
- ½ teaspoon pepper

Slice mushrooms in half, lengthwise, or into small pieces, depending on their size. Put in bowl and set aside. In small saucepan combine remaining ingredients and stir until well mixed. Bring to a boil. Pour over mushrooms. Let cool. Cover and place in refrigerator at least 24 hours. When ready to serve, pour off excess marinade and serve on Melba toast.

Serves 10-12

Leslie Holder

Mushroom Petals

1 stick butter
9 ounces cream cheese
1½ cups flour

Mix butter, cream cheese and flour with a pastry blender. Shape into a ball and chill for 30 minutes.

Filling

3 tablespoons butter
1 medium onion, chopped
2 tablespoons flour
1 6-ounce can mushrooms, finely chopped
¼ teaspoon thyme
½ teaspoon salt
½ cup sour cream
Ground pepper to taste

Sauté onion in butter; add flour, mushrooms and seasonings. Cook for a few minutes; then add sour cream. Roll out pastry to ¼″ thickness and cut into 3″ circles. Use 1 teaspoon filling for each piece of pastry. Fold in half and crimp edges as for fried pies. Bake at 400° for 15 minutes on cookie sheet, or freeze and bake at a later time.

Serves 10

Carolyn Hamel Griffen

Store mushrooms in brown paper bag to last longer.

Stuffed Mushroom Caps

- 3 slices bacon, cooked, drained and crumbled
- ⅓ cup grated sharp Cheddar cheese
- 1 teaspoon chopped chives
- ⅛ teaspoon salt
- Pinch black pepper, onion powder, garlic powder
- 12 medium mushroom caps, washed and dried
- ¼ cup melted butter

Combine bacon with cheese, chives and seasonings. Dip mushroom caps in butter and place on broiler pan. (Place on serving dish if heating in microwave oven.) Fill each cap with rounded teaspoon of bacon-cheese mixture. Place tops of mushrooms 4" from broiler unit. Broil for 6-8 minutes. (In a microwave oven, heat 2-4 minutes.)

Yields 12

Patti Moore Chidlow

Kentucky Pâté

- 8-10 ounces raw chicken livers
- 2 sticks butter
- ⅓ cup sauterne (chicken broth may be substituted)
- 4 eggs
- 1 tablespoon fresh tarragon
- 1 teaspoon salt
- Mayonnaise, parsley, paprika for garnish

Place all ingredients in blender on high. Butter foil; press in loaf pan. Pour in contents from blender. Set loaf pan in pan of water filled to top edge of loaf pan. Bake at 350° for 30-40 minutes, or until firm. Ice with mayonnaise and garnish with parsley and paprika.

Serves 12-15

Susan Sperry Cage

Roasted Pecans

4 cups pecan halves
3 tablespoons butter, melted
1 teaspoon salt

Put pecans 1 or 2 layers deep in a jelly-roll or roasting pan. Roast at 250° for 30 minutes stirring once. Remove from the oven and pour melted butter over pecans. Stir with a wooden spoon to coat each nut. Return to the oven for 30-40 minutes, stirring 2 or 3 times. Remove, add salt, stirring to coat nuts and roast 5-10 minutes more. Store in airtight metal or plastic container.

Caroline Haywood Dickson

Spicy Cashews

2 cups cashews
1½ tablespoons margarine
1 teaspoon salt
¼ teaspoon cayenne
½ teaspoon ground cumin
½ teaspoon ground coriander

Sauté nuts in margarine 3 minutes. Drain. Mix nuts with spices. *Good with cocktails. Hot and spicy.*

Yields 2 cups

Martha Turner Schober

Little Pizzas

1 pound ground beef
1 pound bulk sausage
1 pound cubed Velveeta cheese
Italian seasoning to taste
Garlic powder to taste
Sliced party rye bread

Brown ground beef and sausage. Drain. Add cubed cheese and stir until melted. Add Italian seasoning and garlic powder. Spoon onto party rye slices. Bake at 400° until cheese is bubbly. Freezes well.

Yields 30-40

Jeanne Futch Muslow

Crabmeat Canapés

1 8-ounce package cream cheese
1 3-ounce package cream cheese
½ small onion, chopped
2 tablespoons lemon juice
2 tablespoons Worcestershire sauce
Dash garlic salt
Chili sauce
1 6-ounce can white crabmeat
Parsley

The night before serving, mix cream cheese, onion, lemon juice, Worcestershire sauce and garlic salt. Can be done quickly in food processor. Chill overnight. The next day, spread cream cheese mixture in a plate-size serving dish. Spread a layer of chili sauce over cream cheese. Clean shell out of crabmeat. Crumble crabmeat over chili sauce. Sprinkle parsley over crabmeat. Serve immediately with crackers. *May combine all ingredients and use as a dip for vegetables.*

Serves 10-12

Jack Burroughs

Crabmeat Peggy

½ cup sliced almonds
½ stick butter, melted
1 6½-ounce can Alaskan king crabmeat
½ cup rêmoulade sauce
1 teaspoon Worcestershire sauce
2 tablespoons Miracle Whip

Pan fry almonds in butter until slightly brown. Mix in crabmeat and heat until hot. Stir in rêmoulade and Worcestershire sauce. Serve in chafing dish with Melba toast or crackers. *May use fresh crabmeat.*

Serves 10-12

Michele Armstrong
Qvistgaard-Petersen

Crabmeat Mold

½ 10¾-ounce can mushroom soup
1 8-ounce package cream cheese
1 envelope unflavored gelatin
1 small onion, chopped
½ cup celery, chopped
Dash salt
½ cup mayonnaise
2 6½-ounce cans crabmeat (can be frozen)

Heat soup. Add cream cheese and stir until it melts. Dissolve gelatin in ⅛ cup water. Add to soup and cheese mixture. Add onion, celery, salt, mayonnaise and crabmeat. Pour into greased quart-size mold. Chill several hours. Serve with wafers. *May be served on lettuce as a salad.*

Serves 8 — Janie Harris Tipton

Crabmeat Rockefeller

2 10-ounce packages frozen chopped spinach
1 pound lump crabmeat
4-8 green onions and tops, chopped
1 stick butter
1 8-ounce package cream cheese, softened
Parmesan cheese
Tabasco
Garlic salt

Cook spinach and drain well. Sauté the crabmeat with onions in butter. Add cream cheese and crabmeat mixture to spinach. Mix well. Season with plenty of Parmesan cheese, Tabasco and garlic salt. Serve in chafing dish with Melba rounds.

Serves 20-30 — O. Delton Harrison, Jr.

Crabmeat Remick

1 pound fresh crabmeat
6 slices crisp bacon
1½ cups mayonnaise
½ cup chili sauce
1 teaspoon tarragon
½ teaspoon vinegar
1 teaspoon dry mustard
½ teaspoon Tabasco
½ teaspoon paprika
Salt to taste

Pick crabmeat and then divide into 6 lightly buttered ramekins. Top each portion with 1 slice crumbled bacon. In a bowl, combine remaining ingredients. Top crabmeat with this mixture. Put the ramekins in a preheated broiler for 2 minutes or until bubbly. Do not put too close to heating element or the sauce will burn and the crabmeat will be cold. Can also be served in chafing dish as hot appetizer.

Serves 6

Judith Crow Quinn

Marinated Crayfish

½ cup vegetable oil
2 tablespoons chopped onion
2 tablespoons parsley
2 tablespoons vinegar
1 tablespoon lemon juice
¾ teaspoon salt
¼ heaping teaspoon dry mustard
1 pound boiled, peeled crayfish tails

Mix all ingredients except crayfish in blender. Pour over crayfish in a 1-quart jar. Turn frequently for 24 hours. May also use shrimp.

Serves 12

Ginny Clay Hill

Hot Oysters Supreme

1 cup chopped white onion
1 cup chopped celery
2 sticks butter, divided
2 pints oysters
3 slices bread
Bread crumbs
1 cup snipped green onion tops
1 cup snipped parsley
3 eggs, beaten
Dash cayenne pepper
Salt and pepper to taste

Sautê white onion and celery in 1 stick of butter. Place oysters in a bowl with 3 slices of bread. Let soak. Add enough bread crumbs to absorb all liquid on oysters. Add oysters with bread, green onion tops and parsley to skillet. Remove from fire and slowly add beaten eggs. Cook slowly until mixture is thick, about 10 minutes. After mixture has finished cooking, add cayenne pepper, salt and pepper to taste, and remaining stick of butter. Serve hot in chafing dish with Melba rounds. *May also be served in patty shells for a ladies' luncheon.*

Serves 8-10

Dianne Guy Mapp

Creamy Shrimp Appetizer

1 8-ounce package cream cheese
½ cup mayonnaise
¼ cup French dressing
2 ribs celery, chopped
2 tablespoons chopped green pepper
½ medium onion, chopped
Juice ½ lemon
2 pounds boiled and peeled medium-size shrimp
Salt to taste

Mix cream cheese, mayonnaise and French dressing. Add remaining ingredients in order given, stirring in shrimp last. Chill at least 3 hours before serving.

Yields 4 cups

Carolyn Hamel Griffen

Rice and Shrimp Deviled Eggs

1 dozen hard-boiled eggs
1½ cups raw rice
1 pound raw shrimp
¾ cup chopped celery
½ medium green pepper, chopped
1 large bunch green onions, chopped
½ cup Italian dressing
½ cup mayonnaise
Red pepper to taste
Lemon pepper to taste
Garlic salt to taste

Halve eggs and scoop out yolks. Place halved egg whites on platter and reserve yolks for stuffing. Cook rice in 3 cups of water. Cool. Cook, peel and chop shrimp. Mix shrimp, rice and yolks together. Add the Italian dressing, mayonnaise and seasonings. Stuff egg whites and reserve any remaining mixture to serve on crackers. Serve mixture in center of platter on bed of lettuce. Surround with eggs. *Garnish eggs with paprika, and platter with parsley and lemon slices.*

Yields 24 halves

Jeanne Futch Muslow

Spicy Shrimp

4 pounds shrimp cooked in salted water with shrimp boil
¾ cup olive oil
½ cup white vinegar
3 tablespoons paprika
1½ tablespoons white pepper
1 tablespoon salt
1 cup Creole mustard
½ cup fresh horseradish
8 green onions, sliced
4 diced celery hearts
2 cups mayonnaise

Mix oil, vinegar, paprika, white pepper and salt. Add Creole mustard and horseradish and mix well. Stir in onion, celery and mayonnaise. Add cooked shrimp. Sauce should cover the shrimp. Marinate about 24 hours. The longer it marinates the better it will be. Keep refrigerated. Pour into shells or ramekins.

Serves 6-8 luncheon
15-20 appetizer

Judith Crow Quinn

Shrimp Mousse

6 cups cooked and chopped shrimp or 4 pounds raw shrimp (cooked in crab boil seasoning)
2 cups sour cream
16 ounces cream cheese, softened
1 cup mayonnaise
½ cup finely chopped green pepper
½ cup chopped shallots or green onions
Juice 2 lemons
½ cup boiling water
2 envelopes unflavored gelatin
½ teaspoon Tabasco or more, if desired
1 teaspoon salt or more, if desired
1 tablespoon Worcestershire sauce
Red food coloring

If using raw shrimp, cook in crab boil following package directions. Peel shrimp and chop. Mix sour cream, cream cheese and mayonnaise. Add green pepper, onions and lemon juice. Dissolve gelatin in water; add Tabasco, salt and Worcestershire sauce. Add this mixture and shrimp to sour cream mixture, adding enough food coloring to give a pink color. Pour into a mold immediately. Chill 6-8 hours to set well. May be served with crackers or put in individual molds and served on sliced avocados.

Serves 10-15 appetizer
6 luncheon

Rebecca Strohmaier Roberts

Starting-Gate Shrimp

1 3-ounce bag shrimp boil
5 pounds fresh shrimp
2 onions, thinly sliced
Juice 3 lemons
Lemon slices
1 bunch fresh parsley, chopped
1 quart mayonnaise
Tabasco
Salt
Pepper, freshly ground, to taste

Cook shrimp in shrimp boil until done. Cool and peel shrimp. Add onions, lemon juice and several thin lemon slices. Add parsley and mayonnaise. Add Tabasco, salt and pepper to taste. Toss well. Let sit overnight in refrigerator in covered dish.

Serves 25

Irene Klein Hermer

Shrimp and Artichoke Appetizer

5 pounds raw shrimp
Shrimp boil
5 10-ounce packages frozen artichoke hearts or five 8½-ounce cans, drained
Juice 1 lemon
½ cup capers
¼ cup chopped basil leaves
¼ cup chopped onion
Freshly ground black pepper
2½ cups mayonnaise
Tabasco to taste
1 tablespoon seasoning salt

Place shrimp boil in water and boil 10 minutes. Add shrimp and boil 7 minutes; drain immediately and allow to cool. Cook artichoke hearts according to package directions and cool, or rinse canned artichokes. Peel shrimp and toss with remaining ingredients adding artichokes last. Stir to coat. Serve on lettuce leaf for appetizer or with toothpicks at party.

Serves 12 luncheon
20-30 hors d'oeuvre

Nancy McCullough Humphrey

Liz's Shrimp Mold

1 8-ounce package cream cheese
1½ envelopes unflavored gelatin
½ cup cold water
¾ cup finely chopped celery
1 cup mayonnaise
2 teaspoons finely grated onion
1½-2 cups chopped freshly cooked shrimp
Salt and freshly ground pepper
Cayenne
Seasoned salt
Worcestershire sauce
Paprika
Olive slice
Carrot curls

In food processor or mixer, whip cream cheese. Add gelatin which has been softened in water. Add rest of ingredients and mix on medium speed. Season to taste with salt, freshly ground black pepper, cayenne, seasoned salt and Worcestershire sauce. Lightly butter a large fish mold and pour in shrimp mixture. Chill until firm. After unmolding, sprinkle with paprika and decorate with an olive slice for the eye and carrot curls for fins.

Serves 12-15

Louise Jackson

Steak Tartare

2 pounds freshly ground sirloin
10 minced anchovy filets
2 beaten egg yolks
¼ teaspoon dry mustard
½ cup drained capers
½ cup grated onion
1½ teaspoons salt
¼ teaspoon pepper
Thin pumpernickel bread
Sliced boiled egg
Parsley sprigs

IT IS VERY IMPORTANT THAT YOUR MEAT BE THE FRESHEST POSSIBLE. Grind meat in food processor with on/off motion. Mix in all other ingredients except bread, boiled egg and parsley. Shape in mound. This may be served immediately or put in rectangular baking pan and placed in the refrigerator for 2-3 hours to set. Tap pan and unmold on cold platter. Garnish with parsely and sliced egg and serve with pumpernickel.

Serves 12-15 Martha Turner Schober

Spicy Sausage Balls

2 pounds hot sausage
1 cup catsup
½ cup light brown sugar
2 tablespoons soy sauce
½ cup wine vinegar
1 teaspoon ginger

Roll sausage into balls about the size of pecans. Broil in oven about 10 minutes. Turn while broiling. Drain. Mix sauce in pan and heat until bubbly. Add sausage balls to sauce. Serve in chafing dish. *Men especially love this.*

Yields 80 Edie Broyles Williams

Vegetables with Crabmeat

1 7½-ounce can white crabmeat or 1 6-ounce package frozen king crabmeat
1 8-ounce package cream cheese
1 cup sour cream
2 tablespoons chili sauce or catsup
1 tablespoon grated onion
1 tablespoon lemon juice
¼ teaspoon Worcestershire sauce
Dash Tabasco
Salt to taste
Dash garlic powder

Drain and slice canned crabmeat, or defrost, drain and slice frozen crabmeat. Set aside. Soften cream cheese; blend well with sour cream. Add chili sauce or catsup and rest of ingredients. Blend well. Gently fold in sliced crabmeat. Chill. Serve with vegetable dippers: celery, carrot sticks, cauliflowerettes, radishes, etc. *May use fresh crabmeat.*

Yields 2 cups

Anne Krison Mitchell

Marinated Vegetables

1 pound mushrooms
1 8-ounce can artichoke hearts
⅓ cup chopped green onions
2 ounces stuffed olives
1 tablespoon chopped pimientos

Wash and trim mushrooms; quarter and put in boiling salted water. Boil 1 minute. Drain and put in bowl. Add remaining ingredients. Pour following dressing over vegetables and marinate at least 4 hours. Serve with toothpicks or as a salad on lettuce.

½ cup olive oil
1 tablespoon sherry
¼ teaspoon each: oregano, garlic salt and cracked pepper
½ teaspoon salt
½ cup wine vinegar, white or red

Serves 6 salad
12 appetizer

Mary Brownfield Richard

Bacon-Wrapped Water Chestnuts

- 1 8-ounce can water chestnuts, drained, and cut in half
- Soy sauce
- Brown sugar
- 5 slices bacon, each cut into 4 pieces

Marinate water chestnuts in soy sauce for 30 minutes. Roll in brown sugar and wrap in bacon pieces. Secure with a toothpick. Bake at 400° for 20 minutes in broiler pan so chestnuts will not sit in grease. Can be done ahead and reheated for 5 minutes at 350° before serving.

Serves 8 — Zama Blanchard Jones

Artichoke Soup

- ½ cup chopped shallots
- 1 rib celery, chopped
- 1 carrot, chopped
- 1 bay leaf
- Pinch thyme
- 1 stick butter
- 1 quart chicken broth
- 1 cup frozen artichoke hearts, cooked and chopped
- 2 egg yolks, beaten
- 1 cup whipping cream
- Salt and pepper

Sauté first 5 ingredients in butter. Add broth and simmer 15 minutes. Add artichoke hearts and simmer 10 minutes. Add yolks mixed with cream. Salt and pepper to taste.

Serves 8 — Mary Graham Pate

Chilled Cream of Asparagus Soup

- 1 10¾-ounce can cream of asparagus soup
- 10¾ ounces milk
- ½ cup sour cream
- 3 shakes Tabasco
- 1 teaspoon celery salt
- ½ cup cracked ice

Put all ingredients in the blender and mix. Serve cold. Pretty garnished with thin slices of cucumber or avocado and sprinkled with paprika.

Serves 4 — Ellen Woodruff Reynolds

Chilled Avocado Soup

2 cups chicken broth
1 large garlic clove, minced
1 large or 2 small avocados, peeled and quartered
¼ teaspoon Tabasco
Dash salt
Juice ½ lemon
Chopped chives

Simmer chicken broth and garlic for 5 minutes. Let chill. Put next 4 ingredients in blender and blend well. Add to broth and refrigerate until cold. Sprinkle with chives. Do not prepare this more than 1 day ahead.

Serves 6-8 — Sara Scott Hargrove

Cool-as-a-Cucumber Soup

2 large cucumbers, peeled and sliced
1 green pepper, chopped
½ cup finely chopped onion
3 cups chicken stock
1 cup sour cream or yogurt
1 tablespoon parsley, finely chopped
½ teaspoon fresh dill, finely chopped, or ¼ teaspoon dried dill
Salt and pepper to taste

Place cucumber in saucepan, reserving 4 round slices for garnish. Add green pepper, onion and chicken stock. Simmer covered for 20 minutes. Strain vegetables, reserving the stock. Place sour cream, parsley and dill in food processor or blender. Add the stock, keeping machine running. (Add some cubed raw cucumber at the end for crunch.) Season to taste. Chill. *Serve in crystal long-stemmed goblets, garnished with cucumber, sour cream and chopped dill, if desired. Zucchini squash may be substituted for cucumber.*

Serves 4 — Carolyn Evers Bussey

Corn and Crab Chowder

¼ cup chopped onion
½ stick butter
2 teaspoons flour
½ teaspoon curry powder
2 12-ounce cans shoe peg corn
6 cups milk
1 cup whipping cream
1 teaspoon salt
1 teaspoon pepper
2 tablespoons parsley flakes
2 6½-ounce cans crab meat or ½ pound backfin crab

Sauté onion in butter. Stir in flour and curry powder. Add the remaining ingredients and mix well. Heat, but do not boil. *May be made the day before.*

Serves 10

Virginia Palmer Harris

Cheese Soup

½ stick butter
½ cup diced onions
½ cup diced carrots
½ cup diced celery
¼ cup flour
1½ tablespoons cornstarch
1 quart chicken stock
1 quart milk
⅛ teaspoon baking soda
1½ pounds Old English Kraft Cheese, shredded
Sherry (optional)

Sauté diced vegetables in butter until soft. Add flour and stir. Combine cornstarch with a little stock. Add remaining stock to vegetable mix; stir in cornstarch mix. Add milk, then baking soda. Add cheese and simmer a few minutes. Add sherry to taste.

Serves 8

Judy Lind Chidlow

Five-Star Soup

- 1 pound dried white navy beans
- 6 cups boiling water
- 1 shank end, 3 pound ham, fully cooked, cut up
- 4 cups shredded cabbage (about 1 pound)
- 2 cups thinly sliced carrots (about 7 medium-size)
- 1 cup chopped onion
- 1 cup chopped celery
- 1 clove garlic, minced
- 1 12-ounce package smoked sausage, thinly sliced
- 1 16-ounce can tomatoes
- 6 cups more water
- 1 teaspoon salt
- ½ teaspoon pepper
- 1 cup small elbow macaroni (½ of 8-ounce package)
- Chopped parsley

Pick over beans; rinse and place in large bowl. Pour boiling water over; cover; let stand 1 hour. Trim several small pieces of fat from ham; melt in kettle or Dutch oven. Stir in cabbage, carrots, onions, celery and garlic. Sauté slowly, stirring often, for 20 minutes. Remove and set aside.

Pour beans and liquid into another kettle. Add ham, sliced sausage, tomatoes, salt, pepper and 6 cups more water. Heat to boiling; cover; simmer 1½ hours. Stir in sautéed vegetables and cook 30 minutes, or until beans are tender. Stir in macaroni. Continue cooking 15 minutes longer, until macaroni is tender. Ladle into soup tureen or bowls. Sprinkle with chopped parsley. *Tastes better the second day.*

Serves 8-10

Vicki Longmire Hanna

Thicken soups, gravies and sauces by gradually adding instant potato flakes. The flakes never lump when added directly as flour and cornstarch do, and they add to the texture.

Gazpacho

2 large tomatoes, peeled
1 large cucumber
1 medium onion
1 medium green pepper
1 2-ounce jar pimientos
2 12-ounce cans tomato juice, divided

⅓ cup olive oil
⅓ cup red wine vinegar
¼ teaspoon Tabasco
1¼-1½ teaspoons salt
Pepper to taste

In blender combine first 5 ingredients and ½ cup tomato juice. Blend at high speed. In a bowl mix vegetable purée with remaining tomato juice and the rest of ingredients. Refrigerate. Give time for flavors to blend. Serve with croutons. *This recipe doubles well.*

Serves 10-12

Virginia Doyle Hardy

Gazpacho Seville

1½ ounces sliced almonds
4 slices French bread
1 medium tomato
½ cucumber, peeled
1 small clove garlic

1 tablespoon olive oil
Vinegar to taste (start with 2 tablespoons)
Salt and pepper to taste
Ice water

In blender, pulverize almonds and bread. Add next 4 ingredients and blend until smooth. Adjust vinegar and seasonings to taste. Add enough ice water to fill blender and safely blend without overflowing. If you do not have time to chill in refrigerator, use some crushed ice with the water. Serve with assorted diced garnishes: hard-boiled eggs, croutons, tomatoes, cucumbers, bell peppers or onions.

Serves 4

Marion Wiener Weiss

Maritata
(Italian Wedding Soup)

6 cups hot rich meat broth (all chicken or beef, or combination of these, freshly made or canned)
2 ounces (⅛ of 1-pound package) vermicelli noodles
1 stick unsalted butter, softened
¾ cup freshly grated Parmesan cheese
4 egg yolks
1 cup whipping cream

Let egg yolks, butter and cheese come to room temperature. Bring broth to boiling over direct heat (on a range top or over a denatured alcohol flame). Add vermicelli noodles (broken if desired) and cook uncovered for 5-8 minutes or until noodles are tender.

In a bowl blend the butter, cheese and egg yolks, then gradually beat in the cream. (If you cook at the table, prepare this mixture in the kitchen). Spoon a small amount of the hot broth into the cream mixture, stirring constantly; then pour this mixture back into the hot broth, stirring constantly. Extinguish heat, if in chafing dish, or remove from heat. Serve while piping hot. *This is very interesting prepared and served as a first course from a chafing dish.*

Serves 6 entrée
10 first course

James A. Reeder

Gretl's Soup Stock

3 quarts water
Beef soupbone
3 ribs celery
2 carrots
Onion, chopped

Make soup stock by simmering the above for several hours. Strain to have a clear broth. Season to taste.

Continued...

Liver Dumpling Soup

¼ pound liver, ground in food processor
2 slices onion
1 egg
Salt and pepper
Bread crumbs
1 teaspoon lemon rind

Mix all ingredients into medium hard paste. Let stand 5 minutes or more. With teaspoon drop little dumplings into above broth. Let simmer 10 minutes.

Serves 8-10

Butter Dumpling Soup

2 teaspoons butter
1 egg
Nutmeg
Salt and pepper to taste
Flour

Mix first 5 ingredients well. Add flour until a medium hard paste is formed. Let stand for 15 minutes. With teaspoon, drop little dumplings into above broth. Simmer for 20 minutes.

Serves 8-10

Gretl's Restaurant
Aspen, Colorado

Fresh Mushroom Soup

1 pound fresh mushrooms, sliced
6 cups beef broth (may use cubes)
3 tablespoons butter
1 clove garlic, minced
⅓ cup shallots, chopped
3 tablespoons flour
1 pint whipping cream
Parsley
Whole mushrooms

Cook mushrooms and beef broth for 20 minutes. Meanwhile melt butter and sauté garlic and shallots until soft. Add flour and cook 5 minutes. Do not brown. Add mushrooms and broth. May be prepared ahead to this point. Just before serving add whipping cream. Float parsley and mushrooms on top for garnish.

Serves 6

Peggy Gaffney Shemwell

Minestrone

- 3 pounds ground round or very lean chuck
- 3 heaping tablespoons Italian seasoning
- 3 teaspoons salt
- 1 teaspoon black pepper
- 1 large lemon, halved, reserve juice and rind
- 3 eggs
- 1 cup cooking sherry, divided
- 1 very large frying or baking hen with all excess fat removed and cooked whole
- 4 large onions, chopped
- 4-6 large whole cloves garlic
- 3 large tablespoons solid chicken base, not bouillon cubes
- ½ cup barley
- 3 large green peppers, chopped
- 1 large hot pepper
- 1 large bay leaf
- 2 large stalks celery, use tops and hearts, chopped diagonally in large pieces, and divided
- 2 29-ounce cans whole tomatoes and juice (chop by hand)
- 2 29-ounce cans cut green beans or fresh, reserve juice
- 3 29-ounce cans sliced carrots, reserve juice
- 2 29-ounce cans whole kernel corn, reserve juice
- 2 29-ounce cans LeSueur English peas, reserve juice
- 2 8-ounce cans water chestnuts, sliced or diced
- 3-4 large turnip roots, chopped and diced
- 2 cups chopped fresh mushrooms
- ½ cup chopped fresh dill
- Fresh parsley, snipped
- 1 pound pasta, any form of small variety, or linguine or fettuccine broken into pieces
- Parmesan or Romano cheese
- Fresh or frozen chives

Overnight marinate the ground beef mixed with Italian seasoning, salt, black pepper, juice of lemon (save rind), eggs, ½ cup sherry. Mix well. Cover tightly and place in refrigerator.

In very large soup pot (12 quarts), fill half full with water, adding whole chicken, onions, garlic, chicken base, barley, lemon rind in halves, green pepper, hot pepper, bay leaf and ½ cup cooking sherry. Add 1 stalk of chopped celery. Cover and bring to rolling boil. Turn heat to medium and cook until chicken is tender, about 1 hour.

Continued...

While chicken is cooking, remove ground beef from refrigerator and shape into meatballs, very small, no larger than a dime. Remove chicken when done and let cool. Bone, remove all skin and add chopped chicken to broth, skimming to remove excess fat. Remove whole garlic cloves with slotted spoon. If using fresh carrots, turnip roots or any fresh vegetable, they should be added the same time chopped chicken is returned to stock as they need longer cooking time.

If pot is very full, divide mixture into pot of comparable size. If you do this, everything from this point on is to be halved.

Next add chopped tomatoes and juice and bring to rolling boil as you add meatballs one by one. Add remaining stalk chopped celery. Begin adding canned vegetables and juice in order listed. Add dill, parsley and pasta. Cover and turn off. Let the heat cook the pasta.

After 1 hour, skim for excess fat from meatballs. If you should need to add water, do so until vegetables are added. Be sure to taste for salt. Serve with sprinkled chives or scallions. Let everyone add cheese.

Never reheat entire pot of soup, only amount to be served. Improves with age and freezes well.

Serves 36 Caroline Jones Ellison

A dash of brown sugar won't sweeten the gravy or spoil the flavor, but it will reduce a too-salty taste in gravy or soup. Potatoes will do the same.

Potato-Leek Soup

1 large onion, chopped
3 leeks (washed, peeled, and chopped, saving tops)
1 stick butter
8 cups rich, lean chicken broth
3 large potatoes, peeled and diced into ¼″ pieces
1-2 teaspoons salt
1 teaspoon white pepper
1 teaspoon MSG
2 cups half and half
Leek tops, minced for garnish

Cut off white onion part of leek. Peel outer layer. Rinse thoroughly. Cut into quarters all the way down to the base but not through. Chop. Melt butter in 3-quart saucepan. Add onions and leeks. Sauté until the liquid is clear and not milky. Rinse starch from potatoes. Add chicken stock to onion-butter mixture. Add diced potatoes. Simmer 20-25 minutes, or until potatoes are done. Wash and drain leek tops. Dice very small some of the darkest green and add to the soup as garnish just before serving. Add salt, MSG and pepper. Before serving, blend in half and half (about 1 cup half and half to 4 cups chicken stock). Heat thoroughly and garnish with minced leek tops. If not serving the entire soup at one time but small portions on succeeding days, take out the amount of soup to be served, add half and half, heat and garnish. This avoids reheating the cream several times. This soup will keep about a week. *The secret of this soup is a good, rich, lean chicken stock. Vichyssoise can be made by using less stock and more cream. Serve chilled.*

Serves 10-12 — Norman Kinsey

Freeze meat or chicken stock in ice cube trays. Put in plastic bags and keep in freezer to season soups and sauces.

Matzo Ball Soup

- 2 tablespoons margarine or chicken fat
- 2 green onions, only a little of tops
- 1 cup boiling water
- ¾ cup matzo meal
- 2 eggs, beaten
- ¼-½ cup chopped almonds
- ½ teaspoon salt or to taste
- ¼ cup chopped parsley or to taste
- Chicken broth

Sauté chopped onions in margarine. Add boiling water. Turn off heat; add meal and stir until water is absorbed. Put mixture into bowl and cool. When cooled, add well beaten eggs and almonds, parsley and salt. Mix well. Put in refrigerator. Roll chilled mixture into balls the size desired. Cook in gently boiling broth about 10 minutes. Matzo balls rise to the top and look fluffy when done. Can mix early in day, chill and cook at dinner time. *These are like dumplings and can be precooked in broth and then added to gravy of pot roast or chicken fricassee.*

Serves 3-4

Frances Shohl Peiser

French Onion Soup

- ½ stick butter
- 2½ pounds onions, sliced
- 1½ quarts beef stock
- 1 pint chicken stock
- 2 tablespoons Worcestershire sauce
- 1 bay leaf
- 1½ teaspoons celery salt
- 1 teaspoon black pepper
- 1 teaspoon thyme
- 1 teaspoon basil
- Salt
- Parmesan cheese
- French bread

Heat butter in iron skillet. Add onions and brown well, stirring constantly for about 15-20 minutes. Transfer to large pot. Add beef and chicken stock, Worcestershire, bay leaf, celery salt, black pepper, thyme, basil and salt. Simmer 45 minutes to 1 hour. Remove bay leaf. Sprinkle Parmesan cheese on French bread slices and toast until cheese melts a little. Top each serving of soup with 1 slice.

Yields 2 quarts

Carolyn Evers Bussey

Oyster Bisque

1½ sticks butter
2½ cups milk
1 cup half and half
1 bunch green onions, finely chopped
3 ribs celery, finely chopped
3 tablespoons flour
1 quart shucked fresh oysters
Salt
Red pepper
Paprika

Use a 4-quart soup pot. Melt butter in pot. Heat milk and half and half separately. Add green onions and celery to butter and sauté over low heat until clear, but not brown. Stir in flour. Chop 10 oysters and add to pot. Stir until smooth; then add heated milk and cream; continue stirring. Season with salt, pepper and paprika. Add remaining oysters and juice. Do not let soup boil. When edges of oysters curl, remove pot from heat and cover. Let sit for at least 30 minutes.

Serves 6-8

Patricia Duyer Scarborough

Cream of Tomato Soup

⅓ cup minced onion
2 tablespoons butter
2 tablespoons flour
½ teaspoon basil
½ teaspoon oregano
1¼ teaspoon salt
⅛ teaspoon pepper
1 tablespoon tomato paste
1 tablespoon light brown sugar
1 10½-ounce can condensed beef consommé
1 cup milk
1 1-pound 12-ounce can tomatoes

Stir-fry onion in butter in large, heavy pan until limp (3-5 minutes). Blend in flour, herbs, salt and pepper. Stir in tomato paste, brown sugar, consommé and milk. Heat, stirring constantly until thickened and smooth. Purée tomatoes, a little at a time, in a blender at low speed. Add to pan and simmer uncovered 12-15 minutes. Do not allow to boil.

Serves 6

Melissa LaFleur Simon

Senegalese Soup

5 tablespoons butter, divided
1 medium onion, chopped
1 medium carrot, finely chopped
1 rib celery, finely chopped
1 heaping teaspoon curry powder
4 10-ounce cans chicken broth
2 small cinnamon sticks
2 bay leaves
½ teaspoon whole cloves
1 tablespoon tomato purée
1 tablespoon currant jelly
2 tablespoons almond paste
Salt and white pepper to taste
3 tablespoons flour
2 cups whipping cream
1 3½-ounce can shredded coconut, toasted

Melt 2 tablespoons of butter in large saucepan; add onions, carrots and celery. Sauté gently until vegetables "color". Slowly stir in curry powder and chicken broth until mixture is smooth; add cinnamon sticks, bay leaves, cloves, tomato purée, almond paste, currant jelly, salt and pepper. Bring slowly to a boil and simmer 1 hour. Meanwhile, mix remaining 3 tablespoons butter with flour until smooth paste forms. Add this paste bit by bit to liquid, stirring constantly until smooth. Simmer until soup thickens. *Strain.* Chill for 2 hours. Just before serving, blend in cream and garnish with coconut. To toast coconut, spread evenly on cookie sheet in 250° oven. Shake frequently until brown and crisp. *For curry lovers. Excellent first course with chicken entrée.*

Serves 6-8

Catherine Rhody Bigger

Rice may be powdered in a food processor or blender and added to a simmering soup near the end of cooking to thicken and enrich it.

Cream of Spinach Soup

½ stick butter, divided
½ cup chopped Bermuda onion
1 pound fresh spinach or 1 10-ounce package frozen (defrost and squeeze)
3 tablespoons flour
6 cups chicken stock
Salt and pepper to taste
2 egg yolks
½ cup whipping cream or half and half
Nutmeg to taste

Melt 3 tablespoons butter in saucepan and cook the onion until translucent. Do not brown. Wash and stem spinach. Shred leaves with a knife or chop in food processor. Dry on a towel. Add spinach to saucepan. Cook over low heat, stirring with a fork just until leaves are wilted. Sprinkle with flour. Pour in stock, stirring constantly. Bring to a boil. Purée mixture; add salt and pepper and return to saucepan. In a small bowl combine yolks and cream. Beat lightly; then add a little of the hot soup. When blended, pour the egg mixture into the saucepan stirring rapidly. Heat thoroughly but do not boil or the soup will curdle. Add a little nutmeg and stir in the remaining tablespoon of butter. Serve immediately. May be garnished with chopped parsley or croutons.

Serves 6 — Mary Virginia Saunders Quinn

Rubescent Tisane

6 cups tomato juice
1 14-ounce can beef bouillon
1 small onion, finely chopped
3 ribs celery, minced
Juice 1 large lemon, strained
¼ teaspoon dried basil
¼ teaspoon dried savory
¼ teaspoon dried parsley
¼ teaspoon salt
1 green pepper, coarsely chopped
Black pepper, coarsely ground

Place all ingredients except green pepper and coarse black pepper in a large saucepan. Simmer over low heat for 20 minutes. Serve hot in ceramic mugs and sprinkle with chopped green pepper and coarsely ground black pepper.

Serves 10 — Catherine Rhody Bigger

Cheesy Zucchini Soup

2 medium zucchini, grated
2 medium carrots, grated
1 medium onion, chopped
½ stick margarine or butter
4 tablespoons flour
2 13½-ounce cans chicken broth
4 ounces grated Monterey Jack cheese
1 cup milk
Salt and pepper to taste

Place grated zucchini in a colander; sprinkle with salt and let sit for 30 minutes. Drain well. Sauté grated and chopped vegetables in butter, until slightly limp. Stir in flour and cook over low heat for 5 minutes, stirring constantly. Slowly add chicken broth and stir until smooth. Add grated cheese and stir until melted. Add milk; season to taste. Do not boil.

Serves 6 — Margaret Hunkin Crow

Bayou Apple Salad

2 apples, chopped
2 ribs celery, chopped
½ cup chopped pecans
½ cup mayonnaise
2 tablespoons sugar
2 tablespoons vinegar
1 teaspoon mustard
½ cup whipping cream, whipped

Mix the first 3 ingredients. Combine the last 5 ingredients. Pour over first mixture and stir gently.

Serves 4 — Martha Tomlinson Atkins

To speed ripening, place unripe fruit in a plastic bag along with a ripe apple, or a similar piece of ripe fruit. Ripe fruit exudes a natural gas which speeds up the ripening of the other fruit.

Blueberry Salad

1 3-ounce box blackberry gelatin
1 3-ounce box lemon gelatin
2 cups boiling water
1 teaspoon lemon juice
1 15-ounce can wild blueberries in light syrup, reserve liquid
1 15½-ounce can crushed pineapple in unsweetened juice, reserve liquid

Dissolve both flavors of gelatin in boiling water. Add lemon juice and juice from blueberries and pineapple. Fold in fruits and refrigerate in individual molds or 2-quart rectangular mold.

Topping

2 3-ounce packages cream cheese, softened
¼ cup sugar
1 8-ounce carton sour cream
1 teaspoon vanilla
½ teaspoon salt
½ teaspoon lemon juice
1 cup chopped pecans

Mix first 6 ingredients together. Fold in pecans. Spread topping on unmolded salads at serving time.

Serves 8-10

Cookbook Committee

Hearts of Palm Salad

1 14-ounce can hearts of palm, drained
1 15¼-ounce can pineapple chunks, drained
1 2-ounce jar pimientos, sliced (or more according to taste)
4 ounces poppy seed dressing

Cut hearts of palm in rounds about 1″ thick. Mix with other ingredients and refrigerate for a few hours before serving. *Fresh pineapple can be used. Stuffing these shells with salad is most attractive.*

Serves 6

Elizabeth Friedenberg

Christmas Tree Salad

First Layer

1 3-ounce package lime gelatin
½ cup boiling water
1 8-ounce can crushed pineapple, reserve juice
1 cup pineapple juice

Dissolve gelatin in boiling water and add pineapple and juice. Put into mold and chill until firm before adding second layer.

Second Layer

20 large marshmallows
3 ounces cream cheese
½ pint whipping cream, whipped

Melt marshmallows and cream cheese together over very low fire. Cool. Add whipped cream, mixing well. Add to mold, and chill until firm.

Third Layer

1 3-ounce package cherry gelatin
1⅓ cups boiling water
1 cup chopped nuts
½ cup chopped celery
Non-dairy whipped topping or mayonnaise
Cherries

If bottom of mold is larger than the top *when unmolded,* double all the ingredients for the third layer. Dissolve gelatin in boiling water. Stir in nuts and celery and cool. Add to mold and chill until firm. Unmold and add a dab of non-dairy whipped topping or mayonnaise and a cherry on top. This may be made in a 6-cup mold or small cone-shaped paper cups to look like trees.

Serves 6-8 Sybil Ellis Hamm

Freeze extra bananas in their skins. When ready to use, place under running water, then peal, slice and place in fruit cocktails while still frozen.

Cranberry Salad

- 1-2 oranges
- 2½ cups fresh cranberries
- 1 6-ounce box orange flavored gelatin
- 3 cups boiling water
- 2 tablespoons lemon juice
- 1 cup sugar
- Pinch salt
- 1½ cups finely chopped celery
- 1 cup crushed pineapple, drained
- ½ cup chopped pecans

Peel orange; put peelings and cranberries through a food grinder, or use a food processor to chop finely. Dissolve gelatin in boiling water. Add lemon juice, sugar and salt. Stir until sugar is dissolved. Add cranberry mixture, celery, pineapple and pecans. Mix well. Pour into large (10-12 cup) mold, or a large Pyrex casserole. Let set in refrigerator. Best if made at least 2 days ahead to enhance flavor.

Serves 6-8

Michele Armstrong
Qvistgaard-Petersen

Port Wine Salad

- 1 6-ounce package raspberry gelatin
- 2 cups boiling water
- 1 18-ounce can crushed pineapple
- 1 15-ounce can cranberry sauce
- ½ cup chopped nuts
- 1 cup port wine

Dissolve gelatin in boiling water. Add remaining ingredients and congeal.

Serves 10

Susan Metcalf James

Orange Mold Salad

½ cup sugar or ½ cup honey (If using honey, use ¼ cup less fruit juices.)
½ cup lemon juice
3½ cups orange juice, divided (fresh, frozen or canned)
2 envelopes unflavored gelatin
1½ cups orange sections (mandarin may be used)
¾ cup chopped nuts (pecans or walnuts)
3 bananas, sliced

Add sugar or honey to fruit juices, reserving ½ cup cold orange juice. Heat sugar and juices until sugar melts. Soak gelatin in reserved ½ cup orange juice. Combine with juice and sugar mixture. Cool Add orange sections, nuts and bananas. Place in a 2-quart oiled mold or individual molds. Refrigerate several hours. Serve on crisp lettuce leaves with a dollop of mayonnaise. *This is a delicious tart salad.*

Serves 10-12

Sarah Williams Baird

Melon Mint Cocktail

½ cup sugar
½ cup water
1 bunch mint
Juice 1 orange
Juice 1 lemon
3 cantaloupes or honeydew melons or 1 watermelon, cut in balls

Boil sugar and water 5 minutes. Pour over mint. Cover and let cool. Strain. Add fruit juices and chill. Serve over chilled melon balls or marinate about 1 hour. Garnish with mint.

Serves 12

Mamie Cheairs Rose

Cranberry Chicken Salad

- 2 envelopes unflavored gelatin, divided
- ½ cup cold water, divided
- 1 16-ounce can whole cranberry sauce
- 1 cup crushed pineapple, well drained
- ½ cup pecans
- 1 tablespoon lemon juice
- 1 cup mayonnaise
- 1 cup well seasoned chicken broth
- 2 cups cooked, cubed chicken
- 3 tablespoons lemon juice
- 3 tablespoons sliced, stuffed olives
- ½ cup chopped celery
- 2 tablespoons chopped parsley

Use a 1½-quart flat casserole to make a thick salad or a 2-quart flat casserole for a thinner one. Dissolve over hot water 1 envelope gelatin soaked in ¼ cup cold water. Mix with cranberry sauce, pineapple, pecans and lemon juice. Chill in casserole until firm. Then dissolve over hot water the remaining envelope of gelatin soaked in ¼ cup cold water. Mix with mayonnaise, chicken broth, cubed chicken, lemon juice, olives, celery and parsley. Pour this over the first layer and chill. Cut in squares. *Serve topped with homemade mayonnaise on a bed of red-tipped lettuce. Triples well.*

Serves 10

Caroline Richard McLean

Chicken Salad

- 1 4-4½ pound chicken (3½-4 cups diced chicken)
- 8 eggs, hard-boiled
- 8-10 sweet pickles, chopped
- 6-8 ribs celery, chopped
- 1 1-pound 4-ounce can LeSueur peas
- 1 15½-ounce can Royal Ann cherries, pitted
- 1 cup chopped pecans
- Juice 1 lemon
- Salt and pepper to taste
- 1 cup mayonnaise (approximately)

Boil chicken until tender. Cool. Remove meat from bone and cut into bite-size pieces. Add eggs, pickles, celery, peas and cherries. Just before serving, add pecans, lemon juice, salt, pepper and mayonnaise. *Serve on a bed of lettuce. May substitute fresh pineapple for cherries.*

Serves 8-10

Beth Huckabay Hayes

Molded Chicken Mousse

3 envelopes unflavored gelatin
½ cup cold water
1 10¾-ounce can cream of mushroom soup
2½ cups chicken broth
2 teaspoons salt
¼ teaspoon pepper
1 cup mayonnaise
5 cups cooked, finely diced chicken
1½ cups finely diced celery
1 teaspoon Worcestershire sauce
1½ tablespoons grated onion
2 tablespoons lemon juice
2 tablespoons chopped parsley
1 cup whipping cream, whipped stiff

Sprinkle gelatin on cold water. Combine soup, chicken broth, salt and pepper. Heat until blended and hot. Dissolve the gelatin in the hot mixture; then cool until very syrupy. Stir in other ingredients and fold in whipped cream last. Grease mold as large as a bundt pan with mayonnaise; pour mixture into it and chill at least 5 hours.

Serves 20

Frances Carolyn Wood Pavletitch
Jacksonville, Texas

Potato Salad Poulet

1 0.4-ounce package Hidden Valley Salad Dressing Mix
1 cup mayonnaise
1 cup buttermilk
4 cups cooked chicken, diced
3 cups cooked potatoes, sliced or 2 1-pound cans potatoes
1 10-ounce package frozen baby lima beans, cooked and drained
¼ cup chopped onions
2 tablespoons chopped green pepper
1 teaspoon salt
¼ teaspoon celery salt

Mix salad dressing mix with mayonnaise and buttermilk. Combine chicken, potatoes and 1 cup salad dressing. Cover and refrigerate several hours or overnight. Combine with beans, onions, green pepper, salt and celery salt. This may be served hot by heating in a large saucepan. Do not boil. *Pretty served cold in tomato cups or on lettuce leaves.*

Serves 8

Becky Scaife White

Chicken-Wild Rice Salad

1 6-ounce package long grain and wild rice, cooked
2 cups cooked chicken, cubed
¼ cup chopped green pepper
Salt, pepper, lemon pepper
3 tablespoons Kraft Miracle French Dressing
2 tablespoons lemon juice
¾ cup mayonnaise
Avocado slices
Cherry tomatoes

Combine cooked, cooled rice, chicken, green pepper and seasonings. Be especially generous with the lemon pepper. Add French dressing and lemon juice. You may add the mayonnaise at this point or wait until just before serving. Adding the mayonnaise ahead allows the flavors to blend. Refrigerate. Serve mixture in salad bowl garnished with avocado slices and cherry tomatoes. *Regular orange-colored French dressing may be used in lieu of Miracle French Dressing. Curried rice mix and shrimp may be substituted for wild rice and chicken.*

Serves 6

Dixey Thornton Sanders

Curried Chicken Salad

1 3-3½ pound chicken
Salt and pepper to taste
Seasoned salt to taste
1 onion
1 rib celery
2-3 hard-boiled eggs, chopped
1 onion, chopped
1 4-ounce can water chestnuts, sliced
¼ cup chopped parsley
½ cup chopped celery
2 tablespoons French dressing, oil and vinegar type (optional)
Mayonnaise, enough to bind
1 tablespoon curry powder, or to taste
Salt, red and black pepper to taste

Boil chicken with salt, pepper, seasoned salt, onion and celery rib until tender. (Save stock and freeze for later use.) Remove chicken from bone and cut into bite-size pieces with scissors. Add chopped eggs, onion, water chestnuts, parsley, celery and French dressing. Mix with mayonnaise and seasonings. *Serve on a lettuce leaf or as a sandwich spread.*

Serves 6-8

Nancy McCullough Humphrey

Salmon Salad

1 teaspoon lemon juice
1 7¾-ounce can red sockeye salmon, drained and picked clean of bones and skin
⅓ cup finely chopped celery
¼ cup finely chopped onion (or green onion)
⅓ cup finely chopped cucumber
1 hard-boiled egg, cut up
¼ cup Kraft Creamy Cucumber Salad Dressing
¼ cup mayonnaise
2 teaspoons capers
1 teaspoon dill weed
Salt to taste
Avocado slices
Cherry tomatoes

Combine all ingredients and mix well. Serve on lettuce leaf, garnished with avocado slices and/or cherry tomatoes. *Tuna may be substituted for salmon. Homemade mayonnaise makes it better.*

Serves 2

Margaret Hunkin Crow

Salmon Mousse

2 16-ounce cans salmon
2 envelopes unflavored gelatin
½ cup cold water
1¼ cups water
2 chicken bouillon cubes
¼ cup vinegar
2 tablespoons sugar
1 teaspoon salt
¼ cup lemon juice
2 tablespoons grated onion
1⅓ cups mayonnaise
Green pepper strips
Olive slice

Drain and flake salmon. Soften gelatin in cold water. Heat water to boiling and dissolve gelatin and bouillon cubes in it. Add seasonings and cool until slightly thick. Blend in mayonnaise and salmon. Pour into a 7-cup fish mold. Chill until firm. Unmold and garnish with green pepper strips on the tail and an olive slice for the eye.

Serves 8-10

Barbara Horner Burrell
Naples, Florida

Shrimp Salad

6 ounces egg noodles, cooked
2 pounds cooked shrimp
1 cucumber, chopped
1 tomato, chopped
1 avocado, chopped
3 scallions, chopped
Poppy seeds
Salt and pepper
¾ cup mayonnaise
¼ cup Italian dressing

Cook noodles according to package directions. Mix all ingredients and chill. Serve on lettuce leaf or avocado half. Tomato may be saved for garnish.

Serves 6 Carolyn Hamel Griffen

Oriental Tuna Salad

1 10½-ounce package frozen Italian green beans
1 6½-ounce can tuna, drained
½ cup mayonnaise
1½ teaspoons soy sauce
1 tablespoon lemon juice
1 cup diagonally sliced celery
1 3-ounce can chow mein noodles
Water chestnuts, sliced (optional)

Cook green beans according to package directions; then drain and cool. Add next 5 ingredients; stir well and chill. Right before serving, stir in chow mein noodles. Sliced water chestnuts make a nice addition.

Serves 4 Louise Jackson

Asparagus and Artichoke Salad

2 pounds fresh asparagus
½ cup diced artichoke hearts or bottoms
½ cup diced celery
2 tablespoons diced white onion
¼ cup chopped parsley
½ cup tarragon vinegar
1 cup olive oil
1 teaspoon prepared mustard
½ teaspoon garlic powder
1 tablespoon dried dill
1 teaspoon salt
1 teaspoon oregano
Dash Cavender's All Purpose Greek Seasoning

Snip ends off asparagus and tie in bundles. Cook about 10-15 minutes in boiling water until tender, but still crisp. Drain. Add remaining ingredients and chill for at least 2 hours. *Serve on a bed of lettuce.*

Serves 6-8

Wesley Lambert Richardson

Asparagus Salad

2 envelopes unflavored gelatin
1 cup sugar
1 cup water, divided
½ cup vinegar
½ teaspoon salt
2 14½-ounce cans medium-size asparagus pieces (reserve liquid from 1 can)
½ cup lemon juice
½ cup chopped celery
1 2-ounce jar pimientos
½ cup broken pecans
½ cup grated onion

Soak gelatin in ½ cup water to soften. Boil sugar, remaining water, vinegar and salt. Add softened gelatin to hot mixture. Allow to cool. Add asparagus plus reserved liquid and other ingredients. Pour into greased molds and chill.

Serves 6-8

Katherine Powell Jarrell
Lookout Mountain, Tennessee

Hearts of Artichoke Salad

- 2 10½-ounce cans consommé
- 2 scallions, finely chopped
- 1 small garlic clove (optional)
- 3 tablespoons finely chopped parsley
- ½ teaspoon celery seed
- 1½ envelopes unflavored gelatin, softened in ½ cup cold water
- 1 beef bouillon cube (optional)
- 2 8½-ounce cans artichoke hearts packed in water, drained
- 1 8-ounce carton sour cream
- 1 2-ounce jar black caviar

Simmer first 7 ingredients in a covered saucepan over very low heat for 25-30 minutes, stirring several times to keep gelatin from settling. In the bottoms of well oiled individual salad molds, place a whole heart and a half on top of that. Strain the seasonings from the consommé and discard. Fill the molds with the liquid, cover with wax paper and refrigerate until firm. To serve, unmold on lettuce leaf. (Red tip lettuce is a good compliment for these.) Top with a dollop of sour cream and 1 teaspoon caviar. *Elegant and delicious.*

Serves 10

Jacqueline Labry Nesbitt

To keep refrigerated avocado dip or guacamole from turning dark, place the avocado pit in the center of the dip. Remove at serving time.

Avocado Salad

- ½ head lettuce
- 2 medium tomatoes, cut in wedges
- ½ cup ripe olives, pitted
- ¼ cup sliced onion
- 1 cup corn chips
- 1 ripe avocado, peeled and sliced
- 1 recipe avocado dressing
- ½ cup shredded Cheddar cheese

Combine salad ingredients. Top with avocado dressing and Cheddar cheese.

Continued...

Avocado Dressing

- 1 ripe avocado, peeled
- 1 tablespoon lemon juice
- ½ cup sour cream
- ⅓ cup vegetable oil
- 1 clove garlic
- ½ teaspoon sugar
- ½ teaspoon chili powder
- ¼ teaspoon salt
- ¼ teaspoon pepper

Beat avocado with mixer. Add other ingredients and mix well.

Serves 4-6

Ellen Daniel Brown

Avocado Salad with Herb Dressing

- 1 3-ounce package lemon flavored gelatin
- 2 tablespoons lemon juice
- 1 tablespoon horseradish
- 1 teaspoon grated onion (or onion juice)
- 2 diced avocados (¼″ squares)
- ½ cup minced celery

Dissolve gelatin in ¾ cup boiling water. Add lemon juice, horseradish and onion. Chill until it begins to set. With a rotary beater, beat until gelatin beads. Fold in avocados and celery. Pour into a 6″×10″×1½″ dish. Chill. Make sure all avocado is below jellied surface to prevent discoloration. Cut in squares to serve.

Herb Dressing

- 1 cup mayonnaise
- 1½ teaspoons lemon juice
- Dash salt
- ¼ teaspoon paprika
- 1 teaspoon basil
- 1 tablespoon grated onion
- ⅛ teaspoon curry powder
- ½ tablespoon Worcestershire sauce

Blend all ingredients and chill. Serve on top of salad.

Serves 8-10

Jane Harris Hall

Guacamole

1 clove garlic
2 avocados, medium soft
½ teaspoon lemon or lime juice
2 green onions, chopped
2 medium tomatoes, chopped
1 tablespoon chopped green pepper
Dash Tabasco
Salt
Mayonnaise

Mash garlic in bowl and scrape out. Mash avocados in same bowl and add lemon or lime juice. Add remaining ingredients along with Tabasco, salt and mayonnaise to taste. Serve on shredded lettuce. You may omit tomatoes from salad and serve avocado mixture atop thick tomato slices on a bed of shredded lettuce. *Can be served as a dip with corn chips.*

Serves 6-8

Kathleen Fitzgerald Myers

Broccoli Salad

1 10½-ounce can beef consommé
1 envelope unflavored gelatin
2 tablespoons lemon juice
1 cup mayonnaise
1 3-ounce package cream cheese
1 tablespoon black pepper
1½ teaspoons salt
2 tablespoons Worcestershire sauce
1 teaspoon Tabasco
2 10-ounce packages chopped broccoli, cooked and drained
4 eggs, hard-boiled and chopped
1 2-ounce jar chopped pimientos

Heat consommé. Dissolve gelatin in lemon juice; add to consommé and let cool. In blender mix mayonnaise, cream cheese, pepper, salt, Worcestershire and Tabasco. Add cooled consommé to this mixture. Stir in chopped broccoli, eggs and pimientos. Grease a 9″×9″ mold with mayonnaise and pour mixture into it. Chill until set. May be made 2 days ahead.

Serves 10

Mary Elizabeth Baker Nordyke

Boston Lettuce with Bacon

1 head Boston lettuce
6 slices bacon, fried crisp and crumbled
2 hard-boiled eggs, sliced
1 rib celery, chopped
1 green onion, minced
1 teaspoon bacon drippings
5 teaspoons olive oil
2 teaspoons white vinegar
Salt and freshly-ground pepper
2 drops Tabasco

Wash and drain lettuce and tear into pieces. Combine first 5 ingredients shortly before serving time. Combine bacon drippings (room temperature), olive oil and vinegar. Add salt, pepper and Tabasco to oil mixture and stir well. Pour over salad greens and toss well. Serve immediately.

Serves 4

Margaret Roberts Evans

Garden Broccoli Salad

2 bunches fresh broccoli
1 teaspoon salt
4 green onions, chopped
½ 7-ounce jar stuffed olives, sliced

Cut flowerettes from broccoli stems. Peel and slice stems in small squares and boil in salted water for 10 minutes. Drain well and chill with flowerettes. Add onions and olives. Mix well. *Serve with dressing below.*

1 cup mayonnaise
½ cup grated Parmesan cheese
½ cup Kraft Zesty Italian Dressing
3 hard-boiled eggs, chopped
8 slices bacon, fried crisp and crumbled

Mix mayonnaise, cheese and Kraft Zesty Italian Dressing and pour over broccoli. When serving have a side dish of chopped eggs and bacon to sprinkle on the top.

Serves 8

Margaret Gorton Barnes
Baton Rouge, Louisiana

Molded Gazpacho

2 envelopes unflavored gelatin
3 cups tomato juice or Snap-E-Tom, divided
¼ cup wine vinegar
1 clove garlic, crushed
¼ teaspoon pepper
Dash cayenne
¾ cup chopped cucumber
¼ cup chopped pimientos
2 large tomatoes, chopped
½ cup chopped onion
¾ cup chopped green pepper

Soften gelatin in 1 cup cold tomato juice. Then heat until it simmers. Add rest of tomato juice, vinegar, garlic, pepper and cayenne. Cool in refrigerator until slightly thickened. Add remaining ingredients. Pour into a 6-cup mold. *A lightly oiled bundt pan makes a pretty mold.*

¼ cup sour cream
¼ cup mayonnaise
½ teaspoon salt
1 teaspoon horseradish

Mix all ingredients and serve over salad.

Serves 10-12

Mary Graham Pate

Use mayonnaise to grease molds.

Harmony Salad

1 large outer leaf romaine lettuce
½ cup shredded raw spinach
¼ cup shredded red cabbage
⅓ cup finely grated carrots
¼ cup alfalfa sprouts
½ avocado, sliced
¼ cup grated Monterey Jack cheese
4 slices zucchini
5 cherry tomatoes
2 green pepper rings
2 tablespoons raw sunflower seeds

In a bowl, arrange first 7 ingredients in layers in order given. Decorate with zucchini slices, cherry tomatoes, pepper rings and sunflower seeds. Drizzle with dressing.

Continued...

Dressing

1 0.6-ounce package Good Seasons Italian Dressing
¼ cup tarragon vinegar
2 tablespoons water
⅔ cup vegetable oil
1 tablespoon prepared yellow mustard
2 tablespoons mayonnaise
1 teaspoon celery seeds

Pour package of dressing, vinegar and water in jar. Shake to mix well. Add oil and shake again. Stir in remaining ingredients. Shake immediately before serving.

Yields 2 small salads

Margaret Hunkin Crow

Mama Mia's Salad Mix

1 cup chopped onion
1 cup chopped celery
1 cup chopped green olives
1 cup chopped black olives
2 anchovy fillets with oil
2 6-ounce jars marinated artichoke hearts
8 cloves garlic, minced
¾ cup olive oil
1 teaspoon capers
½ teaspoon Worcestershire sauce
½ cup lemon juice
1 teaspoon each: thyme, oregano, marjoram, savory
1 teaspoon salt
½ teaspoon pepper
4 heads lettuce
Green onions
Parsley
Romano cheese
Celery
Radishes

Mix first 17 ingredients and put into 1-quart airtight container. Marinate 4 days in the refrigerator. This mixture is enough for 4 heads of lettuce. Toss mixture with lettuce and add green onions, celery, parsley, Romano cheese and radishes.

Serves 24

Flora Cooper Langlois
Greenville Springs, Louisiana

South-of-the-Border Salad

- 1 10½-ounce bag corn chips
- 1 large white onion, sliced
- 2 medium cucumbers, sliced
- 1 medium head lettuce, broken up
- 2 medium tomatoes, chopped
- 1 small green pepper, sliced in rings
- 2 ribs celery, chopped
- 8 ounces mushrooms, sliced
- 8 ounces sharp Cheddar cheese, grated
- 1 small jalapeño pepper, chopped (optional)

Layer ingredients in order given in a large glass bowl. Saturate salad with Italian dressing. This salad is colorful and attractive. For added zest, use jalapeño. *This salad may be halved or doubled easily.*

Serves 6

Antoinette Langlois Arceneaux

Marinated Vegetable Salad

- 24 whole cherry tomatoes
- ½ pound fresh mushrooms, sliced
- 1 large green pepper, thinly sliced in rings
- 1 head cauliflower, broken into bite-size pieces
- 1 bunch broccoli, broken into bite-size pieces
- 3 ribs celery, sliced diagonally
- 1 zucchini or yellow squash, sliced, unpeeled

Mix all ingredients and marinate in following dressing at least 5 hours.

- 1½ cups vegetable oil
- ½ cup red wine vinegar
- 1 teaspoon sugar
- ½ teaspoon dry mustard
- 3 tablespoons finely minced onion
- 1½ teaspoons salt
- ½ teaspoon cracked black pepper

Blend dressing ingredients and pour over vegetables. Marinate in refrigerator at least 5 hours. *Serve with or without lettuce. Very colorful and delicious as an appetizer served with toothpicks.*

Serves 10-12

Sandra MacCleary Boyd

Pantry Salad

1 16-ounce can artichoke hearts
1 8-ounce bottle Italian salad dressing
1 head lettuce or several kinds mixed
½ teaspoon McCormick Salad Supreme Seasoning
Croutons, to taste
1 2-ounce can anchovies
Parmesan cheese

Drain liquid from can of artichokes and replace with Italian dressing. Marinate in refrigerator overnight. Wash and drain lettuce, and tear into bite-size pieces. When ready to serve, mix lettuce, artichoke hearts, seasoning and croutons; use only enough dressing for your own taste. When salad is mixed, arrange anchovy strips on top and sprinkle with Parmesan cheese.

Serves 6-8

Ginger Sample Yeatts

Cold Pasta Salad

1 8-ounce package long spaghetti, broken into 2″ pieces, or macaroni shells, cooked
1 8-ounce package Velveeta cheese, cubed
1 small bunch green onions, chopped
1 cup chopped celery
1 large green pepper, chopped
1 4-ounce jar peeled pimientos, chopped (optional)
3 large tomatoes, peeled and chopped
4 tablespoons Worcestershire sauce
Juice ½ lemon
Salt, pepper and red pepper to taste
Tabasco to taste

Stir cheese into warm spaghetti. Add chopped ingredients to spaghetti and cheese mixture; add lemon juice and seasonings.

1 cup + 3 tablespoons mayonnaise
1 8-ounce bottle orange French dressing

Blend these ingredients well. Pour over salad mixture. Mix slightly. Spaghetti will absorb excess dressing. Chill several hours or overnight.

Serves 12

Pam Smith Byrd

Macaroni Salad

- 1 8-ounce package macaroni shells
- 1 cup chopped celery
- ½ cup chopped green pepper
- ½ cup French dressing
- ½ cup mayonnaise
- ½ cup sour cream
- 1 teaspoon prepared mustard
- ½ teaspoon salt

Cook macaroni and drain. Mix with celery, green pepper and French dressing. Toss well and marinate several hours or overnight. Just before serving, mix remaining ingredients and fold into macaroni mixture.

Serves 8-10 — Nita Harrell Braddock

Rice-Potato Salad

- 3 cups hot cooked rice, packed tightly
- 1 medium potato, peeled, boiled, and cut in bite-size pieces
- 6 hard-boiled eggs, chopped
- ½ cup finely chopped dill pickles
- ½ cup finely chopped stuffed olives
- ½ cup finely chopped green pepper
- ¾ cup finely chopped celery
- ½ cup minced green onion tops
- ½ cup minced parsley
- 2 teaspoons minced onion
- 2 teaspoons salt
- ½ teaspoon coarsely ground black pepper
- ½ teaspoon red pepper
- 1 cup mayonnaise (preferably homemade)

Combine all ingredients except rice and potato. Mix well. Add rice and potato *while they are hot,* and mix well. Garnish with sprigs of parsley and sprinkle lightly with paprika.

Serves 12 — Sandra MacCleary Boyd

Rice and Artichoke Salad

1 6-ounce package Chicken Flavor Rice-a-Roni
1 6-ounce jar marinated artichoke hearts, reserve liquid
⅓ cup mayonnaise
¼ teaspoon curry powder
4 green onions and tops, chopped
¼ cup sliced stuffed green olives

Cook Rice-a-Roni according to package directions. Cut artichokes in half and add to rice. Mix mayonnaise, curry powder, green onions and olives with artichoke liquid. Add to rice mixture. Gently mix all ingredients well and refrigerate until served. *Leftovers keep well in refrigerator for several days.*

Serves 8

Anne Krison Mitchell

German Potato Salad

2 pounds boiled potatoes, diced
½ cup crumbled bacon, reserve drippings
½ cup minced onion
¼ cup minced green onion

Sautê minced onions in bacon drippings. Combine potatoes, crumbled bacon and sautêed onions.

Dressing

1½ teaspoons flour
4 teaspoons sugar
1 tablespoon salt
¼ teaspoon pepper
1 tablespoon prepared mustard
⅓ cup vinegar
½ cup water

Mix flour, sugar, salt, pepper and mustard. Add vinegar and water. Cook until flour thickens. Pour dressing over warm potato mixture. Toss lightly and serve. *May add celery and sweet pickles.*

Serves 6-8

Jane Oxford Dobbs
Dallas, Texas

Potato Salad

8 pounds new potatoes
6 hard-boiled eggs, grated
½ cup fresh lemon juice
1 8-ounce jar Kraft Herbs 'n Spices Salad Dressing
2 dill pickles, diced
1 medium green pepper, chopped
1 4-ounce jar diced pimientos
1-2 tablespoons chopped onion
6-8 ribs celery, finely chopped
Dill weed, fresh if possible
½ teaspoon celery salt
1 small hot red pepper, chopped
Parsley, chopped
Salt and pepper to taste
1 quart mayonnaise
Paprika

Wash potatoes. Cover with cold water and cook until tender. Do not overcook. When done, pour off hot water and cover potatoes with cold water. When cool, skin; cut in pieces and set aside in large bowl. Boil eggs. Cool. Peel and refrigerate in plastic bag. Mix lemon juice, salad dressing, pickles, green pepper, pimientos, onion, celery and seasonings, except mayonnaise. Pour over potatoes and refrigerate overnight or at least 4 hours. When ready to serve, or take to the picnic, add mayonnaise and grated egg, reserving a bit of egg to sprinkle over top with paprika. *Crumbled bacon and grated Cheddar cheese also make a nice garnish. For guests who like cucumber, a cup of chopped cucumber stirred into the salad gives a delicious flavor.*

Serves 25

Eleanor Johnson Colquitt

New potatoes should start cooking in boiling water; old potatoes should start cooking in cold water and be brought to the boil.

Summer Salad

1 6-ounce package lemon gelatin
1 cup grated cabbage
1 cup grated carrots
1 cup crushed pineapple, reserve juice
¾ cup chopped nuts
½ cup chopped celery
1 tablespoon vinegar
Salt and pepper to taste

Prepare gelatin according to package directions, except substitute pineapple juice for part of water. Add remaining ingredients. Chill until set. *Can substitute lime or orange gelatin.*

Serves 8

Susan Sigler Updegraff

Sauerkraut Salad

2 16-ounce cans sauerkraut, drained
1 cup diced celery
1 cup chopped green onions
1 8-ounce can water chestnuts, drained and sliced
1 cup diced green pepper
2 tablespoons chopped pimientos (optional)

Combine ingredients and pour dressing over this. Stir to coat all vegetables. Cover and refrigerate overnight. *Keeps well several days. Can be served as relish on hot dogs or po-boy sandwiches.*

Dressing

⅔ cup vinegar
⅓ cup oil
⅓ cup water
1¼ cups sugar

Combine all ingredients and mix well. Set aside.

Serves 10-12

Martha Turner Schober

Salata

1 small head iceburg lettuce
2 ribs celery, chopped
2 green onions, chopped
1 small cucumber, sliced
1 tomato, cut in wedges
Feta cheese, crumbled or cut in cubes
Greek olives

Break lettuce in pieces. Add celery, onions, cucumber and tomato. Lightly coat salad with dressing. Garnish with cubes of Feta cheese and Greek olives. Serve with dressing below.

⅔ cup olive oil
⅓ cup wine vinegar
1 teaspoon salt
¼ teaspoon pepper
1 teaspoon oregano

Put ingredients in jar; shake.

Yields 1 cup

Nancy Pfeiffer Cosse

To crisp freshly washed spinach and lettuce leaves, spread them on a clean dry towel, roll and refrigerate. Also parsley wrapped in a damp dishtowel and refrigerated will become crisp.

Snow Pea Salad with Sesame Dressing

1 7-ounce package frozen snow peas
Boiling salted water
½ head cauliflower
1 5-ounce can water chestnuts, drained and sliced
1 tablespoon chopped pimientos

Cook peas in small amount of boiling salted water until barely tender, about 1 minute. Drain. Separate cauliflower into bite-size clusters, about 2 cups. Cook in boiling salted water about 3 minutes until tender but crisp. Drain. Combine peas, cauliflower, water chestnuts and pimientos. Cover and chill. Just before serving, mix with about 3 tablespoons of sesame seed dressing.

Continued...

Sesame Seed Dressing

- **2 tablespoons sesame seeds, toasted**
- **⅓ cup vegetable oil**
- **1 tablespoon each: lemon juice, vinegar and sugar**
- **½ clove garlic, minced or mashed**
- **½ teaspoon salt**

Place sesame seeds in shallow pan in 350° oven for 5-8 minutes or broil (watch closely) until golden brown. Cool. Combine remaining ingredients. Add seeds. Cover and chill. Shake well before serving.

Serves 4-6 — Vicki Longmire Hanna

Spinach Salad

- **½ head lettuce**
- **1 10-ounce bag fresh spinach, stemmed**
- **10 slices bacon, fried crisp and crumbled**
- **1 white onion, slivered**
- **1 pint cottage cheese**
- **1 pound fresh mushrooms, sliced (optional)**
- **4 hard-boiled eggs, crumbled (optional)**

Mix and serve with following dressing:

Dressing

- **½ cup cider vinegar**
- **¼ cup sugar**
- **1 teaspoon dry mustard**
- **1 teaspoon salt**
- **⅔ tablespoon chopped onion, or 2 teaspoons onion juice**
- **⅔ cup oil**

Put everything except oil in blender. Start it at low speed and slowly add oil. Can be made ahead of time and refrigerated in blender container. Turn blender on again, briefly, before putting on salad.

Serves 10 — Sissy Masters Harper

Spinach and Orange Salad

2 10-ounce bags fresh spinach, washed, dried and torn in bite-size pieces
1 red onion, thinly sliced
1 11-ounce can mandarin oranges, drained

Combine all of the above. *You may add fresh mushrooms and crumbled bacon.* Toss with following dressing:

3 tablespoons lemon juice
2 tablespoons sugar
1 clove garlic, crushed
1 teaspoon salt
½ cup vegetable oil

Place lemon juice in jar with tight lid. Add all other ingredients except oil. Shake until sugar is dissolved; add oil and shake again.

Serves 8 — Mary Graham Pate

Easley's Slaw

1 large or 2 small heads cabbage, shredded
1 large white onion, cut into rings
1 cup less 2 tablespoons sugar

Pour sugar over cabbage and onions. Set aside while making sauce.

2 tablespoons sugar
1 teaspoon celery seed
1 tablespoon salt
1 teaspoon mustard seed
1 cup vinegar
½ cup salad oil

Mix all ingredients in saucepan and bring to a boil. Pour over cabbage immediately. Blend well. Cover and refrigerate at least 12 hours. Just as good up to 1 week later if kept in the refrigerator. *Great with barbecue or fried chicken. Cabbage and onions may be done in food processor and sauce may be boiled in microwave for quick preparation.*

Serves 6-8 — Cynthia Johnson Nowery

Bertha's Cole Slaw

9 cups shredded cabbage (some red makes it pretty)
4 cups grated carrots
1 cup chopped celery
1 cup chopped green pepper
¾ cup chopped green olives, more if desired
1 large red or white onion, chopped
2½ cups mayonnaise
½ cup red wine vinegar
¼ cup sugar
Dash paprika
Salt and pepper to taste

Place all vegetables in large bowl. Add mayonnaise, vinegar, sugar, paprika, salt and pepper. Toss well. Cover and chill. Better if made ahead.

Serves 12

Marie Rountree Rosenfield

Tejas Fresh Vegetable Salad

1 pound fresh string beans, snapped
1 small red onion, thinly sliced
8 ounces fresh mushrooms, sliced
1 medium green pepper, thinly sliced
20 cherry tomatoes, halved
2 green onions, chopped
¼ cup fresh parsley, chopped
3 tablespoons Parmesan cheese, freshly grated
1 teaspoon vegetable salt
½ teaspoon cracked pepper

Steam green beans for 7 minutes and cool at once to prevent further cooking. Put in bowl with the next 6 ingredients. Sprinkle with cheese, salt and pepper. Serve with the following dressing:

½ cup safflower oil
1 tablespoon olive oil
¼ cup tarragon vinegar or cider vinegar with pinch tarragon
⅛ teaspoon dry mustard
⅛ teaspoon paprika
1 teaspoon garlic powder
1 teaspoon honey
1 teaspoon lemon juice

Combine all ingredients in jar and mix well. Pour dressing over vegetables and stir to coat vegetables thoroughly. Marinate at least 4 hours or longer before serving. *Keeps well for 2 days.*

Serves 4-6

Johnette Querbes Barnes

Anchovy-Caper Dressing

½ 3-ounce bottle capers
1 2-ounce can anchovies, chopped
1 bunch green onions, chopped, with tops
1 clove garlic, crushed
1 cup mayonnaise, thinned with 2-3 tablespoons tarragon vinegar

Mix all ingredients. *This is delicious served over lettuce, artichoke hearts, sliced avocado, sliced celery, crumbled bacon and sliced hard-boiled eggs. Shrimp or crab may be added for a luncheon salad.*

Yields 1½ cups — Alice Lee Grosjean Tharpe

Avocado-Yogurt Dressing

2 tablespoons Italian dressing
1 8-ounce carton plain yogurt
1 pint-size package Hidden Valley Ranch Dressing Mix
1 6-ounce can frozen guacamole, thawed

Combine all ingredients. Serve as a dip or as a salad dressing. *Try serving with shrimp or poached fish. You may add mayonnaise for variation, and serve with corn chips or vegetables.*

Yields 2 cups — Margaret Hunkin Crow

Anchovy Dressing

½ tube anchovy paste
¾ tablespoon Worcestershire sauce
2 tablespoons salad vinegar
1 tablespoon lemon juice
3 tablespoons Parmesan cheese
1 tablespoon sugar
⅛ teaspoon Accent
1 cup vegetable oil

Add above ingredients except salad oil in blender. Mix well. Add salad oil. Blend well. Refrigerate at least 1 hour before serving. Serve on romaine lettuce with croutons. *Doubles well.*

Yields 1½ cups — Joan Siegel Roper

French Dressing

2 tablespoons olive oil
1 tablespoon wine or tarragon vinegar
Garlic salt
1 teaspoon dry mustard or Dijon prepared mustard
Coarsely ground pepper
1″ cube blue cheese
Thinly sliced green onion

Put olive oil and vinegar in wooden bowl. Sprinkle with garlic salt, mustard, pepper to taste. Add onion. Combine by using wooden salad server. Add any combination of salad greens and/or vegetables and toss right before serving. *Chopped fresh herbs (parsley, tarragon and/or dill) add interest.* Crumble blue cheese over salad.

Serves 4

Ellen Woodruff Reynolds

Green Mayonnaise Dressing

1 cup mayonnaise
2 tablespoons strained baby food spinach
2 tablespoons capers and juice
¼ teaspoon Tabasco
2 teaspoons chopped green onion
2 teaspoons minced parsley
1 teaspoon tarragon vinegar

Combine all ingredients and blend thoroughly. Chill well. Toss with mixed salad greens. Keeps well in refrigerator for over a week. *Good served as a dip for raw vegetables.*

Yields 1½ cups

Rebecca Strohmaier Roberts

Lemon Cheese Dressing

⅔ cup safflower oil
⅓ cup lemon juice
½ cup Parmesan cheese, grated
1 tablespoon Vege-Sal
Grated onion (optional)

Combine all ingredients in a jar and shake well. Good on mixed green salad. *Vege-Sal may be purchased at health food store.*

Yields 2 cups

Pennye Proctor Jenkins
Coral Gables, Florida

Pennsylvania Dutch Dressing

4 strips bacon, reserve drippings
1 egg, beaten
⅓ cup vinegar
½ cup cold water
1 tablespoon sugar
3 teaspoons sugar

Cook bacon until crisp; crumble into small pieces. Combine egg, vinegar, water, 1 tablespoon sugar and bacon drippings. Return to pan and cook slowly for 1 hour. During cooking, add 1 teaspoon sugar every 15 minutes. Stir frequently. *Add minced onion to lettuce or endive, and pour hot dressing over all. Can substitute spinach and red tipped lettuce.*

Serves 6-8

Mary Ann Bray Therrell

Titania Dressing

⅓ cup chopped green onions
2 cups Hellman's mayonnaise
½ cup chopped fresh parsley
2 cloves garlic
2 tablespoons anchovy paste
1 cup sour cream
½ cup wine vinegar
2 tablespoons fresh lemon juice
½ pound blue cheese
Salt and pepper to taste

Mix all ingredients well. Put in jar and refrigerate. Serve on lettuce or with raw vegetables as a dip.

Yields 1 quart

Antoinette Burt Sentell

Italian Salad Mix

1 onion, chopped
1 green pepper, chopped
1 6-ounce can ripe olives, chopped
1 7-ounce can green olives, chopped
3 dill pickles, chopped
3 cloves garlic, chopped
Capers
1 16-ounce bottle Italian salad dressing

Toss first 6 ingredients. Add a few capers and pour dressing over all. Let stand at least 20 minutes. Serve over your favorite salad greens with croutons. *This keeps well in refrigerator.*

Yields 6 cups

Gail McGregor Mitchell

Plantation Dressing

1 egg yolk
¼ cup sugar
1 tablespoon lemon juice
2 tablespoons orange juice
6-8 marshmallows
3 ounces cream cheese
1 teaspoon grated lemon rind
1 cup whipping cream, whipped

Cook first 4 ingredients until thick, stirring constantly. Remove from heat and add marshmallows and cream cheese. Cool. Add lemon rind and whipped cream. *Good served over fresh or canned fruit.*

Yields 2 cups

Antoinette Burt Sentell

Dried herbs are much stronger by volume than fresh, about 2 to 1.

Blender Mayonnaise

2 eggs
2 tablespoons lemon juice
1 tablespoon vinegar
½ teaspoon dry mustard
1 teaspoon salt
1½ cups vegetable oil

Combine eggs, lemon juice, vinegar and seasonings in blender. Cover and blend at high speed for 30 seconds until mixed. With blender still running, take off the cover and slowly drizzle in the oil. Blend until thick and smooth. Store in refrigerator.

Yields 2 cups

Deegie Schmied Davis

Homemade Mayonnaise

2 egg yolks
2 cups salad oil, divided
1 tablespoon vinegar
2 tablespoons lemon juice
1 teaspoon paprika
1 teaspoon dry mustard
1 teaspoon sugar
1 teaspoon salt
Grated onion (optional)

In mixing bowl, beat egg yolks until lemon colored. Very slowly add 1 cup salad oil. Just let it trickle. When thick, slowly add seasonings which have been mixed with lemon juice and vinegar. Continue to beat while slowly adding remaining 1 cup oil. Beat until thick. If desired, add small amount of grated onion.

Yields 2 cups

Ivy Hedgcock Frierson

Shish Kabob Meat Marinade

1½ cups salad oil
¾ cup soy sauce
¼ cup Worcestershire sauce
2 tablespoons dry mustard
2½ teaspoons salt
1 tablespoon freshly ground pepper
1½ teaspoons parsley flakes
½ cup wine vinegar
1 clove garlic, crushed
⅓ cup fresh lemon juice

Combine all ingredients and heat. Cool. Pour over meat and marinate 4 hours or overnight.

Yields 3½ cups

Linda Tharpe Cann

Shish Kabobs

2-2½ pounds beef or lamb, cut in 2″ cubes, marinated
Green peppers cut in 1″ squares
Cherry tomatoes
Large fresh mushrooms
Whole tiny onions, peeled
Bacon squares

Arrange marinated meat on skewers, alternating vegetables and bacon squares. Have skewers 3″-4″ above fire. Broil 15-20 minutes turning frequently to cook meat evenly. Brush occasionally with marinade.

Serves 6-8

Beef Tenderloin

For a 4-pound tenderloin, marinate for *at least* 8 hours. Remove from marinade and bake on cookie sheet for 35 minutes at 450° for rare.

Serves 4

Cookbook Committee

Steak au Poivre

2 1″-1½″ rib eyes or fillets
Cracked black pepper
¼ cup vermouth
1 tablespoon lemon juice
Dash Worcestershire sauce
4 tablespoons cognac
Salt
2 tablespoons butter
1 tablespoon oil
Watercress (optional)

Place 1 heaping teaspoon of cracked pepper on steaks. Pound in the pepper. Let sit at room temperature 1 hour. In a cup mix vermouth, lemon juice, Worcestershire sauce and cognac. Sprinkle salt in a heavy skillet. Heat skillet. When salt begins to turn brown, add butter and oil. Sear meat on both sides. Cook about 2½ minutes on each side for rare meat. Place meat on warm platter. Add the cognac mixture to the butter in the pan. Heat until bubbly. Pour over meat. Serve at once garnished with watercress. *For Steak au Vert, omit black pepper. Sear meat. Add ¾-ounce green peppercorns, drained, and ⅓ cup whipping cream to sauce.*

Serves 2

Mary Jane Ray Hall

London Broil

1 flank steak
Meat tenderizer
⅓ cup vegetable oil
⅔ cup olive oil
¼ cup wine vinegar
¼ cup lemon juice
½ teaspoon salt
¼ teaspoon pepper
1 teaspoon sugar
½ teaspoon thyme

Sprinkle steak with tenderizer. Combine all ingredients. Pour over steak and marinate at least 1½ hours before broiling. For medium rare, broil 10 minutes on 1 side, basting frequently with marinade. Turn and broil 5 minutes on other side. To serve, slice diagonally. *Marinade is a good basic marinade for sirloin, shish kabob, and any meat cooked on grill.*

Serves 3-4

Carol Tankersley Easley
Denver, Colorado

South Seas Roast

- 2-3 pound roast (eye of round or sirloin tip)
- 1 cup soy sauce
- ¾ cup dry sherry
- 1 teaspoon chopped ginger
- 2 cloves garlic, slivered
- 1 tablespoon sugar
- 4 tablespoons honey
- ¼ cup pineapple juice
- 1 tablespoon freshly ground black pepper
- 2 slices bacon

Marinate beef in the first 7 ingredients for at least 7 hours. Dry marinated beef on paper towels. Pepper outside of beef. Place 1 slice of bacon over meat and 1 slice underneath before cooking. Place in a 400° oven for 10 minutes; reduce the temperature to 350° and allow 15 minutes per pound for medium rare, 12 minutes for really rare.

Serves 4

Sharon Jenkinson Boddie

Beefrouladen

- 1 large round steak ½"-¾" thick (1 steak makes 2 rouladen)
- Salt and pepper to taste
- 2 tablespoons (approximately) Dijon mustard or German mustard
- 5-6 strips bacon
- ½-¾ cup chopped onions
- 3 dill pickles, sliced lengthwise
- 2 carrots, sliced lengthwise (optional)
- 1½ cups water, or 1 12-ounce can beer
- 1-2 bouillon cubes
- 8 ounces sour cream

Cut round steak in half and pound out with mallet. Season both halves and spread them with mustard. Lay bacon strips, onions, pickles and carrots on meat. Roll up steaks and secure with toothpicks or twine. Roll in flour. Brown meat in skillet on all sides; add water or beer and bouillon cubes. Simmer covered for 1-1¼ hours or until tender. Take rouladen out; add sour cream to thicken sauce. Place back into sauce and let sit for a while. Serve hot over noodles or rice. *One-fourth cup sherry may be added to sour cream if rouladen was not cooked in beer.*

Serves 4-6

Carol Tankersley Easley
Denver, Colorado

Beef and Mushroom Ratatouille

1 tablespoon oil
2½ pounds boneless chuck, cubed
1 cup chopped onion
1 clove garlic, minced
1 28-ounce can tomatoes, cut in pieces, reserve juice
1 tablespoon oregano
2 teaspoons salt
¼ teaspoon black pepper
2 6-ounce cans sliced mushrooms, drained
1 medium eggplant, peeled and diced
2 zucchini, sliced, unpeeled

Brown beef well in oil in Dutch oven. Remove beef and set aside. In drippings, sautē onion and garlic. Return beef to pot. Add tomatoes, juice, oregano, salt and pepper. Bring to boil, stirring occasionally. Reduce heat and simmer covered for 1½ hours. Add mushrooms, eggplant and zucchini and bring to a boil again, stirring. Reduce heat and simmer covered for 30 minutes. *Serve over rice or noodles.*

Serves 6

Nancy Hudson Ketner

Beef Stew

3 onions, sliced
2 tablespoons bacon drippings
2 pounds lean stew meat, floured (can use sirloin tip roast)
1½ tablespoons flour
1 cup beef bouillon, divided
1½ cups dry red wine, divided
¼ teaspoon each: marjoram, thyme, oregano
1 teaspoon salt
½ teaspoon pepper
1 8-ounce can mushrooms, drained and sliced

Sautē onions in bacon drippings. Remove from pan and set aside. Dust meat with flour and brown in skillet. Add ¾ cup bouillon, 1 cup wine and all seasonings. Simmer covered 2 hours on low heat or bake in oven at low temperature. Add onions, ½ cup wine, ¼ cup bouillon and mushrooms. Cook 30 minutes longer. *Serve over poppy seed noodles.*

Serves 6

Brandon Taylor Stephens

Wine has a considerable amount of salt, which becomes stronger when cooked down. When cooking with wine, use salt sparingly.

Electric Skillet Stroganoff

2 pounds sirloin cut in strips
4 tablespoons butter
½ cup tomato juice
Dash garlic salt or powder
1 8-ounce can mushrooms, stems and pieces
2 teaspoons salt
½ teaspoon pepper
1 10¾-ounce can cream of mushroom soup
1 8-ounce carton sour cream

Heat skillet to 400°. Trim meat well and brown slightly in the butter, about 5-8 minutes. Add tomato juice and garlic. Cover (leave vent open) and when steaming, turn control to simmer, (200°-225°) for 45 minutes to 1 hour. Stir mushrooms, seasonings, soup and sour cream into meat mixture. Turn off. Can be reheated when served. *Serve over rice.*

Serves 4-6

Nell Ray Tugwell McClure

Piquant Piccata

4 beef cutlets, pounded paper thin
Flour
Salt and pepper
6 tablespoons butter, divided
2 tablespoons olive oil
3 tablespoons lemon juice
2 tablespoons chopped parsley
2 tablespoons chopped green onion tops
1 8-ounce package green noodles

Dust cutlets with flour, salt and pepper. Heat 4 tablespoons of the butter plus olive oil in large skillet over medium heat until bubbly. Quickly brown cutlets, about 5-8 minutes on each side. Remove cutlets to warm plate and cover loosely with skillet top. For butter sauce add parsley, lemon juice and green onion tops to same skillet. Remove from heat and stir in remaining butter. Prepare noodles according to package directions. Arrange cutlets on noodles on serving platter or individual plates. Pour hot butter sauce over all. *Garnish with lemon slices and additional chopped parsley, if desired.*

Serves 2-3

Sider French Krison

Sauerbraten

- 4-5 pound beef roast (boneless chuck, round or rump)
- 2 tablespoons pickling spice
- 15 whole cloves
- 4 bay leaves
- 1 teaspoon peppercorns
- 2 cups cider vinegar
- 2 cups water
- 1 teaspoon salt
- ½ cup sugar
- 3 cloves garlic, minced
- 3 large onions, chopped
- 1 lemon, sliced
- 3 tablespoons margarine
- 10 or more gingersnaps, crushed

Wipe roast with a damp cloth. Put pickling spice, cloves, bay leaves and peppercorns in a cheesecloth and tie well.

Combine vinegar, water, salt, sugar, garlic, onion and spice bag in saucepan and heat. Do not boil. Put meat and lemon slices in a large glass bowl and pour hot mixture over meat and set in refrigerator. Marinate for 4 days, turning meat once each day. Remove meat and drain thoroughly, reserving the marinade.

Heat margarine in a heavy Dutch oven. Add roast and brown slowly on all sides over medium heat. Add 2 cups marinade and bag of spices and bring to a boil. Reduce heat; cover and simmer for 2½-3 hours. Be sure the liquid around the meat is always simmering. Remove meat and add rest of marinade. Remove spice bag. Bring to a boil; reduce heat and cook 10 minutes. Add gingersnaps slowly, and stir constantly until gravy thickens. Add more gingersnaps if needed to thicken gravy. Serve sliced on platter with a little gravy on top and extra on the side.

Serves 6-8

Jean Spurlock Schaumburg

Baked Beef Brisket

1 4-7 pound boneless beef brisket
2 cloves garlic
Salt to taste
Red or black pepper to taste
Red wine vinegar
2 large onions, sliced

Cut garlic in slivers and insert in both sides of meat. Salt and pepper generously. Sprinkle with red wine vinegar. Let marinate for 30 minutes to 1 hour. Slice onions and place on top of meat in pan. Cover tightly with foil. Place in 400° oven. When meat is hot (about 20 minutes) turn oven to 250° and cook for 4 hours. Do not peek. Let cool thoroughly in juices before slicing.

Serves 8-10

Jane Colley Cochran
Lafayette, Louisiana

For gravy without lumps, place appropriate quantity of flour and water in jar; cover and shake until mixed; add to pan and proceed as usual.

Steak 'n Spaghetti

2-3 pounds heavy beef chuck steak, cut in serving pieces
1 1.4-ounce envelope onion soup mix
1 16-ounce can peeled Italian tomatoes
1 teaspoon oregano
Freshly ground pepper to taste
Garlic powder to taste
Dash Tabasco
1 tablespoon Worcestershire sauce
2 tablespoons vegetable oil
2 tablespoons wine vinegar
Spaghetti or vermicelli
Parmesan cheese

Arrange meat in large skillet and cover with soup mix and tomatoes with juice. (Tomatoes may be sliced or broken, if desired.) Sprinkle with remaining ingredients, except spaghetti and Parmesan cheese. Simmer covered, 1½ hours, or until meat is fork tender. Serve with spaghetti or vermicelli, cooked *al dente* (slightly firm), and Parmesan cheese.

Serves 4

Joan Yarbrough Gresham

Corned Beef Brisket Kosher Style

1 whole corned beef brisket

Soak corned beef overnight in water. (This is to reduce salt flavor.)

3 heaping tablespoons mixed pickling spices
4 cloves garlic, crushed
1 cup sugar
1 cup vinegar

Put brisket in pot filled with water (about 3 times the volume of the brisket) along with above ingredients. Pickling spices and crushed garlic could be tied in cheesecloth. Cook brisket slowly 4-4½ hours covered until fork-tender. Serve with horseradish sauce or mustard. *Always slice brisket on diagonal. Can be sliced very thin with electric knife. Potatoes, cabbage and carrots can be cooked in broth from meat.*

Josephine Walker Williams

Spicy New England Corned Beef

1 5-6 pound raw corned beef brisket
½ cup brown sugar
½ cup prepared mustard

Place brisket, fat side down, in roasting pan in approximately ½" water. Seal pan with heavy foil and cook at 350° for 2½-3 hours until tender, keeping small amount of water in pan. When brisket is done, drain liquid from roasting pan and pour into a large stock pot. Make a paste with brown sugar and mustard. Spoon glaze over and under brisket. Return to oven at 300° for 30 minutes.

Continued...

Vegetables

5 quarts water
Salt and pepper to taste
2 tablespoons liquid crab boil
2 pounds new potatoes
1 pound carrots, peeled
1 pound small white onions, peeled
7-8 ribs celery, quartered
1 large or 2 small heads cabbage, quartered

Pour water and liquid reserved from brisket into large stock pot. Add salt, pepper and crab boil. Boil potatoes uncovered until done. Remove, set aside and keep warm. Boil carrots uncovered until tender; remove and keep warm. Boil onions and celery for 5 minutes; add cabbage and boil 5-10 minutes more, according to desired tenderness.

To serve, slice brisket on large platter placing all vegetables around it in an attractive manner. *Serve with rye bread, horseradish and hot mustard.*

Serves 6

Carl Wiley Jones

Bar-B-Qued Beef Brisket

1 cup catsup
1 cup chili sauce
1 cup water
½ cup lemon juice
¼ cup brown sugar, packed
1 tablespoon Worcestershire sauce
1 tablespoon Dijon mustard
1 1.4-ounce package onion soup mix
1 5-6 pound brisket

Mix first 8 ingredients and simmer 10 minutes or longer. Trim most of fat off meat, leaving a thin layer. Put meat on grill about 8″ from coals. Cook 4-5 hours or until meat is tender. Turn meat every 20 minutes and baste with sauce each time you turn it. *Regular mustard may be used instead of Dijon. Sauce is good on ribs or chicken.*

Serves 6-8

Rose Salky Vedlitz

Mini-Reuben Tarts

¼ cup mayonnaise
¼ cup chili sauce
½ cup sauerkraut or 8-ounce can, thoroughly drained and squeezed
1 cup cooked corned beef, loosely packed, finely chopped
¾ cup grated Swiss cheese, loosely packed
Unbaked tart shells
Mayonnaise and paprika

In a small bowl whisk the mayonnaise and chili sauce. Add the sauerkraut (separating the lumps), corned beef and cheese; mix well. Spoon 1 level tablespoon of the mixture into each tart shell, filling to the top but not over the edges. Spread the filling with a little extra mayonnaise; sprinkle with paprika. Bake in 350° oven until browned, about 30 minutes. With a small metal spatula loosen edges on all tarts. Insert the spatula at one side of a shell and tilt the tart; lift out, with the spatula and your fingers, to a hot serving plate or electric tray. Quickly remove all the tarts the same way. Serve at once.

Unbaked Tart Shells

1 stick butter, softened
1 3-ounce package cream cheese
1 cup all-purpose flour

Beat the butter and cream cheese until blended. Gradually stir in the flour to form a dough. If very soft, cover tightly and chill. Using a scant tablespoon of dough for each, shape into 24 balls. Press each ball over the bottom and sides (up to but not over the top) of a small ungreased muffin cup, each 1 ¾ " across the top and ¾ " deep. (These muffin pans come with 12 cups in each.) If not used at once, cover tightly and chill; may be kept refrigerated before filling as long as 1 or 2 weeks.

Yields 24

Cecily Brownstone
Associated Press Food Editor

Beef and Broccoli Wok

- ⅓ cup soy sauce
- 2 tablespoons cider vinegar
- ¾ teaspoon sugar
- 1 beef bouillon cube
- ⅓ cup water
- 2 teaspoons cornstarch
- 3 tablespoons peanut oil, divided
- 2 cloves garlic, halved
- 1 pound beef flank steak, cut in ⅛″ diagonal slices
- 1 large onion, halved and cut in ¼″ slices
- 1½ cups peeled broccoli stems, cut in ⅛″ diagonal slices
- 2½ cups broccoli flowerettes
- ¼ pound fresh mushrooms, cut in ⅛″ slices
- 1 8½-ounce can water chestnuts, drained and sliced

Mix soy sauce, vinegar and sugar in a measuring cup. Mix bouillon cube, water and cornstarch in another cup. In a large wok or heavy skillet heat 1½ tablespoons oil over high heat. Add garlic and cook a few minutes to season oil. Add meat and stir-fry for 2 minutes. Remove meat and juices to a dish and wipe out wok. Discard garlic. Add 1 tablespoon oil and when hot add onion and broccoli stems. Stir-fry 2 minutes. To this, add remaining tablespoon of oil around edge of wok and add flowerettes and mushrooms. Stir-fry 2 minutes. Add water chestnuts. Add meat and juices and soy-vinegar mixture. Stir; cover and cook 2 minutes. Stir corn-starch mixture (be sure bouillon cube is broken up) and add to wok. Cook stirring constantly 2-3 minutes, until thickened. Serve immediately with rice. *To prepare this successfully, you must have everything measured and prepared before you begin.*

Serves 4 — Donna Banks Curtis

Japanese Hot Pot

Chicken broth
1 pound flank steak, freeze slightly and slice very thin on the diagonal
1 pound boned chicken breasts, cut in strips and marinated several hours in 2 tablespoons soy sauce; 2 tablespoons salad oil; 1 teaspoon fresh ginger root, chopped; and 1 clove garlic, chopped
¼ small head Chinese cabbage, separated into leaves
1 small bunch broccoli, cut into bite-size pieces
1 pound lean lamb, thinly sliced
1 pound medium shrimp, shelled and deveined (optional)
1 pound tofu (fresh soy bean cake), cut in ½" squares
½ pound fresh mushrooms, sliced
½ pound fresh snow peas (may use frozen, but defrost and do not cook)
Cauliflower broken into bite-size pieces
Sliced turnips
Green onions, sliced
Cooked rice

Prepare all ingredients as described above and arrange some of each on a plate, using 1 plate of ingredients for each 2 guests. Heat chicken broth in a wok in the center of the table. Wok must be easily accessible for all guests, so more than 1 wok may be needed; (6 can eat from 1 wok). Wok should be about ¾ full of broth. Bring broth to a boil and bring the guests to the table. Each person cooks his own meal holding a piece at a time with chopsticks in the broth and eating with rice. (Can use oriental wire ladle to hold several items at once, or even kitchen tongs for those who cannot manage chop sticks.) Each item cooks for less than 1 minute. *Have a slotted spoon handy to fish out food that drops into broth. When everyone has finished the meats and vegetables, serve the soup remaining in the wok in individual bowls. This is delicious since the broth has been seasoned by all the ingredients being cooked in it. Before serving soup one may want to add sizzling rice.*

Continued...

Sizzling Rice

1 cup regular rice
4 cups water
2 teaspoons salt
Oil

A day or more in advance combine rice, water and salt in a large pan. Let stand 30 minutes. Bring to a boil. Cover and simmer for 30 minutes. Drain. Spread evenly on a greased cookie sheet. Bake at 250° for 8 hours. Turn occasionally with a spatula. Before serving in soup heat 2″ of oil to 425° in a frying pan and fry large bite-size pieces of rice about 4 minutes until golden. Drain and take immediately to hot soup and pour in; it will sizzle. Serve soup and rice mixture. *Accompaniments to serve with meats and vegetables could be soy sauce, Chinese mustard (mix Colman's dry mustard and water to a paste), and Hot Pepper Oil*—see Index.

Serves 6

Lecie Roos Resneck

Pepper Steak

2 pounds round steak, cut into thin strips on slant
2 tablespoons vegetable oil
Salt to taste
1 green pepper, cut in thin strips
1 onion, cut in thin half circles
3 ribs celery, cut in slanted ½″ pieces
½ pound snow peas (optional)
1 cup sliced fresh mushrooms
⅓ cup slivered almonds
1 tablespoon soy sauce
1 tablespoon sherry
⅛ teaspoon garlic powder
¼ teaspoon ground ginger
2 tablespoons cornstarch
6 tablespoons water

Quickly brown meat in hot oil in deep skillet or wok. Add salt, vegetables, mushrooms, almonds, soy sauce, sherry, garlic powder and ginger. Cover and cook over low heat 10 minutes. Combine cornstarch and water. Stir until cornstarch is dissolved. Add to meat mixture, stirring constantly until slightly thickened. Cover and simmer about 15 minutes. Additional water may be added if needed. Serve over rice.

Serves 6

Betty Gunn Arceneaux

Stir-Fried Broccoli and Beef

Broccoli

- 1 small clove garlic
- 1½ tablespoons oil
- 1 pound fresh broccoli, (slice stems in ⅛" pieces and break off flowerettes)
- ¼ pound fresh mushrooms, sliced
- ¼ cup water
- ¼ teaspoon MSG
- Salt and pepper to taste

Brown garlic in oil, over high heat. Remove garlic and add broccoli stems. Fry, stirring until broccoli changes to brighter green. Add flowerettes and mushrooms and stir a few more minutes. Add water and cover and cook 3 minutes. Sprinkle with MSG, salt and pepper. Pour in serving dish and place in warm spot.

Beef

- 1 tablespoon oil
- 1 pound sirloin steak, sliced 1½" long and ⅛" thick
- 1 teaspoon cornstarch
- 1 teaspoon sugar
- ⅓ cup water
- 1 tablespoon sherry
- 1 tablespoon soy sauce

Heat oil in skillet. Add beef and fry quickly while stirring. Make a smooth paste with cornstarch, sugar and water. Add sherry and soy sauce. Add to beef in the skillet and cook just until thickened. Pour over broccoli. *Serve with rice and more soy sauce at table.*

Serves 4

William Landon Yauger

Gourmet Hamburgers

4 pounds ground meat
1 tablespoon salt
1 teaspoon black pepper
1 teaspoon lemon pepper
1 tablespoon minced onion
1 teaspoon dry mustard
4 tablespoons Worcestershire sauce
1 tablespoon Pickapeppa Sauce
1 tablespoon Cavender's All Purpose Greek Seasoning
1 tablespoon garlic powder
1 tablespoon dill weed
1 tablespoon paprika
1 tablespoon catsup
2 whole eggs
¼ pound Cheddar cheese, finely grated
¼ pound Swiss cheese, finely grated
¼ pound blue cheese, finely crumbled
¼ pound Gruyère cheese, finely grated
(Add other cheeses if desired; or use other cheese in place of above.)
2 11-ounce cans Cheddar cheese soup (undiluted)
1 tablespoon Worcestershire sauce
½ cup commercial barbecue sauce
8 English muffins, split
Mayonnaise
Mustard
Lettuce
Tomatoes
Pickles
16 crisp bacon slices

In a 4-quart mixing bowl add first 14 ingredients, and then stir until well mixed. (Adjust any special seasonings you prefer.) Make 8 hamburger patties from mixture. As you mold patties, add cheeses mixed together in center of patty and form hamburger around cheeses. Make sure patty is well molded around cheese. Cook hamburger preferably on barbecue pit over medium fire, making sure 1 side is browned lightly before turning over. (These are as good rare as they are well done.) While hamburgers are cooking, heat soup and Worchestershire sauce in a double boiler, and heat barbecue sauce. Toast English muffins after spreading them with mayonnaise and mustard. Add lettuce, tomatoes and pickles. Put 1 hamburger atop 2 muffin halves, then cheese sauce, barbecue sauce, crisp bacon slices. Serve open face.

Serves 8 Wesley Lambert Richardson

Greek Eggplant Casserole

2 tablespoons butter
1 cup finely chopped onion
1½ pounds lean ground meat
1 clove garlic, crushed
½ teaspoon oregano
1 teaspoon basil
½ teaspoon cinnamon
1 teaspoon salt
Dash pepper
2 8-ounce cans tomato sauce
2 tablespoons dry bread crumbs
2 1¼ pound eggplants, peeled
1 stick butter or margarine, melted

In a 3½-quart Dutch oven, melt butter and sauté onion, ground meat and garlic until brown. Add oregano, basil, cinnamon, salt, pepper and tomato sauce. Bring to a boil, stirring constantly. Reduce heat; simmer uncovered for 30 minutes, until thickened. Add bread crumbs. Set aside. Halve eggplants lengthwise. Slice crosswise ½" thick. Sprinkle lightly with salt; brush with melted butter. Broil until golden on each side.

2 tablespoons butter or margarine
2 tablespoons flour
½ teaspoon salt
Dash pepper
2 cups milk
2 eggs
8 tablespoons grated Parmesan cheese, divided
8 tablespoons grated Cheddar cheese, divided

In a medium saucepan melt butter. Remove from heat. Stir in flour, salt and pepper. Add milk gradually. Bring to a boil, stirring constantly until thickened. Remove from heat. Beat eggs. Beat some of hot cream mixture into eggs. Return egg mixture to saucepan. Mix well; set aside. In the bottom of a shallow 2-quart baking dish, layer half the eggplant, overlapping slightly. Sprinkle with 2 tablespoons each cheese. Spoon meat sauce evenly over eggplant. Sprinkle with 2 tablespoons each cheese. Layer remaining eggplant slices. Pour cream sauce over all. Sprinkle top with remaining 4 tablespoons each cheese. Bake at 350° for 35-40 minutes or until light golden brown and top is set. Cool slightly. Cut in squares.

Serves 8

Gail Kelley Shell

Meat-Stuffed Artichokes with Sauterne Sauce

4 whole fresh artichokes
1 pound ground chuck
¾ cup chopped onion
2 tablespoons cooking oil
½ cup fine, dry bread crumbs
¼ cup snipped parsley
2 eggs, beaten
½ teaspoon salt
¼ teaspoon pepper
¼ teaspoon ground nutmeg

Wash artichokes and cut off stems close to base. Cook in boiling salted water for 25-30 minutes or until stalks are fork-tender or leaf can be pulled out easily. Drain upside down. Cut off top third of leaves with kitchen shears; remove center leaves and chokes. Lightly brown meat and onion in oil; drain well, and place mixture in large mixing bowl. Add crumbs, parsley, eggs, salt, pepper and nutmeg; mix well. Spread artichoke leaves slightly; fill centers of artichokes with meat mixture. Place in a 9″ × 9″ × 2″ baking dish. Pour hot water around artichokes to a depth of 1″. Bake uncovered at 375° for 30-35 minutes or until heated thoroughly.

Sauterne Sauce

¼ cup sauterne
1 tablespoon minced onion
¾ cup mayonnaise
2 tablespoons snipped parsley
1 tablespoon lemon juice

In a small saucepan, combine sauterne and onion; let stand 10 minutes. Add mayonnaise, parsley and lemon juice; mix well until combined. Cook and stir over low heat until mixture is heated thoroughly. Do not boil. To serve, drizzle each artichoke with sauce.

Serves 4 — Anne Krison Mitchell

To keep artichokes and cauliflower from darkening when cooking, add a little milk or sugar to cooking water.

Moul Tousch

1 pound ground round
1 teaspoon salt
1 teaspoon pepper
1 teaspoon poultry seasoning
¼ teaspoon Accent
¼ cup chopped parsley
¼ cup chopped green onions
¼ cup chopped green pepper
1 egg
¼ cup tomato sauce
Dash Worcestershire sauce

Mix all ingredients together and shape into 1″ balls.

Noodle Dough

2 cups flour
2 eggs, beaten
¼ teaspoon baking powder
¼ teaspoon salt
2 tablespoons water

Mix dough in order given. Divide into small portions and roll very thin on floured board. Cut into 2½″ squares and place meatballs in center. Bring corners together and with moistened fingers roll in palm of hand. Drop in boiling salted water for 20 minutes.

Sour Lettuce

1 head lettuce, finely chopped
Tart oil and vinegar dressing
Salt and pepper

Mix above ingredients. Serve noodle balls over sour lettuce with melted butter on top. *This is a complete meal. Very unusual, but delicious.*

Serves 3-4

Peggy Daab Morgan

Spicy Chili

- 3 tablespoons butter or margarine
- 1½ cups thinly sliced onions
- 1 cup chopped green pepper
- 2 pounds lean beef, cut in ½" cubes
- 1 28-ounce can tomatoes, undrained
- ½ cup dry red wine
- 3-4 tablespoons chili powder
- 1 or 2 cloves garlic, crushed
- 1 teaspoon oregano
- 1 teaspoon paprika
- ½ teaspoon cumin seed
- ½ teaspoon pepper
- 2 teaspoons salt
- 1 15-ounce can chili beans

Melt butter in large pot or Dutch oven. Sauté onion and green pepper; add beef and brown. Add remaining ingredients except beans. Simmer covered until beef is tender, about 2 hours. Add beans and reheat. *Serve with salted crackers or over rice or noodles. For added ease when cubing round steak, have your meat partially frozen or have the butcher grind the meat coarsely.*

Serves 6

Joan Yarbrough Gresham

Chili de Señor Pico

- 1 pound ground chuck
- 2 tablespoons flour
- 5 teaspoons chili powder
- 1 8-ounce can tomato sauce
- 1 bunch green onions, chopped
- 1 6-ounce can ripe olives, sliced
- 1 cup boiling water
- 1 teaspoon ground cumin
- Salt and pepper to taste
- Pinch oregano
- 1 pound Cheddar cheese, cut in bite-size pieces
- 1 15-ounce can red kidney beans

Brown ground chuck. Drain. Add flour, chili powder, tomato sauce, green onions, ripe olives, boiling water and seasonings. Simmer a few minutes and add cheese and beans. Heat until cheese melts. *As a dip, omit beans and serve in chafing dish. Keep heated for dipping with corn chips. As main dish, add beans and serve over corn chips.*

Yields 1-1½ quarts

Rosemary Cherry Futch
Winnfield, Louisiana

Thrill Hill Chili

6 pounds ground chuck
4 large yellow onions, chopped
3 large ribs celery, chopped
1 green pepper, chopped
4 cloves garlic, chopped
8 tablespoons chili powder
1 tablespoon salt
1 tablespoon black pepper
2 16-ounce cans tomatoes, chopped
3 15-ounce cans tomato sauce
1 cup catsup
1 cup chili sauce
4 cups water, divided
Grated cheese
Chopped green onions
Corn chips

Add chopped vegetables to meat and brown. Add seasonings, tomatoes, tomato sauce and 2 cups water. Let simmer for at least 3 hours. Strain off grease. Add 2 cups water for a little more sauce. Garnish with grated cheese, chopped green onions and corn chips. *Children love this. Adults might want to add cayenne pepper to taste for more spice. For Sloppy Joes, add ½ cup barbecue sauce to 1 quart of meat sauce.*

Serves 25

Ann Olene Covington Querbes

Chili-Frito Casserole

3 pounds lean ground meat
3 cups chopped onion
2 cups water
3 12-ounce cans tomato sauce
⅓ cup Gebhardt's chili powder
3 1-pound cans kidney beans, drained
1 10½-ounce package regular corn chips
¾ cup sliced ripe olives
2½ cups shredded sharp Cheddar cheese

Brown meat and onion. Drain excess grease. Add water, tomato sauce and chili powder. Simmer for 30 minutes. In a 4-quart casserole (about 3½" deep), layer beginning with meat mixture, then kidney beans, corn chips, olives, cheese, ending with chips and cheese. Bake at 325° for 50-60 minutes.

Serves 10

Shirley Willman Skipworth

Cabbage Rolls

1 pound ground round
2 slices white bread
Salt and pepper
½ 10½-ounce can onion soup
1 head cabbage leaves, wilted

Run hot water through bread and squeeze out excess. Add to meat. Add salt and pepper and soup. Mix well.

Freeze the cabbage ahead of time and then run hot water over it to wilt cabbage leaves—no odor. In each wilted leaf, roll a small ball of meat. Tuck in the ends and place in roaster, seam side down. Continue until all meat is used. Make sauce below.

Sauce

2 10¾-ounce cans tomato soup
¾ cup brown sugar
3 teaspoons lemon juice
1 teaspoon Kitchen Bouquet
Salt and pepper to taste
1½ soup cans water

Mix all ingredients together and pour over cabbage rolls. Bake at 400° for 30 minutes. Turn oven down to 325°; cover roaster and continue cooking 3 hours until sauce thickens. Add more onion soup if sauce is too thick.

Serves 6

Phyllis Hinchin Selber

Add caraway seeds to boiling water to remove odor when cooking cabbage and shrimp. NO caraway taste when cooked.

Rub hands with parsley or lemon to remove the odor after chopping onions or garlic.

Dolmades with Avgolemono Sauce

30-40 grape leaves (16-ounce jar)
1½ pounds lean ground chuck
1 tablespoon salt
½ teaspoon pepper
1 tablespoon crushed fresh or dried mint leaves
1 teaspoon oregano
1 small onion, grated
1 egg, beaten
½ teaspoon baking soda
2 tablespoons dry white wine
2 tablespoons hot water
½ cup raw rice
2 tablespoons butter

To prepare grape leaves: rinse 3 times in a colander under cold water, then drop into a large kettle of boiling water. Turn off heat and soak for an hour.

To prepare filling: sauté onions, mint, parsley and seasonings in butter or oil. In a large bowl combine meat, soda, water, wine, eggs, oregano and raw rice. To this, add sautéed mixture and mix thoroughly by hand.

To assemble ingredients: in a heavy pot, suitable for top of stove, melt 2 tablespoons butter and line with the larger of the rinsed grape leaves. (The large leaves are tough and not really suitable for good dolmades; so line the pan with these.) Separate the remaining leaves; remove the thick stem from each, and drape over the side of the pan in which they were cooked. Using 1 tablespoon of filling for each leaf, place the filling at the stem end of the leaf *being absolutely sure that the shiny side is down.* (The filling is placed on the dull side.) Fold the sides of the leaf in over the filling and roll tightly. Place the rolled, filled leaves in *tight* layers in the buttered pot. Now measure 2 cups or more of beef or chicken broth and pour over the dolmades. Place a heavy plate over them in the kettle to keep them from unrolling. (The stock will cover the plate.) COVER the kettle and cook over medium heat 30-45 minutes. Shake (do not open) the pan occasionally.

Continued...

Avgolemono Sauce

- 2 cups stock from dolmades pot, adding water if necessary
- 2 teaspoons flour
- 3 eggs
- ½ cup lemon juice

Prepare sauce at serving time and add at the moment the meal is to begin. Make a paste of ½ cup of stock and the flour and combine with remaining stock in a saucepan and simmer gently 5 minutes. Using an electric beater, beat the eggs in a large bowl until very thick. By the spoonful, gradually add the hot stock and the lemon juice alternately while continuing to beat. Pour the sauce over the dolmades and shake the pan to distribute the sauce evenly. Serve immediately and do not stir, cover or reheat.

The dolmades can be made early in the day. Also, they may be served at room temperature with a little olive oil drizzled over as an hors d'oeuvre.

Serves 8-10 — Christine Sidaris Svolos

Italian Casserole

- 1 8-ounce package crescent dinner rolls
- 1 pound ground meat
- 1 onion, chopped
- 1 16-ounce can stewed tomatoes
- 1 tablespoon Italian seasoning
- ½ teaspoon seasoned black pepper
- 1 teaspoon salt
- ½ pound fresh mushrooms, sliced
- 2 cups grated Mozzarella cheese
- Parmesan cheese

Spread package of crescent rolls in an 8″ × 11″ Pyrex dish. Brown meat and drain. Add onions, tomatoes and seasonings. Cover and cook 35-40 minutes. Spread this on dough. Layer mushrooms over meat. Top with Mozzarella, then Parmesan cheese. Bake at 350° until hot. Let sit 10 minutes before serving.

Serves 4-6 — Carolyn Hamel Griffen

Tufoli

1 5-ounce package tufoli
3 quarts boiling water
1 tablespoon salt
1 tablespoon oil
1 pound ground chuck
1 teaspoon salt
½ teaspoon pepper
¼ teaspoon cayenne
1 clove garlic, finely chopped
Dash Tabasco
6 ounces small-curd cottage cheese
1 egg, well beaten
3 tablespoons Parmesan cheese
1 15½-ounce jar spaghetti sauce
1 cup grated Monterey Jack cheese

In a large pot bring water and salt to boil; add tufoli slowly. Cook uncovered until tender, approximately 10 minutes, stirring occasionally. Drain and cool. Brown ground chuck and drain. Season with salt, peppers, garlic and Tabasco. Add the cottage cheese, egg and Parmesan cheese. Stuff tufoli and arrange in a shallow rectangular baking dish. Cover with spaghetti sauce and bake at 375° for 25 minutes. Sprinkle with cheese and serve. *Add ½ package frozen chopped spinach (cooked) for variety. May use your own homemade spaghetti sauce instead.*

Serves 4-5

Cherrie McCrory Iles

Italian Meatballs with Tomato Sauce

1 pound ground round
¼ cup chopped parsley
1 teaspoon vegetable salt
¼ teaspoon white pepper
1 egg, slightly beaten
1 clove garlic, finely chopped
1 cup soft whole wheat bread crumbs
3 tablespoons water
2 tablespoons grated Parmesan cheese
2 tablespoons safflower oil

Combine ingredients except oil in a bowl. Mix stirring with a fork until blended. Shape into medium-size balls. Brown balls in oil in 12″ skillet turning to brown on all sides. When all are browned, add following sauce.

Continued...

Tomato Sauce

3 tablespoons safflower oil
⅓ cup diced onion
1 clove garlic, minced
½ cup diced celery
1 28-ounce can tomatoes, crushed and strained
2 6-ounce cans tomato paste
1 4-ounce jar sliced mushrooms with liquid
1½ teaspoons vegetable salt
⅛ teaspoon pepper
¼ teaspoon nutmeg
¼ teaspoon allspice
½ teaspoon oregano
2 teaspoons sugar
3 tablespoons chopped parsley
4 tablespoons Parmesan cheese

Heat oil and sautē the onion, garlic and celery until tender. Add the remaining ingredients. Bring to boil and simmer for about 1 hour. For thicker sauce, simmer uncovered until desired consistency is obtained. Bring meatballs and sauce to a boil; then cover and simmer for 30 minutes. Serve over hot cooked and drained spaghetti sprinkled with grated Parmesan cheese.

Serves 6 Nettie Mae Gravelle Walden

Spaghettini with Italian Sausage

2 tablespoons oil
½ pound mushrooms, sliced
1 carrot, sliced
1 clove garlic, crushed
½ cup chopped celery
1 large onion, sliced
2 large green peppers, cut in strips
1 pound Italian sausage, casings removed
1 12-ounce can tomato paste
12 ounces water
1 teaspoon sugar
½ teaspoon Italian seasoning
¼ cup dry red wine (optional)
1½-2 12-ounce packages spaghettini

Use black iron Dutch oven to sautē mushrooms, carrot, garlic, celery, onion and green pepper in oil. Add sausage; cook until sausage loses redness. Drain fat. Add remaining ingredients. Cover and simmer for 40 minutes to 1 hour, stirring occasionally. Serve hot, over cooked spaghettini. *When casings are removed from sausage, sausage will crumble in sauce. It's supposed to!*

Serves 6 Dee Jackson Bustillo

Lasagne

8 ounces whole wheat lasagne noodles
1 teaspoon olive oil
1 teaspoon vegetable or sea salt
1½ tablespoons olive oil
2 cloves garlic, minced
1 cup chopped onion
½ cup chopped celery
½ cup chopped green pepper
½ pound ground round
1 13½-ounce can Italian tomatoes, chopped
2 6-ounce cans tomato paste
1 6-ounce jar sliced mushrooms
¼ cup minced parsley
1 bay leaf, crushed
⅛ teaspoon oregano
⅛ teaspoon basil
⅛ teaspoon crushed red pepper
Pinch thyme
1 teaspoon salt
1 14-ounce carton low-fat cottage cheese
1 14-ounce package Mozzarella cheese
Parmesan cheese, freshly grated if possible
Parsley
Paprika

Prepare the lasange noodles by placing them into plenty of boiling water to which 1 teaspoon each of olive oil and salt has been added. When tender (about 7 minutes) rinse with cold water to keep from sticking together and set aside.

In heavy skillet sauté minced garlic, onion, celery and green pepper in olive oil for 5 minutes. Add ground round to vegetables and continue to sauté until the meat loses its redness. Add the Italian tomatoes and tomato paste. Stir in the mushrooms. Add parsley, bay leaf, oregano, basil, red pepper, thyme and salt. Stir sauce well and simmer for 30 minutes over low heat.

To prepare the lasagne, line the bottom of a well oiled 2-quart oblong pan with 4 noodles. Spread half of the meat sauce on top of the noodles; then layer with half the cottage cheese; then layer with half the Mozzarella cheese. Sprinkle with Parmesan cheese. Repeat the procedure putting layer of noodles, meat sauce, cottage cheese, Mozzarella; then sprinkle generously with Parmesan. Garnish with minced parsley and paprika. Bake in 350° oven for 30 minutes. Remove from oven and let stand for a few minutes before cutting into squares. Serve on warm plates.

Serves 6-8

Johnette Querbes Barnes

Tamale Bake

1 14½-ounce can tamales
2 tablespoons all-purpose flour
1 teaspoon chili powder
Garlic salt to taste
3 eggs, beaten
1 16-ounce can cream style corn
½ cup sliced ripe olives
½ cup sharp Cheddar cheese, shredded

Drain tamales, reserving sauce. Slice tamales crosswise; set aside. Combine reserved tamale sauce, flour, chili powder and garlic salt in mixing bowl. Add eggs, corn, olives and sliced tamales. Turn into a 6″×10″×2″ baking dish. Bake uncovered at 350° for 40 minutes. Sprinkle with cheese. Bake 3 minutes longer until cheese melts. Cut into squares.

Serves 4

Rosemary Cherry Futch

Beef-Chili Relleños Casserole

1 pound ground beef
½ cup chopped onion
1 teaspoon salt
½ teaspoon pepper
3 4-ounce cans whole green chilies
1½ cups grated Cheddar cheese
4 eggs, beaten
1½ cups milk
¼ cup flour

Brown beef and onion; drain grease. Sprinkle meat with salt and pepper. Cut green chilies in half, lengthwise, and remove seeds. Arrange half of chilies in a 6″×10″×1½″ greased baking dish. Sprinkle chilies with grated cheese and top this with meat mixture. Place remaining chilies over meat. Beat eggs, milk and flour until smooth; pour batter over chili and meat mixture. Bake uncovered in 350° oven for 45-50 minutes or until inserted knife comes out clean. Cool 5 minutes and cut into squares for serving. *Serve Mexican hot sauce, spooned on top if desired, as this dish is not "pepper" hot.*

Serves 6-8

Vera Williams Calvin
Hot Springs, Arkansas

Moussaka

1 large eggplant, peeled and sliced
1½ teaspoons salt
1½ pounds ground chuck
1 large onion, chopped
2 cloves garlic, minced
½ teaspoon thyme
¼ teaspoon oregano
¼ teaspoon nutmeg
2 tablespoons parsley, chopped
1 teaspoon sugar
1 16-ounce can tomato sauce
¼ cup white wine
½ cup bread crumbs, divided
Olive oil
2 tablespoons grated Parmesan cheese

Season eggplant slices with salt and allow to stand for 30 minutes. Meanwhile, brown meat with onion and garlic. Add seasonings, parsley, tomato sauce and wine. Cover and simmer for 30 minutes. Add half the bread crumbs.

Sauce

⅓ cup flour
⅓ cup butter, melted
1½ cups milk
¼ cup sherry
3 eggs, well beaten
½ teaspoon salt
½ teaspoon pepper

Melt butter in saucepan; stir in flour and salt. Gradually add milk and sherry, and cook over medium heat until thickened. Remove from heat. Stir a few tablespoons of sauce into beaten eggs in a small bowl. Gradually stir the eggs into sauce.

To assemble, pat eggplant slices dry and brown in olive oil. Sprinkle bottom of large rectangular casserole with remaining bread crumbs. Place some slices of eggplant in casserole. Spoon layer of meat sauce over eggplant. Repeat layers of eggplant and meat sauce until all are used. Cover evenly with cream sauce, sprinkle with Parmesan and bake at 350° for 40 minutes or until nicely browned. Let sit 20-30 minutes before slicing.

Serves 6-8

Carolyn Clay Flournoy

Tomato juice used to soak a hopelessly black frying pan for 30-45 minutes will let you wash it clean as new.

Beef and Eggplant Casserole

1½ pounds ground chuck
1 teaspoon chili powder
½ teaspoon ground cumin
2 medium onions, coarsely chopped
2 medium green peppers, coarsely chopped
Salt and pepper to taste
1 medium eggplant, pared, cubed and boiled
½ teaspoon oregano
1 large bay leaf, crumbled
Sprinkle anise seed
2 tablespoons flour
3 large slice or diced fresh tomatoes or may substitute 1 16-ounce can tomatoes, drained
1 teaspoon basil
Dots butter
Seasoned croutons
Parmesan cheese

Using no grease, brown meat in a heavy skillet, mixing in chili powder and cumin. Add onions, green peppers, salt and pepper to the browned mixture. Cook until onions and peppers are barely tender. Set aside. Boil eggplant in a small amount of salted water until barely fork tender; drain well and spread eggplant over a greased 2-quart flat casserole. Cover the eggplant with the meat mixture; sprinkle evenly with oregano, bay leaf, anise seed and flour. Layer with tomatoes and sprinkle with basil, butter, croutons and cheese. Bake uncovered in 350° oven for 30 minutes or until the mixture bubbles and the croutons are slightly browned.

Serves 4 generously

Runette Martindale Longmire
Arlington, Texas

To "dice" is to cut into cubes, evenly shaped. When appearance counts, dice.
To "chop" is to cut up in a less careful way with pieces about the same size. Shapes may be irregular.
To "mince" is to chop finely into small pieces.

Cranberry Meat Loaf

¼ cup brown sugar
½ cup cranberry sauce
1½ pounds ground beef
½ pound ground smoked ham
¾ cup milk
¾ cup cracker crumbs
2 eggs
1½ teaspoons salt
⅛ teaspoon pepper
2 tablespoons diced onion
3 bay leaves

Spread brown sugar over bottom of greased loaf pan. Mash cranberry sauce and spread over sugar. Combine remaining ingredients except bay leaves; shape into loaf and place on top of cranberry sauce. Place bay leaves on top of loaf and bake at 350° for approximately 1 hour. Remove bay leaves before serving.

Serves 8-10 Margaret Scott Burks

Sicilian Twirl Meat Loaf

¾ cup soft bread crumbs
½ cup tomato juice or V-8
2 eggs, beaten
2 tablespoons snipped parsley
1 clove garlic, minced
½ teaspoon salt
¼ teaspoon pepper
2 pounds lean ground beef
8 thin slices boiled ham
6 ounces grated Mozzarella cheese
3 slices Mozzarella cheese, halved diagonally

Combine first 7 ingredients. Mix with ground beef. Pat meat into a 10″ × 12″ rectangle on foil or wax paper. Arrange ham slices on meat, leaving ½″ margin. Sprinkle grated cheese on ham. Using foil to lift, roll meat, starting from short side. Seal ends and seam. Place meat roll seam side down in baking pan. Bake at 350° for 50 minutes for medium rare and 1 hour and 15 minutes for well done. Place cheese triangles on top and return to oven for 5 minutes.

Serves 6-8 Marion Wiener Weiss

Tate's Meat Loaf

1 pound ground beef
¼ pound ground ham
½ pound ground pork
(Meat should be ground together.)
2 tablespoons brown sugar
2 cups fine bread crumbs
1½ cups milk

Combine all ingredients until thoroughly mixed. Bake in loaf pan at 350° for 1½ hours. Serve with mustard sauce.

Mustard Sauce

1 tablespoon dry mustard
2 eggs, beaten
2 tablespoons vinegar
2 tablespoons water
1 cup sour cream

Place mustard, eggs, vinegar and water in the top of a double boiler. Cook until thick, stirring while cooking. Add sour cream. Serve with meat loaf.

Serves 6

Chef Henry Tate

Dilled Veal en Crème

¼ cup sour cream
½ cup whipping cream
2 teaspoons dill weed
1½ pounds veal scallops
3 tablespoons butter
Juice ¼ lemon
1 teaspoon salt

Combine sour cream, whipping cream and dill. Cover and let sit in refrigerator for at least 4 hours. Pound veal scallops between wax paper until thin and tender. Sauté veal in butter until done. Squeeze lemon juice over meat and stir. Remove meat to heated dish and keep warm in oven. Keep juices in pan. Stir cream mixture and salt into pan juices. When warm, pour over veal and serve.

Serves 4

Margaret Hunkin Crow

Veal Patrician

1 10-ounce package chopped frozen spinach, cooked and drained
1 cup grated ricotta cheese
1 cup grated Parmesan cheese, divided
1 egg yolk
½ teaspoon nutmeg
8 slices veal (milk fed, sliced ¼" thick)
8 slices prosciutto (or other unsmoked ham, sliced wafer thin)
1 cup milk, beaten with 2 eggs
Flour
1 stick butter, divided
2 tablespoons olive oil, divided
1 clove garlic, crushed
½ yellow onion, chopped
¼ pound ground meat
½ teaspoon salt
1 teaspoon white pepper
1 1-pound can Italian plum tomatoes, coarsely chopped
¼ cup vermouth

Prepare filling of chopped spinach, ricotta cheese, ¾ cup of the Parmesan, egg yolk and nutmeg. Mix and set aside. Pound veal flat and face with prosciutto Place an eighth of the filling at end of veal/prosciutto and roll, securing with a toothpick. Slide veal rolls through milk and egg mixture, dredge in flour, and sautē until golden in half of the butter and olive oil. Remove and place in oven proof casserole. In clean skillet, use remaining butter and oil to sautē garlic and onion until transparent. Add ground meat and salt and pepper. Cook until done, but not brown. Add tomatoes and vermouth. Simmer until vermouth aroma is gone. Pour this sauce over veal. Prepare bēchamel sauce below.

4 tablespoons butter
4-5 tablespoons flour
2 cups scalded milk
Salt

Melt butter; blend flour and add milk and salt to taste. Stir until thick and smooth. Pour over red sauce and sprinkle top with remaining ¼ cup of Parmesan. Bake at 400° for 15-20 minutes or until bubbly and brown. Salt carefully as prosciutto is cured, and *very* salty when cooked. *This recipe is not difficult if done in steps.*

Serves 8

Patricia Welder Robinson
Houston, Texas

Veal Picante

4 ounces prime veal strip per serving
Flour
Salt and pepper
Freshly drawn butter
Lemon juice
Parsley, chopped

Cut veal into 3 equal-size portions. Pound until approximately ⅛" thick. Season lightly with salt and pepper; dredge in flour and shake off excess. Sauté gently in butter without browning. Move veal to platter and sprinkle with lemon juice and parsely. *For Veal Scallopini Marsala, after moving veal to platter, add to skillet more freshly drawn butter, 3 ounces sliced-mushrooms and 3 tablespoons Marsala wine. Simmer until creamy. Pour over veal and garnish with parsley.*

Serves 1

Chef Shorty Lenard

Veal with Capers

8 veal scallopini
¾ teaspoon salt
¼ teaspoon pepper
Flour
4 tablespoons butter, divided
2 tablespoons vegetable oil
½ pound fresh mushrooms, sliced
2 tablespoons red or white wine vinegar
2 tablespoons water
½ cup chicken broth
2-4 tablespoons capers, drained
2 tablespoons chopped parsley
4 cups cooked vermicelli

Pound veal very thin. Salt, pepper and flour scallopini, and sauté in 2 tablespoons butter and oil. Sauté mushrooms in remaining 2 tablespoons butter in a different pan. Add water and vinegar to veal pan and deglaze. Add mushrooms, capers and chicken broth. Cook until syrupy. Add parsley. Pour sauce over veal and serve atop vermicelli.

Serves 4

Cookbook Committee

Cannelloni Milanese

White Sauce

- 4 tablespoons butter
- 4 tablespoons flour
- 1 cup milk
- 1 cup evaporated milk
- ¼ teaspoon salt
- ¼ teaspoon white pepper
- 2 teaspoons dry chicken stock base

Melt butter in a saucepan and add flour. When well blended, add the 2 milks, stirring with a whisk. Add salt, pepper and chicken stock base. Cook, stirring until it thickens.

Red Sauce

- 2 tablespoons olive oil
- ½ cup chopped onion
- 1 16-ounce can tomatoes, chopped, and juice
- 1 15-ounce can tomato sauce
- 4 tablespoons tomato paste
- 1 teaspoon Italian herb seasoning
- ½ teaspoon basil
- 1 teaspoon sugar
- ¼ teaspoon salt
- 1 teaspoon seasoned pepper

Heat oil. Add onions and sauté until clear. Add the remaining ingredients and cook 40 minutes.

Filling

- 2 tablespoons olive oil
- 2 tablespoons butter
- ½ cup chopped onion
- ½ teaspoon minced garlic
- 1½ pounds ground veal
- 1 10-ounce package frozen chopped spinach, defrosted and squeezed
- ½ cup grated fresh Parmesan cheese, divided
- 3 eggs, beaten slightly
- 2 tablespoons whipping cream or evaporated milk
- ½ teaspoon Italian herb seasoning
- 1 8-ounce package manicotti noodles, cooked and drained
- or 1 8-ounce package lasagne noodles, cooked and drained
- or 16 cooked crêpes

Heat oil and butter and sauté onion and garlic until clear. Add meat and sauté 2-3 minutes. Add spinach and continue cooking 3-4 minutes until mixture is thick. Put in a mixing bowl. Add remaining ingredients, reserving ¼ cup Parmesan cheese to use later.

Continued...

Stuff each manicotti tube with filling, or put 1 tablespoon of filling on a 3½" lasagne rectangle and roll to cover, or fill crêpes and roll up. Layer a third of the red sauce in a 9" x 13" x 2" baking dish. Put the canneloni side by side in 1 layer, seam side down. Put white sauce over that; then add the rest of the red sauce. Sprinkle with remaining ¼ cup of Parmesan cheese. Bake at 375° for 20 minutes. Broil 30 seconds to brown. *See Index for crêpe recipe.*

Serves 8 — Cookbook Commitee

Munchen Veal Stew

2 pounds veal shoulder
Flour
3 tablespoons butter (or more)
1 large onion, sliced
3 tomatoes, peeled and quartered
1 bay leaf
5 whole cloves
¼ teaspoon thyme
1 teaspoon marjoram
¼ teaspoon cayenne pepper
Salt and pepper
2½ cups light beer
5 ginger snaps
Juice 1 lemon

Cut veal shoulder into about 1" cubes; roll in flour, and fry lightly in 3 tablespoons butter. Remove from pan and set aside. Sauté onion slices in the same butter. Return meat to onions in pan; add tomatoes, bay leaf, cloves, thyme, marjoram, cayenne pepper, salt and pepper to taste. Add beer. Cover pan tightly and cook slowly 2 hours. Moisten 5 ginger snaps with water; crush and add to contents of pan. Recover pan and continue cooking slowing for 30 minutes more. Just before serving add the lemon juice. *With this stew, serve mashed potatoes and cold beer.*

Serves 6 — Carolyn Clay Flournoy

Veal Cutlets with Mushrooms

- **6 veal cutlets, ¼" thick**
- **⅓ cup flour**
- **½ stick butter or margarine**
- **1 clove garlic, halved**
- **½ pound mushrooms, sliced**
- **½ cup dry vermouth**
- **¼ cup water**
- **1 teaspoon salt**
- **1 tablespoon chopped parsley**

On cutting board, pound veal cutlets lightly on both sides until ⅛" thick. On wax paper, coat cutlets lightly with flour. In a 12" skillet over low heat, melt butter; add garlic and cook until golden; discard garlic. Increase heat to medium high; add 3 cutlets and cook until lightly browned on both sides, turning once. Remove cutlets to platter, keeping warm. Repeat with other 3 cutlets, adding butter if necessary. Reduce heat to medium. To drippings in skillet, add mushrooms, vermouth, water and salt. Cook, stirring until mushrooms are tender, about 5 minutes. Spoon mixture (which will not be thick) over meat and garnish with parsley. *May want to plan on 2 cutlets per person because veal will shrink. Can substitute lemon juice for dry vermouth.*

Serves 6 Kay Arceneaux

Pork Loin Roast Vineyard Style

- **4-6 pound pork loin roast**
- **½ teaspoon salt**
- **¼ teaspoon seasoned pepper**
- **¼ teaspoon sage**
- **¼ teaspoon nutmeg**
- **1 clove garlic, minced**
- **2 tablespoons oil**
- **¼ cup chopped parsley**
- **¼ cup chopped onion**
- **1 bay leaf**
- **2 cups red wine (not dry)**
- **1 cup beef consommé**

Rub meat with salt, seasoned pepper, sage and nutmeg. Brown in skillet with oil and garlic. Place roast in a baking dish and add parsley, onion, bay leaf and wine. Bake uncovered at 350° for about 2 hours, turning twice. Add consommé for last 20 minutes of cooking time. Strain gravy to remove vegetables. Serve over rice.

Serves 6 Clarisse Kennon Sullivan

Pork Chops 'n Stuffing

4 pork chops
2 tablespoons chopped green onion
¼ cup melted butter or margarine
¼ teaspoon poultry seasoning
⅔ cup water, divided
3 cups seasoned bread crumbs
1 10¾-ounce can cream of mushroom soup

Brown pork chops on both sides. Place them in a shallow baking dish; set aside. Lightly mix onion, butter, poultry seasoning, ⅓ cup water and bread crumbs. Divide this into 4 portions and mound atop each pork chop, lightly pressing together. Blend soup and ⅓ cup water. Pour over chops. Bake at 350° for 1 hour or until tender.

Serves 4 Rebecca Strohmaier Roberts

Sherried Pork Chops

6 ½"-¾" thick pork chops
Salt and pepper
Flour
3-4 tablespoons vegetable oil
⅔ cup sherry
⅓ cup water
⅔ cup chopped green onions
½ pound fresh mushrooms or 1 3-ounce can, sliced

Salt and pepper pork chops to taste. Dust lightly with flour and brown in oil. Arrange chops in casserole dish or iron skillet. Cover with mushrooms, onions, sherry and water. Cook at 350° for 35-45 minutes depending on thickness of the chops. *This makes a nice gravy and could be served over rice or potatoes.*

Serves 4-6 Suzanne Musgrave Duggan

Applesauce and horseradish are good accompaniments for pork.

Sweet-Sour Pork

2 tablespoons bacon drippings
1½ pounds lean boned pork shoulder, cut into thin strips
1 1-pound 4-ounce can pineapple chunks, reserve syrup
½ cup water
⅓ cup vinegar
¼ cup brown sugar, packed
2 tablespoons cornstarch
½ teaspoon salt
1 tablespoon soy sauce
½ cup thinly sliced onion
¾ cup thinly sliced green pepper
Cooked rice

In hot bacon grease, in a large skillet, cook meat until golden brown on all sides. Combine ¾-1 cup of pineapple syrup, water, vinegar, brown sugar, cornstarch, salt and soy sauce. Cook 2 minutes until clear and slightly thickened. Add meat; cook covered 1 hour or until meat is fork tender. Add onion, pineapple and pepper; cook for 7 minutes. Serve with ring of rice.

Serves 4

Dorothy Davies Miller

Sausage Supreme

1 pound sausage
1 cup chopped celery
½ cup chopped onion
½ cup chopped green pepper
¼ cup chopped pimientos
1 10¾-ounce can cream of mushroom soup
1½ cups milk
½ cup raw rice
½ teaspoon poultry seasoning
¼ teaspoon salt
1 cup soft bread crumbs
2 tablespoons butter, melted

Brown sausage; drain off excess grease. Add celery, onion and green pepper; cook until tender, but do not brown. Stir in pimientos, soup, milk, rice and seasonings. Put in a 2-quart casserole. Bake uncovered at 350° for 50 minutes, stirring occasionally. Mix crumbs and butter; sprinkle over casserole. Bake 20 minutes longer, uncovered. *Good with black-eyed peas.*

Serves 6

Janie Harris Tipton

Sangor

1 stick butter
1 clove garlic, crushed
1½ large onions, chopped
½ pound mushrooms, sliced
1 pound pork, cubed
1 pound sirloin tip, cubed
½ cup raw wild rice
½ cup raw white rice
2 10½-ounce cans consommé, divided
4 teaspoons soy sauce
2 cups chopped celery
1 8-ounce can sliced water chestnuts
2 tablespoons seasoned salt
½ cup slivered almonds, sautéed
Almonds for garnish

Sauté garlic, onions and mushrooms in butter. Remove from pan and put into casserole. Brown meat well and add to casserole with garlic, onions and mushrooms. Add wild and white rice, soy sauce, celery, water chestnuts, seasoned salt and 1 can consommé. Bake at 350° for 2½ hours. Then stir in the second can of consommé and the almonds. Bake 30 minutes longer. Garnish with a few almonds.

Serves 6

Janell Maeder Falter

Curried Ham Roll

3 tablespoons butter, melted
2 tablespoons cornstarch
2 teaspoons curry powder
3 cups milk
½ teaspoon MSG
1 cup blond seedless raisins

Add cornstarch and curry to melted butter to make a paste. Slowly blend in milk; add MSG and raisins. Cook sauce slowly until thickened, stirring constantly.

3 cups chicken broth
1 cup raw long-grain rice
1 tablespoon minced onion
1 tablespoon minced parsley
6-8 slices center cut ham

Cook rice in chicken broth and drain; add onion, parsley and 1 cup curry sauce. Fill ham slices with rice mixture. Roll. Place in shallow dish seam side down. Pour remaining sauce over these and bake at 300° about 30-40 minutes. *Prepare ahead and put in oven at last minute, if desired.*

Serves 6-8

Gladys Bozarth Lincoln

Ham Balls

2 pounds ham
1 pound pork
4 eggs, beaten
2 cups bread, broken
1½-1¾ cups milk

Grind ham and pork together. Add eggs, bread and milk to meat. Shape into 16 large balls. Bake in oven at 350° for 30 minutes. Drain.

1 cup water
1 cup cider vinegar
3 cups brown sugar
4 teaspoons dry mustard

Bring water, vinegar, brown sugar and dry mustard to a boil in a pan and simmer 10 minutes. Pour syrup over balls and bake at 350° for 1 hour. Serve hot.

Serves 8

Gail Kelley Shell

Special Egg Rolls

½ pound lean pork, chopped
¼ pound raw shrimp, shelled, deveined and chopped
3 tablespoons peanut or vegetable oil
2 cups chopped Chinese cabbage, or 2 cups fresh or canned bean sprouts
1 cup chopped celery
4 green onions, chopped
½ teaspoon salt
¼ teaspoon MSG
1 teaspoon cornstarch
1 tablespoon soy sauce
1 package egg roll skins
1 egg, beaten
Oil for frying

Heat 3 tablespoons oil in large skillet over high heat. Add pork. Cook, stirring until meat loses its color. Add shrimp. Cook 1 minute. Add vegetables and seasonings. Cook 2 minutes, stirring often. Sprinkle with cornstarch. Mix well. Stir in soy sauce. Cook 1 minute. Turn into colander; set in bowl. Cool completely.

Remove egg roll skins one at a time. Place 1 square with a corner pointing toward you. Put 2-3 tablespoons cooled fill-

Continued...

ing on dough, slightly below center. Brush edges of dough with beaten egg. Fold the corner nearest to you up and over the filling. Fold the left corner over; then fold over the right one. Roll toward top corner to form a cylinder. Repeat with rest of squares. Cover with a damp towel until ready to use. Heat 2″ of oil or shortening to 375° in deep heavy pan or in a skillet. Cook rolls, 3 or 4 at a time, until crisp and golden. Drain. *Serve with a sweet sauce and hot mustard.*

Yields 12 — Joe B. Boddie

Choucroute Frankfurt Style

4 pounds fresh or canned sauerkraut, well drained
2 tablespoons bacon drippings or rendered pork fat
1 large onion, chopped
2 cloves garlic, chopped
1 pound slab bacon
4 pig knuckles
½ teaspoon caraway seeds
1½ teaspoons juniper berries, slightly bruised or ⅓ cup gin
2 bay leaves
Salt and pepper to taste
2 cups Moselle wine
2 cups water or chicken stock
8 frankfurters
1 pound bratwurst

Rinse sauerkraut in cold water; then press it out by hand until dry and shake it loose to remove lumps. Heat drippings in an 8-quart Dutch oven and sauté onions and garlic until golden; remove and set aside. Place a third of sauerkraut in pot. Layer with half each of the bacon, pig knuckles, onions, garlic and caraway seeds. Combine half of the juniper berries and 1 bay leaf in a cheesecloth bag; place on top of mixture. Add salt and pepper to taste. Repeat layers and seasonings, topping with remaining third of sauerkraut. Add wine and water. Cover and bake at 375° for 3 hours. After 3 hours, slice bratwurst into 8 pieces. Arrange with frankfurters on top of sauerkraut. Cover and continue cooking 30 minutes. Taste for seasoning.

To serve, arrange sauerkraut in a dome shape on a large heated platter, discarding seasoning bags. Place meats on sauerkraut. *Accompany with German mustard, bowl of horseradish, pumpernickel bread, Reisling wine and beer.*

Serves 6-8 — Carolyn Clay Flournoy

Roast Lamb Athenian Style

8 pound leg of lamb
1½ teaspoons salt
Pepper
3 garlic cloves
½ cup melted butter, divided
¼ cup lemon juice
1 teaspoon dried rosemary
3 pounds new potatoes, pared
Paprika

Wipe lamb with damp paper towel. Rub with salt and pepper. Peel garlic and cut into slivers. Cut 12-16 slits about 1" deep into lamb. Insert garlic slivers. Place lamb in shallow roasting pan without rack. Brush lamb with ¼ cup melted butter. Pour lemon juice over lamb and sprinkle with rosemary. Arrange potatoes around meat; roast uncovered and baste often for about 2½-3 hours or until thermometer registers 170° for medium. Turn potatoes 3 or 4 times during roasting. Remove lamb to a heated platter and let stand for 20 minutes before carving. Serve with lemon egg sauce.

Lemon Egg Sauce

2 tablespoons butter
3 tablespoons flour
¾ teaspoon salt
1 cup chicken broth
3 tablespoons lemon juice
4 egg yolks
1 tablespoon chopped parsley

Melt butter in top of double boiler over direct heat. Remove from heat; stir in flour and salt until smooth. Gradually stir in broth and lemon juice. Cook over low heat, stirring until mixture boils. Place over hot, not boiling water. In a small bowl beat egg yolks. Slowly beat in a small amount of hot mixture. Slowly add to rest of mixture in double boiler stirring constantly. Cook over hot water until thick. Remove from heat and stir in chopped parsley.

Serves 6

Michele Armstrong
Qvistgaard-Petersen

Chicken Supreme

¼ cup flour
1 teaspoon paprika
1 teaspoon salt
Dash pepper
3 large whole chicken breasts, skinned, halved
¼ cup butter or margarine
2 tablespoons water
2 tablespoons flour
½ teaspoon salt
1¼ cups half and half
1 3-ounce can sliced mushrooms, drained
1 tablespoon lemon juice
2 ounces Swiss cheese, grated (about ½ cup)

At least a day ahead combine first 4 ingredients; coat chicken breasts with flour mixture and brown in butter. Add water and simmer covered for 25-30 minutes. Remove chicken to an 7½″×11¾″×1¾″ baking dish and reserve drippings. Combine flour, salt and half and half. Stir into reserved drippings in skillet. Cook and stir until thick and bubbly. Add mushrooms to sauce. Then add lemon juice and pour over chicken. Cover. Chill up to 24 hours. Bake covered at 350° until hot, 50-60 minutes. Sprinkle with cheese. Bake uncovered until cheese melts, 1-2 minutes.

Serves 6

Glenda Futch Farmer

Chicken Breasts in Sour Cream

6 chicken breast halves
1 stick butter
1 10¾-ounce can mushroom soup
1 cup sour cream
¼ cup sherry
Season to taste

Sautē chicken in butter until barely brown. Remove chicken from skillet. Turn fire off. Add soup, sour cream and sherry to drippings in skillet. Add seasonings of your choice. Pour mixture over chicken in a flat casserole. Bake at 350° for 1 hour. *You may prepare and bake this ahead, and reheat before serving.*

Serves 4-6

Dixey Thornton Sanders

Chicken Breasts Scallopini

3 whole chicken breasts, boned, skinned, halved
¾ teaspoon salt
½ teaspoon pepper
6 teaspoons cornstarch
6 teaspoons vegetable oil
2 egg whites, unbeaten

Pound chicken breasts until ¼″ thick. Put in a 9″×13″ shallow Pyrex baking dish; sprinkle with salt and pepper and let stand for 20 minutes. Sprinkle with cornstarch and oil. Let stand 30 minutes. Brush with unbeaten egg whites and let stand 30 minutes.

Flour
Salt and pepper to taste
6 tablespoons butter
8 ounces fresh mushrooms, sliced
1 clove garlic, minced
3 tablespoons lemon juice
⅓ cup water
1 lemon, thinly sliced

Coat marinated chicken with flour, salt and pepper. Shake off excess. Sautē in butter until golden brown and opaque throughout (about 5 minutes). Remove from pan and keep warm. Add mushrooms and garlic to pan and cook 5 minutes. Add lemon juice and water; cook 5 minutes. Add lemon slices and pour over sautēed chicken breasts. Serve immediately.

Serves 4-6

Susan Stewart Hall

Baked Imperial Chicken with Cumberland Sauce

2 2½-3½ pound fryers, cut up; or boned chicken breasts
1 stick butter, melted
½ cup grated Parmesan cheese
2 cups seasoned bread crumbs
3 tablespoons sesame seeds

Dip chicken in melted butter. Mix next 3 ingredients. Roll chicken in mixture and place in shallow baking dish. Refrigerate or freeze. Bring to room temperature; dot with butter. Bake at 350° for 1 hour or until done.

Continued...

Cumberland Sauce

1 cup red currant jelly
1 6-ounce can frozen orange juice concentrate
4 tablespoons dry sherry
1 teaspoon dry mustard
⅛ teaspoon ground ginger
¼ teaspoon Tabasco

Combine and simmer until smooth. Serve over chicken. Good served with rice, using sauce as gravy.

Serves 6-8 — Cece Wheless Fearon

Chicken, Almonds 'n Peaches

4 whole chicken breasts, halved and skinned
⅔ cup flour, divided
1½ teaspoons paprika
1 teaspoon Accent
1 teaspoon salt
½ teaspoon black pepper
½ cup corn oil
½ cup slivered almonds
1 29-ounce can peach halves, drained, reserve liquid
Water, enough to make 1½ cups liquid using peach liquid
1 10½-ounce can beef broth
2 tablespoons catsup
1 cup sour cream
½ cup grated Parmesan cheese

Mix ⅓ cup flour with paprika, Accent, salt and pepper. Roll chicken pieces in flour. Heat oil in skillet over medium heat. Add chicken and cook until brown on all sides, turning as needed. Remove chicken and place in a large casserole or baking dish. Slightly brown almonds in skillet; stir in remaining ⅓ cup flour. Add water-peach juice mixture and broth, stirring constantly. Add catsup; cook until thickened. Remove from heat; stir in sour cream. Pour over chicken. Cover with foil. Bake at 350° for 1 hour. Remove from oven; uncover. Arrange peach halves, cut side up, over top of chicken; sprinkle with cheese. Return to oven; bake uncovered 10 minutes or until chicken is done. *Serve with egg noodles; garnish with parsley.*

Serves 8 — Kay Jacobs Wendell

Chicken in Orange Sauce

4 chicken breasts
2 teaspoons salt
⅛ teaspoon pepper
8 ounces fresh mushrooms, sliced
¼ cup chopped onions
2 cups orange juice
1 teaspoon sugar
1 beef bouillon cube, dissolved in ¼ cup boiling water

Sprinkle chicken with salt and pepper. Brown in butter in a large skillet. Remove chicken to paper towel. Quarter mushrooms and add to skillet. Cook until brown. Remove and set aside. Cook onions in skillet a few minutes. Add juice and sugar and cook over high heat until mixture reduces by half. Lower heat and stir in beef bouillon. Arrange browned chicken in sauce. Cover and cook over low heat until tender, about 1 hour, on top of stove. Add mushrooms last 10 minutes.

Serves 4 — Virginia Ferguson Chastain

Chicken Breast Casserole

6 whole chicken breasts, split and skinned
Salt and pepper to taste
1 stick margarine
¾ cup vegetable oil
2 onions, finely chopped
¼ cup minced parsley
4 tablespoons flour
2 cups chicken consommé
¾ cup tomato juice
½ cup sherry

Salt and pepper chicken. Heat oil and margarine. Brown chicken and place in large baking pan. Sauté onions and parsley in about 4 tablespoons of the oil and margarine mixture. Add enough water to the flour to make a thin paste. Add paste, consommé and tomato juice; simmer 10 minutes. Pour over chicken breasts and bake covered at 275° for 3 hours. Add sherry last 30 minutes.

Serves 8 — Cherrie McCrory Iles

Marinated Char-Broiled Chicken Breasts

4 large chicken breasts, boned and skinned
1 bottle teriyaki sauce

Put chicken breasts in plastic container; pour sauce over; cover and marinate in refrigerator for at least 2 hours. Cook on grill over medium flame 4-5 minutes on each side or until done, basting frequently with remaining sauce. *Excellent low-calorie entrée.*

Serves 4 — Charles M. Hutchinson, III

Yogurt Broiled Chicken

2-4 chicken breast halves
2 tablespoons lemon juice
2 cloves garlic, chopped
1 teaspoon salt
1 teaspoon chopped fresh mint
1 cup plain yogurt

Sprinkle lemon juice over chicken. Let stand 10 minutes in glass dish; turn once. Combine rest of the ingredients; add to chicken and marinate 1 hour. Place skin down. Broil 8-10 minutes on each side.

Serves 2-4 — Sherrill Womack Palmer

Instant Sweet and Sour Chicken

1 whole chicken, cut up
1 16-ounce can whole cranberry sauce
1 8-ounce bottle Russian salad dressing
1 1.4-ounce package dry onion soup

Place chicken in casserole. Mix sauces with dry onion soup. Pour over chicken and bake at 375° for 30 minutes covered, and 30 minutes more uncovered.

Serves 4 — Jeanne Futch Muslow

Sherried Artichoke Chicken

1 fryer, cut up, or 6-8 chicken breasts
Salt, pepper and paprika to taste
6 tablespoons butter, divided
1 16-ounce can artichoke hearts, drained
¼ pound fresh mushrooms
3 tablespoons chopped scallions
2 tablespoons flour
⅔ cup chicken broth
¼ cup sherry
½ teaspoon dried rosemary

Sprinkle chicken pieces with salt, pepper and paprika and brown well in 4 tablespoons butter. Place the browned chicken pieces in a 2-quart casserole and arrange the artichoke hearts between the chicken. Add the remaining 2 tablespoons butter to the drippings in the pan, and add mushrooms and scallions; sautē until tender. Sprinkle the flour over the mushrooms and stir over low heat for at least 1 minute. Stir in broth, sherry and rosemary. Cook stirring often for 5 minutes and pour over chicken. Can be refrigerated at this point. Bring back to room temperature; cover and bake at 375° for 45 minutes.

Serves 6-8

Carolyn Lozietz Huff

Chicken Breasts Piquant

6 whole chicken breasts, halved, skinned and boned
¾ cup Burgundy
¼ cup soy sauce
¼ cup vegetable oil
1 4-ounce can sliced mushrooms, undrained
1 teaspoon ginger
¼ teaspoon oregano
1 tablespoon brown sugar
½ medium onion, minced

Breasts are easily boned when barely frozen. Place boned chicken breasts in 9″ × 13″ casserole. Mix all ingredients and pour over chicken. Bake at 350° for 1½ hours or until tender. *The sauce may be thickened with flour after chicken is cooked.*

Serves 8-10

Betsy Devereaux Gahagan

Savory Crescent Chicken Squares

- 1 3-ounce package cream cheese, softened
- 3 tablespoons margarine, melted and divided
- ¼ teaspoon salt
- ⅛ teaspoon pepper
- 2 tablespoons milk
- 1 tablespoon chopped green onion
- 1 tablespoon chopped pimientos (optional)
- 2 cups cubed chicken or turkey or 2 5-ounce cans boned chicken
- 1 8-ounce can refrigerated quick crescent rolls
- ¾ cup Italian bread crumbs

In medium bowl blend cream cheese and 2 tablespoons margarine until smooth. Add salt, pepper, milk, green onion, pimientos and chicken last. Mix well. Separate crescent rolls into 4 rectangles, pressing seam together firmly. Put a fourth of the mixture in the middle of each rectangle. Pull 4 corners of each rectangle to the center, twisting slightly together at the top. Brush with remaining margarine, sprinkling bread crumbs over top. Bake on an ungreased cookie sheet at 350° for 20-25 minutes until golden brown. Reheat in foil.

Serves 4 — Rebecca Strohmaier Roberts

Chicken Cacciatore

- 6 tablespoons vegetable oil
- 2 2½-3 pound fryers, cut up
- 1 cup minced onion
- ¾ cup minced green pepper
- 4 cloves garlic, minced
- 1 1-pound 13-ounce can tomatoes
- 1 8-ounce can tomato sauce
- ½ cup Chianti
- 3¾ teaspoons salt
- ½ teaspoon pepper
- ½ teaspoon allspice
- 2 bay leaves
- ½ teaspoon thyme
- Dash cayenne pepper

In hot oil in large skillet, sautē chicken until golden. Add onions, pepper and garlic; brown. Add remaining ingredients and simmer uncovered for 30 minutes. Arrange chicken on platter and pour sauce over. *Serve with rice.*

Serves 8 — Frances Schnick Manderson

Chicken Vermicelli

- 1 large (6-7 pound) hen, with 2-3 pounds extra breasts and thighs
- 4 large onions, chopped, divided
- 1 red sweet pepper, chopped
- 3 green peppers, chopped, divided
- 4 cups celery, chopped, divided
- 10-12 tablespoons chicken fat
- 3 10¾-ounce cans mushroom soup
- 3 3-ounce cans sliced mushrooms, drained
- 2 4-ounce jars chopped pimientos, drained
- 2 8-ounce packages cream cheese, cut in chunks
- 3 12-ounce packages vermicelli
- 2 4-ounce packages slivered almonds
- 1½ pounds sharp Cheddar cheese, diced
- 3 6-ounce cans pitted ripe olives, drained
- 3 8½-ounce cans water chestnuts, sliced and drained

Simmer hen, 2 cups onions, 2 cups celery, sweet red pepper and 1 green pepper in water, covering hen until it is almost done. Remove hen from broth; cool; bone; cut in large pieces. Reserve the broth for cooking vermicelli. Sauté remaining onions, celery and green pepper in chicken fat. Add chicken pieces, mushroom soup, mushrooms and pimientos to onions, peppers and celery that were sautéed in chicken fat. Mix well and add cream cheese to these ingredients; turn off heat. Boil vermicelli in 12 cups chicken broth for 3 minutes. Turn off heat and let stand until all broth is absorbed. To vermicelli add almonds, Cheddar cheese, olives and water chestnuts. Toss vermicelli mixture and chicken sauce together until well mixed.

Serves 25-30

Janey Lawley Monzingo

Store leftover poultry giblets and trimmings in one large ziplock bag in the freezer, beef and veal scraps in another. A sufficient amount makes soup stocks—wonderful base for stews as well.

Chicken Spaghetti

- 1 6-pound hen, cooked
- 4 cups chicken broth
- 1 20-ounce can tomato juice
- 3 medium onions, chopped
- 3 cloves garlic, chopped
- 1 cup chopped celery
- 4 small bay leaves
- 2 12-ounce packages spaghetti, cooked
- 1 pound Velveeta cheese, grated and divided
- 1 10¾-ounce can mushroom soup
- 1 3-ounce can mushrooms, drained

Bone hen and cut in small pieces. Mix tomato juice, onions, garlic and celery with broth. Cook slowly for 1 hour. Add bay leaves to mixture. Grease bottom of a heavy pot that has a lid. Layer spaghetti, chicken, sauce, half the grated cheese, dabs of mushroom soup and mushrooms. Make 2-3 layers and top with remaining cheese. Cover and bake at 350° for 45 minutes.

Serves 12 — Jan Dyar Braswell

Chicken Tortillas

- 1 large fryer
- 1 large onion, chopped
- 2 tablespoons butter
- 1 10¾-ounce can cream of celery soup
- 1 10¾-ounce can cream of mushroom soup
- 1 10-ounce can Rotel tomatoes
- 1 8-ounce package tortilla chips
- 3 cups grated American cheese
- 1-2 jalapeños, chopped (optional)

Boil and bone fryer. Sauté onion in butter. Add celery soup, mushroom soup, tomatoes and simmer until mixture is smooth. In a large casserole arrange 1 layer tortilla chips, 1 layer soup mixture, 1 layer chicken and 1 layer grated American cheese. Repeat. Top with paprika. Bake at 350° until bubbly.

Serves 8 — Mary Tullie Wyrick Critcher

Chicken Olé

2 cups cooked, diced chicken
4 cups cooked wide noodles
¼ cup chopped onion
1 4-ounce can green chilies, chopped
1 10¾-ounce can cream of chicken soup
½-¾ cup chicken broth
½ cup sour cream
1 teaspoon salt
½ teaspoon pepper
1½ cups grated Cheddar cheese, divided

Mix all ingredients together with 1 cup grated Cheddar cheese. Use ½ cup chicken broth at first and add a little more if you think the mixture might need more liquid, but don't make it soupy. Put in greased 2-quart casserole. Sprinkle the remaining Cheddar cheese on top. *For an extra touch also use freshly grated Parmesan cheese on top.* Bake at 350° for 45 minutes to 1 hour.

Serves 6

Linda Tharpe Cann

Chicken Enchiladas

12 whole chicken breasts
2-3 carrots
2-3 sprigs parsley
Salt to taste
1 13¼-ounce package sharp Cheddar cheese, grated
1 pint sour cream
1 8-ounce package cream cheese, softened
15-20 frozen flour tortillas

Put chicken, carrots, parsley and salt in a pot and cover with water. Bring to a boil and cook slowly until chicken is tender, about 1 hour. Cool. Remove skin and bones from chicken. Cut chicken in small pieces and put in bowl. Season with a small amount of salt and pepper. Add Cheddar cheese, sour cream and cream cheese. Mix thoroughly. This should be quite moist. Fry the tortillas in hot oil until soft (about 10 seconds on each side). Fill each tortilla with chicken mixture; roll and place in greased casserole. Cover and refrigerate until ready to cook. Remove from refrigerator a few hours before heating. Make chili sauce.

Continued...

Chili Sauce

3 tablespoons olive oil
1 clove garlic, chopped
1 6-ounce can tomato paste
2½ cups canned green chilies
5 ripe tomatoes, peeled and chopped (may use canned)
2 large onions, chopped
Pinch salt
½-¾ cup hot jalapeño green sauce (optional)

In heavy skillet, fry garlic in oil. Add next 4 ingredients and salt. Cover with water and cook over low heat. Stir constantly until thick. Cool and refrigerate until ready to use. Add jalapeño green sauce, if desired, and pour over enchiladas. Cover with foil and bake at 350° for 15 to 20 minutes, or until hot throughout. *This is time consuming, but worth the effort. Delicious and spicy.*

Serves 12-16

Judy Jackson Peavy

Jimmy's Hung Yen Gai Ding

2 ounces snow peas
2 ounces celery
2 ounces onions
1 ounce mushrooms
2 ounces water chestnuts
2 ounces bamboo shoots
2 ounces Chinese cabbage (bok choy or celery cabbage)
4 ounces raw white chicken meat
½ ounce vegetable oil
1 tablespoon salt
2 cups chicken stock
1 tablespoon cornstarch
¼ cup water
2 ounces toasted almonds
Steamed rice

Wash and finely dice vegetables; dice chicken in squares. Heat oil in heavy frying pan or wok for 3 minutes. Add salt and diced chicken and fry 2 minutes or until golden brown. Add vegetables and cook for 3-4 minutes. Add chicken stock and simmer until it comes to a boiling point. Mix cornstarch in water and stir into mixture in pan until well blended and thickened. Top with almonds and serve over steamed rice. *According to Jimmy Joe, these proportions are enough for 1 casserole to serve 1 very hungry person. Hung Yen Gai Ding translates to Diced Chicken with Almonds and Vegetables.*

Chef Check Wing Joe

Stir-Fried Chicken

4 chicken breasts, boned, skinned and thinly sliced
3 tablespoons soy sauce
2 tablespoons cornstarch
1 8-ounce can pineapple chunks, reserve juice
1 teaspoon sugar
½ cup chicken broth
1 teaspoon curry powder, or less to taste
Corn oil
1 onion, sliced
1 green pepper, sliced
3 ribs celery, sliced
½ pound fresh mushrooms, sliced
1 6-ounce package frozen Chinese pea pods
½ cup sliced almonds, toasted
Cooked rice

Marinate chicken in soy sauce for 2 hours or more. Dissolve cornstarch in pineapple syrup. Add pineapple chunks, sugar, chicken broth, soy sauce (drained from chicken) and curry. Set aside. Heat oil (start with 2 tablespoons) in wok or large skillet. Stir-fry chicken in oil 5 minutes. Remove chicken. Stir-fry onions, pepper, celery, mushrooms and pea pods until crisp and tender. Put chicken back in skillet with vegetables. Add sauce made with pineapple juice and pineapple. Heat to boil, add almonds and serve over rice. *As a variation, use brown rice.*

Serves 4-6

Mary Graham Pate

Southern Home-Fried Chicken

1 whole chicken, cut up
Garlic salt and pepper
2 eggs, beaten
½ cup milk
Flour
Corn oil

Wash chicken and season with garlic salt and pepper. Combine eggs and milk. Dip seasoned chicken in egg mixture, then in flour. Fry in corn oil until done.

Serve- 4

Marie Rountree Rosenfield

Bami

2 3-pound chickens
1 5-ounce bag egg noodles
¼ cup chicken fat or 2 tablespoons margarine
3 cloves garlic
2 medium onions, minced
1 pound fresh mushrooms, sliced or 12 ounces canned chopped mushrooms
1 16-ounce can bean sprouts, drained
2 8½-ounce cans water chestnuts, drained and sliced
1 tablespoon salt
½ teaspoon red pepper, or to taste
½ teaspoon Tabasco
1 tablespoon Worcestershire sauce

Boil chicken and tear into small pieces. Save stock. Cook noodles in chicken stock. In chicken fat or margarine, brown garlic and onions. Add all other ingredients except noodles. Simmer about 10 minutes until almost done. Combine mixture with noodles. Let it sit overnight for best flavor. Heat in 350° oven for 30 minutes. Serve with soy sauce.

Serves 8 — Doris Thomas Brown

Plantation Chicken Shortcake

1 pound fresh mushrooms, sliced
6 tablespoons butter, divided
2 cups half and half
4 tablespoons sherry
2 tablespoons flour
1 teaspoon salt
White pepper
Cornbread squares
Sliced baked ham
Cold sliced chicken breast
Grated Parmesan cheese

Saute mushrooms lightly in 4 tablespoons butter. Add half and half and sherry. Cook 6-8 minutes. Thicken the above mixture with 2 tablespoons butter, flour, salt and white pepper. Split and butter 3″ squares of cornbread, and in a shallow casserole dish layer cornbread with ham and chicken. Pour sauce over all. Sprinkle with Parmesan cheese and place under broiler until hot and bubbly.

Serves 6 — Virginia Hodges Jeter

Poulet de Normandie

1 8-ounce package Pepperidge Farm Herb Dressing
1 stick margarine, melted
1 cup chicken stock
2 tablespoons butter or margarine
½ cup chopped onion tops or chives
½ cup celery
½ cup mayonnaise
2½ cups diced chicken
¾ teaspoon salt
2 eggs, beaten
1½ cups milk
1 10¾-ounce can cream of mushroom soup
Grated cheese

Mix first 3 ingredients. Put half of this mixture into a buttered 8" × 12" casserole dish. Sauté onion tops and celery in 2 tablespoons butter. Mix this with mayonnaise, chicken and salt. Pour this mixture over casserole mixture. Add milk to beaten eggs and pour over remaining half of bread mixture. Pour this over casserole. Cover with foil and refrigerate overnight. Take out about 1 hour before baking. Pour mushroom soup over top and bake at 325° for 40 minutes. Sprinkle with grated cheese and bake for 10 minutes more.

Serves 6-8

Doris Johnson Herndon

Chicken Croquettes with Mushroom Sauce

1 pound chicken breasts, boned and skinned
½ cup bread crumbs
½ cup milk
2 egg yolks
Salt and white pepper
Flour
2 whole eggs, beaten
Bread crumbs
3 tablespoons butter
3 tablespoons vegetable oil

Chop chicken as fine as ground meat in food processor with steel blade, or use meat grinder. Soak bread crumbs in milk. Squeeze out. Mix chicken, crumbs, egg yolks, salt and pepper. Make 6 patties. Roll in flour; dip in beaten eggs; roll in bread crumbs. Fry in butter and oil 5 minutes on each side.

Continued...

Mushroom Sauce

½ pound fresh mushrooms, sliced
½ cup chopped onions
2 tablespoons butter
2 tablespoons flour
½ cup half and half
½ cup sour cream
½ teaspoon salt
White pepper to taste

Sauté mushrooms and onions in butter. Stir in flour and cook over low heat 2-3 minutes. Slowly add half and half and sour cream. Cook over low heat until thickened. Do not boil. Add salt and pepper. You may keep warm over hot water. Pour over chicken croquettes and serve.

Serves 4-6 Susan Stewart Hall

Spinach Noodle-Chicken Casserole

1 6-pound hen, boiled until tender, boned and chopped
1 pound spinach noodles, boiled until tender
1 cup chopped onion
1 cup chopped green pepper
1 cup chopped celery
6 tablespoons butter
¾ pound Velveeta cheese, grated
2 10¾-ounce cans cream of mushroom soup
1 cup chopped water chestnuts
1 cup chopped fresh mushrooms
6 shakes Worcestershire sauce
1 5-ounce jar stuffed olives, sliced
Garlic salt to taste
1 3-ounce can French fried onion rings

Sauté onions, green pepper and celery in butter until golden. Melt cheese with soup and add sautéed vegetables. Combine this mixture with water chestnuts, mushrooms, Worcestershire sauce, olives and garlic salt. Add noodles, chicken and mix well. Top with onion rings and bake at 350° for 30 minutes.

Serves 16 Nancy Stutsman Lewis

Chicken Tarragon

½ stick butter
1 tablespoon dried chives
1 tablespoon soy sauce
1 tablespoon dried parsley
1 teaspoon Kitchen Bouquet
Dash rosemary
2 teaspoons tarragon leaves
Dash garlic powder
½ teaspoon Worcestershire sauce
Dash Tabasco
1 teaspoon salt
1 tablespoon lemon juice
½ teaspoon Cavender's All Purpose Greek Seasoning
½ teaspoon black pepper
1 3-3½ pound whole chicken with giblets
1 16-ounce jar Durkee Boiled Onions
¾ cup white wine

Mix the first 14 ingredients and simmer on stove a few minutes until blended. Stuff chicken with boiled onions and pour 2 tablespoons of basting sauce into chicken cavity. Truss chicken. Place chicken on rack in shallow baking pan. Chop giblets and place on rack and in bottom of pan. Pour 2 tablespoons basting sauce and white wine into pan. Bake at 400° for 1 hour, basting every 20 minutes. Skim grease from gravy.

Serves 2-4

Don K. Joffrion, M.D.

Chicken-Wild Rice Casserole

1 1.4-ounce package dry onion soup
1 pint sour cream
1½ cups raw wild rice
3 2½-pound chickens
2 cups dry sherry or white wine
1 cup water
1 teaspoon salt
Dash pepper
½ teaspoon dried basil
Pinch thyme
1 teaspoon curry powder
6 tablespoons minced fresh parsley
1 cup sliced mushrooms
2 cans water chestnuts, sliced
1 10¾-ounce can cream of mushroom soup
Paprika and bread crumbs

Blend dry onion soup and sour cream. Chill 2 hours. Cook raw wild rice per instructions (about 1 hour); drain. Place

Continued...

chickens, sherry, water, and next 6 ingredients in large roaster. Cover *tightly* and bake at 300° for 1½ hours. When done, remove chicken from pan to cool. Strain pan juices and simmer down to 2 cups. Meanwhile, slice water chestnuts and mushrooms; skin, bone and chop chicken into small pieces. Slowly add 2 cups pan juices to mushroom soup; heat. Slowly add sour cream mixture to sauce, stirring constantly. Toss chicken, rice, water chestnuts and mushrooms together. Pour sauce over mixture; toss lightly. Turn into large buttered casserole (larger than 4-quart size) or several smaller dishes. Top with bread crumbs and paprika and heat at 250° for 40 minutes.

Serves 10 — Sissy Masters Harper

Chicken Crêpes

16 crêpes*
3 whole chicken breasts, boiled and cut in bite-size pieces, reserve broth
¼ cup chopped green pepper
¼ cup chopped onion
¼ cup chopped celery
2 tablespoons butter
⅓ cup butter
¾ cup flour
1 cup warm cream
1 cup warm milk
1 cup warm broth, reserved from chicken
Salt and pepper
2 tablespoons sherry

Sauté vegetables in 2 tablespoons butter. Remove from pan. Melt ⅓ cup butter; stir in flour with a whisk. Add cream, milk and broth. Stir with whisk until smooth and thick. Add vegetables and chicken. Season to taste; add sherry. Fill crêpes. Place in buttered casserole. Can be frozen or heated and served immediately. Heat at 325° for 20 minutes. *Keep some of filling in saucepan to heat on top of stove. Thin a little with cream or broth and spoon over crêpes after they are on plates.* *See Index for recipe.

Serves 8 — Susan Elgin Rice

Chicken and Broccoli Crêpes

20 crêpes*
1 small fryer boiled in a small amount of water, salt, pepper, onion, garlic and celery
2 10-ounce packages frozen chopped broccoli
2 tablespoons butter
½ onion, chopped
8 ounces fresh mushrooms, sliced
2 tablespoons flour
½ cup half and half
¼ cup chicken broth
2 tablespoons grated Parmesan cheese
1 8-ounce can water chestnuts, sliced and drained
1 teaspoon salt
Pepper to taste

Make crêpes. While boiling chicken, cook broccoli according to package directions and drain. Sauté onion and mushrooms in butter until lightly browned. Stir in flour. Add half and half and chicken broth slowly until thick. Add remaining ingredients including broccoli and chicken which has been boned, skinned and cut into bite-size pieces. Mixture will be very thick. Refrigerate mixture or fill crêpes and serve with the following sauce. *See Index for recipe.

Sauce

½ stick butter
¼ cup flour
1½ cups half and half
2 cups milk
1½ cups grated Parmesan cheese
1 tablespoon prepared mustard
1 teaspoon salt
Parsley

Melt butter, stir in flour. Add half and half and milk and stir until thickened. Add remaining ingredients and stir until cheese has melted. Pour over filled crêpes, seam side down in greased shallow casseroles. Sprinkle with parsley. Bake at 350° for 30 minutes.

Serves 10 — Sandra MacCleary Boyd

Chicken Crêpes Merrimac

- 4-5 chicken thighs, cooked and boned
- 4-5 chicken breasts, cooked and boned
- 4 carrots, sliced
- ¾ stick butter
- 1 green pepper, chopped
- ½ pound fresh mushrooms, sliced
- ⅓ cup sherry
- 1½ sticks butter
- ½ cup flour
- 3 cups chicken broth
- Salt and white pepper to taste
- 24 entrée crêpes*
- Grated Swiss cheese
- Hollandaise sauce (optional)*

After boiling chicken, reserve broth. Sauté carrots in ¾ stick butter. Add green pepper, mushrooms and sherry. Allow to cook a few more minutes. Make a white sauce with butter, flour and broth. Season to taste. Add chicken and vegetable mixture. Fill crêpes and roll. Place in buttered Pyrex dish and bake at 350° for 20-30 minutes. Sprinkle with grated cheese the last 10 minutes of baking. Drizzle with hollandaise sauce before serving. *Can freeze before baking.* *See Index for recipe.

Serves 12 — Cynthia Johnson Nowery

Chicken Livers with Artichokes

- ¼ cup chopped onion
- 2 tablespoons butter
- 1 pound chicken livers, halved
- 1 1⅛-ounce envelope hollandaise sauce mix
- ½ teaspoon dried dill weed
- ¼ teaspoon salt
- ⅔ cup water
- 1 7-ounce can artichoke hearts, drained and quartered
- 3 cups cooked rice

Cook onion in butter until tender, but not brown. Add livers; cook quickly until just browned, about 3 minutes. Remove from heat. Push livers to one side. Blend dry sauce mix into pan drippings in skillet; add dill weed and salt. Stir in water. Cook over medium heat until thick and bubbly. Add artichokes; reduce heat and simmer 4-5 minutes. Serve over hot cooked rice.

Serves 4 — Holly McGee Pippen

Skewered Chicken Livers

Chicken livers
Bacon, cut in 1″ pieces
Olive oil
Seasoned bread crumbs
Salt
Seasoned Pepper

Clean, wash and pat livers dry. Cut in half. Alternate liver halves and bacon pieces on skewers, beginning and ending with bacon. Salt and pepper. Brush with olive oil and roll in bread crumbs. Broil about 4 minutes on each side. Check for doneness; cook until pink in center. *You may substitute oysters for livers. Water chestnuts also make a nice addition.*

Martha Turner Schober

Chicken or Seafood and Artichoke Hearts

2 5-6 pound hens, cooked, boned and cut up; or 3 cups each crab, shrimp and lobster
4 sticks margarine
1 cup flour
7 cups milk
1 teaspoon salt
1 cup tomato sauce, heated
½ teaspoon red pepper
2 teaspoons Accent
2 small cloves garlic, crushed
½ pound American cheese, grated and divided
10 ounces Gruyère cheese, grated and divided
5 6-ounce cans button mushrooms, drained
5 8½-ounce cans artichokes drained
8 cups chow mein noodles or 30 patty shells

Melt margarine; add flour and brown. Add milk and cook until medium thick. Add salt, tomato sauce, red pepper, Accent, garlic, half the American cheese and half the Gruyère cheese. Cook until cheese melts. Add chicken or seafood, mushrooms and artichokes. Place in several (2-3) buttered casseroles. Mix remaining cheeses and top casseroles. Bake at 350° until bubbly, about 40 minutes. Serve over ¼ cup chow mein noodles or in patty shells. *This divides or doubles well.*

Serves 30

Mary McGee Boggs

Chicken-Sausage Pot Pies

- 1 medium onion
- 8 ounces pork sausage
- 4 tablespoons butter
- ⅓ cup flour
- ¼ teaspoon salt
- ⅛ teaspoon pepper
- 2 cups chicken broth (may use canned broth)
- 1 cup milk
- 1 3-pound chicken, boiled, boned and cut into small pieces
- 1 10-ounce package frozen English peas and carrots

In saucepan brown sausage and onions; drain on paper towel. Pour out fat. In same saucepan, melt butter. Blend flour, salt and pepper. Stir in chicken broth and milk. Stir and cook until thickened and bubbly; cook about 1 minute more. Add chicken, sausage, onions, peas and carrots; heat thoroughly. Divide into 6 or 8 individual casseroles. Top with pastry.

Pastry

- 1 cup sifted flour
- 1 teaspoon sesame seeds
- ½ teaspoon salt
- ½ teaspoon paprika
- ⅓ cup shortening
- 2 tablespoons water

Combine flour, sesame seeds, paprika and salt; cut in shortening. Sprinkle water in, 1 tablespoon at a time, mixing with a fork until all flour is moistened and dough clings together. Gather dough in a ball. Pinch into 6 or 8 equal parts. Roll ⅛" thick on a floured surface. Put dough on top of each filled casserole. Cut slits in center of dough. Place casseroles on baking sheet. Bake at 425° for 25-30 minutes. *Roll dough between 2 sheets plastic wrap. Peel off 1 side placing dough-side on casserole. Then peel off other side of plastic wrap. Dough never tears.*

Serves 6-8

Shirley Willman Skipworth

Turkey â la King

6 tablespoons butter, divided
2 tablespoons flour
½ small bay leaf
½ teaspoon salt
Pinch freshly ground pepper
Dash powdered nutmeg
1 cup milk
¾ cup mayonnaise
¼ cup half and half
3 cups cooked turkey, diced
1 cup chopped green pepper
1½ cups sliced fresh mushrooms
3 tablespoons chopped pimientos
3 ounces dry Madeira wine

Melt 3 tablespoons butter in a saucepan over medium heat. Then blend in flour, bay leaf, salt, pepper and nutmeg. Remove pan from fire and slowly stir in milk. Return pan to fire and cook 10 minutes, stirring constantly, until sauce has thickened. Remove from heat; take out bay leaf and gently stir in mayonnaise. Add cream and stir. Add turkey. In a frying pan melt 3 tablespoons butter; sauté green pepper and mushrooms until tender. Add these to cream sauce and simmer stirring constantly 10 minutes. Remove from heat; add pimientos and Madeira. Blend well and serve over rice or patty shells.

Serves 6 — Virginia Hodges Jeter

Turkey Breasts with Cherry Sauce

1 16½-ounce can pitted black bing cherries, reserve juice
2 tablespoons cherry juice
1 teaspoon cinnamon, cloves, ginger and nutmeg
2 tablespoons sugar

Put cherries in a saucepan with their juice, the mixed spices and sugar. Cook slowly until cherries are reduced to a pulp. Put into blender or processor and purée.

Continued...

Firm slices turkey breast
Salt and freshly ground pepper
2 tablespoons butter
3 ounces Madeira wine

Salt and pepper the turkey slices. Sauté them in a mixture of bubbling butter and Madeira. Turn the slices at least once and when they are hot, remove to a heated dish. Place cherry sauce in center of dish. When serving turkey, place some sauce on each dish. *This is very unique—a nice way to use leftover turkey.*

Serves 6

Virginia Hodges Jeter

Baked Cornish Hens

2 1-pound Cornish hens
Salt, freshly ground pepper and lemon pepper
2 tablespoons slivered almonds
2 tablespoons finely chopped onion
1 4-ounce can chopped mushrooms, drained, or 6-8 fresh mushrooms, chopped
⅓ cup uncooked rice
3 tablespoons butter
1 cup water
1 chicken bouillon cube
1 teaspoon lemon juice, more for tartness
½ teaspoon salt
Melted butter to brush hens

Season hens inside and out with salt, pepper and lemon pepper. In small saucepan, slowly brown almonds, onions, mushrooms and rice in butter, 5-10 minutes, stirring constantly. Add water, bouillon cube, lemon juice and salt. Bring to a boil. Reduce heat, cover and simmer slowly until rice is fluffy. Lightly stuff hens with rice and brush with melted butter. Place breast up in shallow baking pan. Roast covered in 400° oven for 30 minutes. Uncover and roast 1 hour longer at 350° or until drumstick can be easily twisted. *May be cooked ahead and reheated, but be careful not to overcook.*

Serves 4

Louise Jackson

Game Hens with Hot Tamale Stuffing

½ cup chopped onion
¼ cup chopped celery
¼ cup chopped green pepper
1 stick butter, divided
4 frozen hush puppies, thawed, or equivalent amount cornbread—about 2 muffins
4-6 hot tamales, crumbled
Sliced water chestnuts (optional)
Salt, pepper, and chili powder to taste
Chicken broth if needed for moisture
2 game hens

Sauté onion, celery and green peppers in small amount of butter until soft and clear. Add all other ingredients, moistening with canned chicken broth, if necessary. Clean game hens and stuff loosely. Mound leftover stuffing around birds. Bake at 350° for 1 hour or until birds are tender and golden brown, basting occasionally with melted butter.

Serves 2-3

Lucretia Taylor Miller

Regal Roasted Cornish Hens

2 sticks butter, melted
¾ cup lemon juice
1 teaspoon garlic salt
2 tablespoons paprika
2 teaspoons oregano
½ teaspoon salt
½ teaspoon pepper
Lemon pepper and seasoned salt to taste
½ cup white wine
2 teaspoons liquid smoke
8 Cornish game hens or broiler halves

Mix all ingredients except Cornish hens. Place hens in shallow dish and pour mixture over them. Marinate overnight in refrigerator. Remove from marinade. Roast at 350° for 1 hour, basting several times with reserved marinade. These may also be cooked slowly on the outdoor grill for 1-1¼ hours, brushing with marinade. *To test for doneness, the leg should twist easily from the joint.*

Serves 6-8

Dixey Thornton Sanders

Sauce Piquante Ducks

4 wild ducks, skinned
4 tablespoons baking soda
2 tablespoons salt
Seasoned salt

Skin ducks and wash well inside and out. Place ducks in cold water to cover. Add baking soda and salt to cold water. Let soak for 1 hour. Wash again. Season ducks inside and out with salt and seasoned salt. Place in roasting pan, breast side down. Add enough water to barely cover ducks. Bake at 350° for 2 hours or until very tender. Cool. Bone and reserve broth from ducks. Set meat aside. Refrigerate broth for several hours in order to skim the fat.

2 medium onions, chopped
1 bunch green onions, chopped
1 green pepper, chopped
4 ribs celery, chopped
2 cloves garlic, minced
½ stick butter or bacon drippings
Duck meat
4 cups broth
¼ cup dried parsley flakes
½ pound bulk sausage
4 tablespoons sausage grease
4 tablespoons flour
1 tablespoon Worcestershire sauce
1 teaspoon Tabasco
½ teaspoon green pepper sauce
¼ cup red wine
½ teaspoon Accent
¼ teaspoon salt
1 2¼-ounce can ripe olives, chopped
1 8-ounce can sliced mushrooms or ½ pound fresh mushrooms

Chop onions, green pepper, celery and garlic. Sauté these ingredients in butter or bacon drippings. Add duck meat and broth to this mixture. Let simmer on very low fire for 40 minutes. Add parsley. Pan fry sausage. Reserve 4 tablespoons grease from sausage. Pat sausage dry to drain grease. In sausage drippings add flour to make a light roux. Add roux and sausage to duck mixture. Next add seasonings to taste. Add ripe olives and cook 15 minutes over very low fire stirring constantly. Shortly before serving add canned or raw mushrooms. Heat to bubbling and serve over rice. Better made a day ahead so all ingredients have a chance to season. *Sauce may be thickened with 1-2 tablespoons flour mixed with a little water added to sauce. Freezes well.*

Serves 8-10

Knox McGuffin Goodman

Canards dans la Soupière

Wild duck, 1 per person
For each 2 ducks:
1 10½-ounce can beef consommé, full strength
½ soup can dry cocktail sherry
½ 6-ounce can frozen orange juice concentrate
½ 10-ounce jar currant or red plum jelly
2 tablespoons cornstarch, dissolved in ½ cup water
Wild or brown rice

Clean ducks. Cut in half, if necessary, to fit in large covered casserole. Pour consommé and sherry over ducks. Cover and bake in 325° oven for 3 hours, basting every 15 minutes. Remove ducks from liquid and take meat off bones. Discard skin; stir orange juice and jelly into liquid. Thicken with cornstarch and water. Return meat to gravy. Serve in tureen. Serve over wild or brown rice.

Margaret Hunkin Crow

Wild Ducks

4 wild ducks
Salt and pepper
4 cloves garlic
4 onion slices
4 apple slices
2 tablespoons pickling spices
4 tablespoons orange juice concentrate
2 tablespoons flour
2 tablespoons vegetable oil
Orange slices
2 cinnamon sticks
Sherry

Clean, wash and dry ducks. Salt and pepper inside and out. Mix pickling spices with apple and onion slices. Place 1 clove garlic, 1 onion slice, 1 apple slice and 1 tablespoon orange juice concentrate inside each duck. Dust ducks with flour and place in roasting pan. Make a roux with 2 tablespoons flour and oil. Add water to make a gravy. Pour in with ducks. Tuck orange slices and cinnamon sticks in with ducks. Cook covered at 325° for 3 hours. Baste with sherry every 30 minutes.

Serves 4

Garland Houck Guth

Smoky Roasted Geese, Ducks, Quail or Doves

3-4 geese or 6-8 ducks or 18-20 quail or doves
Salt and pepper
2 oranges
2 apples
2 medium onions
2 medium white potatoes
4 ribs celery
6 links smoked sausage
2 pounds bacon

Salt and pepper cavities of birds. Chop vegetables and fruit into sizes appropriate for the bird being used. Mix and stuff cavities of birds. Slice sausage and put slice in each bird. Wrap birds with bacon and secure with toothpicks. Brown over medium fire on barbecue pit. Watch very carefully as fire will flame up because of bacon. Larger birds may take as long as 30 minutes. Birds should be browned nicely all over. Remove toothpicks; place birds on tray and set aside. *Have water available at barbecue pit to help control flame.*

6 sticks butter
1 cup chopped onions
1 6-ounce can chopped mushrooms
1 cup chopped celery
4 lemons, cut in half
¾-1 cup Worcestershire sauce
Salt and pepper to taste
Garlic powder to taste
1 fifth red Burgundy

Melt butter in a large Dutch oven and sauté onions, mushrooms and celery for about 5 minutes. Squeeze lemon juice over mixture and drop lemons into the pot. Add Worcestershire sauce. Simmer 10 minutes, stirring occasionally. Add salt, pepper and garlic powder. (This is best if salty.) Add wine. Place birds in Dutch oven and bake covered at 350° for 3 hours or longer. The meat should just about fall off the bone when done properly. Carefully remove birds to serving plate. Reserve sauce to pass. May be made day before and reheated in Dutch oven, but is best when served immediately. *Sauce may be thickened with 1-2 tablespoons flour and simmered until good consistency.*

Serves 12-15

Wesley Lambert Richardson

Fillets of Duck

Large wild ducks
Worcestershire sauce
Lemon pepper
Salt
Bacon

Remove breasts from ducks. Remove all skin. Wrap each breast in bacon and secure with toothpick. Marinate in Worcestershire sauce, plenty of lemon pepper and salt for about 30 minutes. Cook over charcoal or gas grill about 20 minutes or until bacon is nearly done. Breasts will be slightly pink in the middle.

Lea R. Hall

Roast Duck

4 wild ducks, cleaned and washed thoroughtly
Seasoned salt to taste
Pepper to taste
Accent to taste
1 apple, cut in small pieces
4 ribs celery, cut in small pieces
3 large onions, chopped, divided
½ stick margarine
¼ cup sherry
¼ cup soy sauce
2 tablespoons chopped parsley
Paprika
4 pieces bacon

Season ducks generously with salt, pepper, Accent, inside and out. Put one-fourth chopped apple, one-fourth chopped celery and one-fourth of 1 chopped onion inside each duck. Sautê remaining onions in roaster until light brown. Place stuffed ducks, breast side down, on top of sautêed onions. Sprinkle ducks with sherry and soy sauce. Sprinkle parsley and paprika on ducks. Place 1 piece of bacon on each duck. Cover and bake at 375° for 1½ hours. Baste often. Remove cover; turn ducks over. Sprinkle with paprika, baste and bake another 30 minutes. *A flour and cold water paste may be added to thicken the nicely browned gravy.*

Serves 8

Connie Roos Posner

Fried Breast of Teal Duck or Doves

12 teal duck or 24 doves
3 12-ounce cans beer or enough to cover meat
1 teaspoon cayenne pepper
2 or more cups flour
1¼ teaspoons salt
1 teaspoon lemon pepper
2-3 cups vegetable oil

Remove breast meat with skin from bone of ducks. For doves, remove the whole breast, including breast bone. Rinse with cold water; pat dry. Place in glass bowl; cover with beer and cayenne. Let sit 6 hours or refrigerate over night. Drain off beer. Roll breast in flour mixed with salt and lemon pepper. Drop breasts, 1 at a time, into deep fat, medium high temperature. Fry until browned but not hard. Great finger food for hors d'oeuvres or picnics.

Serves 6

Francais Glassell Lambert

Potted Doves

25-30 doves
Salt and pepper to taste
25-30 slices bacon
3 tablespoons Worcestershire sauce
1 tablespoon butter
1 6-ounce can orange juice concentrate
18 ounces water
1 10½-ounce can chicken broth
½ cup sherry (optional)
1 teaspoon Kitchen Bouquet

Clean, wash and dry whole doves. Season with salt and pepper. Wrap each dove with bacon and secure with toothpicks. Place doves in roaster lined with heavy-duty aluminum foil large enough to fold over the top to seal. Mix remaining ingredients and pour over doves. Seal foil. Roast covered at 350° for 1 hour. During the last 10 minutes, open foil and turn up heat so bacon will crisp. The drippings make delicious gravy. *Mallard ducks are delicious prepared this way.*

Serves 8-10

Lurene Owens

Southern Fried Quail

18 quail
2 tablespoons soda
2 tablespoons salt
Milk to cover quail
2 eggs
2 cups flour
2 tablespoons salt
Pepper to taste
Cooking oil

Pick quail clean. Dissolve soda and salt in enough water to cover quail and soak for 2 hours or longer. Drain and rinse. Then soak in milk to cover 1 hour or longer. Beat eggs with 2-3 tablespoons of milk quail is soaking in. Put flour, salt and pepper in medium-size paper bag; shake to mix. Take 2-3 quail at a time from milk; dip in egg and shake in bag of flour. Remove to cookie sheet or wax paper. After all quail are floured, fill 12″ × 2½″ black iron skillet half full with cooking oil. Heat oil until very hot. Add 9 quail and brown on 1 side. Turn; cover; reduce heat to low and cook 5 minutes. Remove lid; turn heat to high and cook 1 minute to crisp. Turn and crisp other side for 1 minute. Remove and drain.

Serves 12-14

Jerry Bettis Trichel

Venison Stew

2 pounds venison, cut in 1″ cubes
4 tablespoons bacon drippings
Water
1 teaspoon garlic salt
1 teaspoon Worcestershire sauce
1½ teaspoons salt
½ teaspoon black pepper
¾ cup chopped onion
4 medium potatoes, cut in cubes
6 medium carrots, sliced
1 green pepper, chopped
2 cups sliced celery
3 tablespoons flour
¼ cup cold water

Brown venison cubes in hot bacon drippings in heavy Dutch oven. Add water to cover venison; add seasonings and onion. Cover and simmer for about 2 hours. Add vegetables and cook 20-30 minutes or until tender. Dissolve flour in ¼ cup cold water and stir into stew. Cook approximately 5 minutes. Serve hot.

Serves 6-8

Martha Hatchell Rigby

Montmorency Sauce for Hens or Ducks

3 cups ruby port
1½ teaspoons grated orange rind
3 cloves
1 teaspoon nutmeg
1 teaspoon allspice
1 teaspoon thyme
¾ cup chicken broth
1½ cups red currant jelly
4 tablespoons butter, divided
⅔ cup orange juice
4 teaspoons cornstarch
½ cup cherry juice
2 16½-ounce cans pitted black bing cherries, drained, reserve juice
6-8 Cornish hens
Salt and pepper
6-8 garlic cloves

Combine port, rind and spices. Simmer until reduced by half. Add broth, currant jelly, 1 tablespoon butter, and stir until dissolved. Add orange juice and 3 tablespoons butter. Bring to a boil. Add cornstarch that has been dissolved in cherry juice and stir constantly until thickened. Add cherries. May be frozen. Roast Cornish hens, which have been salted and peppered and have a garlic pod in their cavities, at 400° for about 1 hour. When done, place on platter garnished with red grapes, crabapples and watercress or parsley. Pour some of the sauce over each hen. Serve the remainder in a sauce boat. *The sauce may also be served over chicken breasts or ducks. The cavities may be filled with wild rice, sausage, livers or water chestnuts. Serve hens atop half a pineapple shell.*

Serves 8

Mary Jane Ray Hall

When using wine and liquor in cooking, the alcohol cooks away and only the taste remains, an enhancement to the dish.

To remove a stubborn cork wrap a cloth dipped in boiling water around the neck of the bottle. After a few minutes, the cork will come out easily.

Red Fish

1 2-ounce can pimientos
1 pound Cheddar cheese, grated
½ onion, grated
Salt and pepper, divided
2 tablespoons mayonnaise
Juice 1 large lemon
¼ teaspoon each thyme, marjoram, nutmeg and allspice
½ teaspoon sweet basil
2 bay leaves, broken
Celery salt to taste
1 clove garlic, minced
3 pounds red fish fillets
1½ cups olive oil
2 tablespoons butter
2 tablespoons flour
1 large onion, chopped
1 1-pound can tomatoes
2 tablespoons Worcestershire sauce
3 cups Chablis
1-2 cups water
Squares of toast, fried in butter

Day before, prepare pimiento cheese. Combine chopped pimientos, grated cheese, grated onion, salt and pepper and mix with mayonnaise. Refrigerate. About 2 hours before serving, mix lemon juice with spices, salt, pepper, celery salt and garlic. Pat into fish slices. Place fish into shallow pan with olive oil. Cover and refrigerate. Melt butter; add flour slowly to make a roux. Sauté onion in roux. Add tomatoes, Worcestershire sauce, white wine and water. Cook for 10 minutes. Remove fish from olive oil; dredge in flour and brown in butter. Then place fish in wine and tomato sauce and cook until tender. Do not overcook fish. Remove fillets and place on squares of toast. Cover with layer of pimiento cheese. Pour hot tomato sauce, which has cooked down to thick gravy, over all.

Serves 6

James M. McLure

Baked Red Snapper

1 5-pound red snapper
1 lemon, thinly sliced
Chopped green onion tops
Chopped parsley

Season fish with salt and pepper and place in baking dish. Spoon sauce over fish and bake at 325° for 30-40 minutes. Cut 1 lemon in thin slices and serve on fish. Sprinkle chopped green onion tops and parsley on top of fish and sauce.

Continued...

½ cup vegetable oil
1 cup chopped onion
½ cup chopped celery
4 cloves garlic, minced
2 8-ounce cans tomato sauce
1 1-pound can tomatoes
2 cups cold water
Salt, black pepper, red pepper to taste

Put oil in heavy pot with chopped onions, celery and garlic. Cook slowly uncovered until vegetables are wilted. Do not brown. Stir often. Add tomatoes and tomato sauce. Cook over medium heat 40 minutes. Add water, salt, black pepper and red pepper. Cook 20 minutes; do not cover pot at any time. Sauce should be medium thick. Put sauce in jar and keep in refrigerator.

Serves 3-4 Jeanne Futch Muslow

Flounder Rolls with Shrimp Newburg Sauce

6 flounder fillets
Salt
2 tablespoons butter
½ teaspoon Tabasco
Paprika

Sprinkle salt on both sides of fish; roll up from the narrow end and place seam side down in shallow baking pan. Combine melted butter and Tabasco; drizzle over fish. Sprinkle with paprika. Bake at 400° for 20 minutes. *Serve with cooked long grain wild rice and Shrimp Newburg Sauce below.*

2 tablespoons butter
2 tablespoons flour
½ teaspoon salt
⅛ teaspoon nutmeg
¼ teaspoon Tabasco
1 cup milk
2 egg yolks
½ cup half and half
1 pound cooked, cleaned shrimp
2 tablespoons sherry (optional)

While fillets are baking, melt butter in saucepan. Blend in flour, salt, nutmeg and Tabasco. Add milk and stir constantly over medium heat until it comes to a boil and is thick. Reduce heat. Beat egg yolks and cream; stir into sauce. Add shrimp and cook over low heat until thickened and shrimp is heated. Stir in sherry.

Serves 4-6 Sara Stuart Burris

Red Fish Supreme

1 6-pound red fish, boned and cut into fillets or 2½-3 pounds red fish fillets
1 large lemon
½ teaspoon Accent
½ teaspoon seasoned salt
¼ teaspoon white pepper
½ stick butter
¼ cup flour
¼ cup vermouth
Fresh parsley, chopped

Marinate fish in pan with juice of lemon, Accent, seasoned salt and white pepper for about 2 hours in refrigerator. Melt butter in skillet. Shake flour over fish and cook in skillet until lightly browned. Add vermouth and simmer until flaky. Sprinkle with parsley. *A good low-calorie recipe.*

Serves 4-6

Knox McGuffin Goodman

Cook frozen fish while it is still a bit icy in the middle. Fish takes only a few minutes longer to cook and stays moist and juicy.

Caper Sauce Fish

3-4 pounds red snapper
1 onion
2 ribs celery
¼ teaspoon pepper
1 teaspoon salt

Poach fish with ingredients until done (about 15-20 minutes). Be sure to use head when poaching so that stock will gel. Remove fish from bones and place on platter in shape of fish; fill in with small pieces. Boil stock down to about 1 cup and pour over fish. Cover with plastic wrap and place in refrigerator until it congeals.

Continued...

Caper Sauce

1 dozen eggs, hard-boiled
4 cups mayonnaise
1 2½-ounce bottle small imported capers
1 tablespoon lemon juice
5 drops Tabasco

Mash egg yolks and add to mayonnaise with remaining ingredients. Cover fish with a portion of sauce, reserving some to pass when serving. Be sure to have plenty of sauce, even if you have to make more. Decorate fish with some of the grated egg whites. A stuffed olive may be used for the eye, strips of pimiento for the mouth and tail, and parsley to make gills. *Garnish the platter with lettuce and tomato or beets.*

Serves 6-8

Mary Loeb Fogel

Red Snapper Firenze

3 portions red snapper fillets
2 tablespoons flour
3 tablespoons butter
Salt, pepper to taste
Sliced pimiento
Capers
Banana butter
Almonds
Chopped parsley

Flour fish fillets; sauté in melted butter in skillet. Salt and pepper fillets; when they are brown take out and put in shallow casserole. Add a little more butter to skillet and sauté pimiento and capers and sprinkle on top of fish. Slice banana butter and put on top of fish. Bake at 500° for 4 minutes. Sauté almonds and parsley and put on top when you are ready to serve.

Banana Butter

½ banana
½ stick butter
Pinch cayenne pepper
Pinch tarragon

Purée banana and butter. Add cayenne pepper and tarragon and mix well. Put butter on a piece of tin foil and roll up to make a tube. Freeze. When ready to use, cut in slices.

Serves 3

Chef Guiseppe Brucia

Electric Skillet Trout

2 tablespoons butter or margarine
1 large onion, chopped
1 10¾-ounce can cream of mushroom soup
¼ teaspoon black pepper
¼ teaspoon thyme
8 large trout fillets
1 large green pepper, chopped or cut in strips
Paprika
Parsley flakes

Heat electric skillet to 300°. Melt butter and sauté chopped onion. Stir in mushroom soup, pepper and thyme. (May use more more pepper and thyme if desired.) Turn skillet to 200°. Place fish on top of mixture with the skin side down. Cover with thin strips of green pepper. Put top on skillet with vent closed and cook for 3 hours at 200°. Sprinkle with paprika and parsley flakes and cook 5 minutes.

Serves 6-8

Linda Hamel Bird

Trout Chablis

1½ pounds trout fillets or other mild fish
1 teaspoon salt
1 4½-ounce jar sliced mushrooms, drained, or 1 cup thinly sliced fresh mushrooms
3 tablespoons butter
2 teaspoons fresh or dried minced onion
1 cup dry white wine
1 tablespoon cornstarch
⅓ cup water
2 tablespoons lemon juice
1 tablespoon parsley
1 7-ounce can shrimp or 5 medium fresh shrimp per serving

Divide trout into 4 servings. Sprinkle each with salt. Place in double thick foil. Cook mushrooms in butter until tender, but not brown. Add onions; stir in wine. Mix cornstarch and water. Add and mix until smooth. Cook until thick; boil slowly for 1 minute. Stir in lemon juice; add parsley. Divide shrimp and place evenly on trout. Cover with sauce. Wrap securely in foil to prevent juices from escaping. Cook in oven at 350° for 30 minutes or 25 minutes over coals.

Serves 4

Rebecca Strohmaier Roberts

Bass Bake

Bread crumbs
1 stick butter
1 tablespoon vinegar
1 tablespoon Worcestershire sauce
1 tablespoon lemon juice
⅛ teaspoon pepper
1 teaspoon salt
1 teaspoon prepared mustard
Paprika
Bass fillets

Cover bottom of square baking pan with bread crumbs. Make sauce by melting butter and adding the next 6 ingredients. Place bass fillets over bread crumbs, and pour sauce over top. Sprinkle with paprika. Bake at 450° for 20 minutes.

Serves 2-4

Lucretia Taylor Miller

If cooking fish without liquid, place a lettuce leaf or two under it to prevent sticking.

Fried Fish

Fillets of fish
Black pepper
Red pepper
Worcestershire sauce
Tabasco
Creole mustard
Yellow corn meal
Oil for frying

Season both sides of fillets with black pepper, red pepper, Worcestershire sauce and Tabasco. Put generous dab of Creole mustard on each fillet. Roll in corn meal. Fry in 400° oil until golden brown. To check oil temperature, place a kitchen match in oil and when match lights, the oil is correct temperature. *You must use a wooden kitchen match.* Freshwater fish need heavier seasoning than salt-water fish. Be sure to bring oil back to 400° before starting second batch of fish.

Anne Donnes Scarborough

Seafood Mornay

Shrimp

2 pounds raw, medium shrimp
1 box crab boil
2 lemons
2 bay leaves
1 onion, quartered
5 drops Tabasco
Scant ¼ cup salt
1 teaspoon black pepper
2 quarts water

Put crab boil, lemons, onions, Tabasco, salt, pepper and bay leaves in large pot with water. Bring to boil and add shrimp. Let come to hard boil again. Quickly remove from heat; cover and let stand 5-7 minutes. Peel. Set aside. (It is most important to cook shrimp correctly and not too long.)

Sauce

1½ sticks butter
¾ cup flour
⅓ cup grated onion
¾ cup chopped white part of leeks, reserve tops
¼ cup chopped fresh parsley
3 cups whipping cream
1½ cups white wine
3 teaspoons salt
¼ teaspoon cayenne
1 teaspoon white pepper
2 tablespoons Worcestershire sauce
Tabasco to taste
3-4 ounces Swiss cheese, grated
1 2-ounce jar chopped pimientos
3-4 tablespoons lemon juice

In a 3-quart heavy pot, melt butter and stir in flour. Stir and cook until smooth. Add onions, leeks and parsley; cook until wilted. Slowly add cream, stirring constantly. Add wine, salt, pepper, cayenne, Tabasco and Worcestershire. Continue stirring. Add Swiss cheese and stir until smooth. Set aside to cool. Add small jar pimientos and lemon juice when cool. (This is the time to correct seasoning to suit your taste. Remember the sauce needs to be good and rich because of the addition of crabmeat and mushrooms.)

Continued...

Assembly

4 8½-ounce cans artichoke hearts, drained
1 pound fresh mushrooms, sliced
1 pound fresh lump crabmeat
6 tablespoons Romano cheese

In a 5-quart casserole, layer as follows: shrimp, sauce, mushrooms, sauce, crab, mushrooms, sauce, shrimp, artichokes and sauce. Sprinkle with Romano cheese. Casserole needs to be at room temperature when you put it in the oven. If sauce is too thick, add additional cream. The sauce needs to be a little on the thin side. Cook covered at 350° for 30-45 minutes. *As an extra pretty touch, sprinkle grated Swiss and Cheddar cheese on top. Sprinkle chopped leek tops over this and run in oven until cheese melts, about 5 minutes. This may be cooked a day in advance and brought to room temperature before cooking. It also freezes well.*

Serves 10

Beverly "Nan" Smith Stewart

Scallops à la Meunière

2 pounds sea scallops
Cold milk
Salt and pepper
Seasoned flour
2 sticks butter, divided
Minced chives (optional)
Lemon wedges

Salt and pepper scallops. Cover with cold milk and let stand 2 minutes. Drain and dry scallops; coat with seasoned flour.

In a large skillet, sauté scallops in 1 stick of butter until they begin to brown. Brown remaining stick of butter in a separate pan. Arrange scallops on plate and pour hot foamy brown butter over them. Sprinkle with minced chives and serve with lemon wedges. *Recipe doubles well.*

Serves 4-6

Martha Turner Schober

Lobster Thermidor

4 1-pound lobster tails
2 tablespoons butter
2 tablespoons flour
1 teaspoon paprika
1 teaspoon salt
1 teaspoon sugar
1 teaspoon prepared mustard
⅛ teaspoon cayenne pepper
2 teaspoons Worcestershire sauce
Dash Tabasco
1½ cups half and half
2 cups grated Cheddar cheese
½ cup fresh mushrooms, sliced
¼ green pepper, minced
Butter
Bread crumbs and Parmesan cheese

Boil lobster tails in salted water about 10 minutes or until lobster meat turns pink. Remove meat from shells and cut in chunks. In double boiler blend butter and flour; add seasonings, grated cheese and cream. In a small skillet sauté mushrooms and green pepper, and add to cheese sauce. Add lobster meat; mix well. Place mixture in ramekins or patty shells. Top with melted butter, bread crumbs and Parmesan cheese. Bake at 375° until crumbs are browned.

Serves 4 Clarisse Kennon Sullivan

Frozen Pepperidge Farm patty shells may be defrosted and rolled out to make a quick flaky pastry.

Crabmeat Patties

2 sticks butter, softened
2 3-ounce packages cream cheese, softened
2 cups sifted flour

Beat butter and cream cheese until smooth. Add flour, ½ cup at a time. Unless you have a processor, use hands to smooth dough. Shape into ½" balls. Make a deep impression in each ball with thumb. *The pastry may be frozen at this point. Thaw and fill with crabmeat mixture.*

 Continued...

Crabmeat Mixture

1 pound crabmeat, diced
2 bunches chives, chopped
Mayonnaise
Ripe olives, sliced

Add crabmeat, olives and enough mayonnaise to hold together. Fill pastry and garnish with olives. Bake at 350° for 10 minutes or until lightly browned. *An equal amount of lobster can be substituted for crabmeat for variety.*

Yields 3 dozen

Michele Armstrong
Qvistgaard-Petersen

Crabmeat Soufflé

16 slices bread, crust removed, divided
1 pound lump crabmeat
1 bunch green onions, chopped
1 cup chopped celery
¼ pound fresh mushrooms, sliced and sautéed in butter
½ cup mayonnaise
10 ounces grated Cheddar cheese, divided
4 eggs
3 cups milk
Salt and cayenne pepper to taste
Paprika

Place 8 slices of bread into a 9″×15″ Pyrex baking dish. Mix crabmeat, green onion, celery, mushrooms and mayonnaise. Spread over sliced bread. Sprinkle half the grated cheese over crabmeat mixture. Place remaining bread over cheese. Sprinkle remaining cheese on top layer of bread. Mix eggs, milk, salt and cayenne pepper and pour over mixture. Sprinkle with paprika. Place dish in refrigerator for at least 2 hours. Bake at 325° for 1 hour. Remove from oven. Let sit for 10 minutes before cutting into squares.

Serves 12

Evelyn Humphreys Quinn

Crabmeat-Shrimp Casserole

- 1 cup chopped onion
- 1 cup chopped celery
- 1 large green pepper, chopped
- 1 stick butter or margarine, melted
- 1 6-ounce box Uncle Ben's Long Grain & Wild Rice, cooked according to package directions
- 2 pounds cooked shrimp, peeled
- 2 6-ounce packages frozen crabmeat, thawed and drained
- 3 10¾-ounce cans cream of celery soup
- 2 4-ounce cans sliced mushrooms, drained
- ½ cup slivered almonds
- 1 2-ounce jar pimientos, drained
- 1 cup bread crumbs, divided

Sauté onion, celery and green pepper in butter until tender, but not brown. Add remaining ingredients except bread crumbs. Spoon mixture into 2 lightly greased 2-quart casseroles. Sprinkle each with ½ cup bread crumbs. Bake at 350° for 30-45 minutes or until bubbly.

Serves 12-14

Sara Stuart Burris

Crabmeat Mornay

- 1 stick butter
- 1 small bunch green onions, chopped
- ½ cup finely chopped parsley
- 2 tablespoons flour
- 1 pint half and half
- ½ pound Swiss cheese, grated
- 1 tablespoon sherry
- Red pepper to taste
- Salt to taste
- 1 pound lump crabmeat

Melt butter in heavy pot and sauté onions and parsley. Blend in flour, cream and cheese until cheese is melted. Add other ingredients and gently fold in crabmeat. Serve hot. This can be served in chafing dish for a hot hors d'oeuvre or in patty shells for the main course.

Serves 6

Leigh Kelley Dieffenbach
New Orleans, Louisiana

Stuffed Eggplant

- 4 1-pound eggplants
- 1 cup minced onion
- 4 tablespoons chopped parsley
- 2 sticks margarine or butter, divided
- 1 pound backfin crabmeat
- 2 cups chopped boiled shrimp
- 2 cups béchamel sauce*
- 8 tablespoons freshly grated Parmesan cheese
- 8 tablespoons bread crumbs
- Salt, pepper, red pepper and Worcestershire sauce to taste

Halve eggplants lengthwise. Put cut side down in pan just large enough to hold them. Cover with foil and bake at 350° for 45 minutes or until tender. Scoop out pulp and reserve shells. Chop the pulp. Sauté onions and parsley in 1 stick butter and stir in eggplant pulp. Add seasonings to taste. Cook covered for 5 minutes or until eggplant is very soft. Add crabmeat, shrimp and béchamel sauce. Put in shells and place in baking dish just large enough to hold shells. Sprinkle each with 1 tablespoon each Parmesan cheese, bread crumbs and melted butter. Bake at 400° for 10-15 minutes until top is golden. *See Index for recipe.

Serves 8

Georgia Adams Cook

Crab Clarisse

- 4 tablespoons butter
- 2 tablespoons flour
- Grated nutmeg
- 3 shakes Beau Monde
- 1 teaspoon sugar
- 1 cup half and half
- ½ cup sauterne
- 3 dashes Tabasco
- 2 teaspoons Worcestershire sauce
- 2 tablespoons chopped parsley
- 1 pound fresh lump crabmeat

Blend butter and flour in skillet. Add seasonings, cream and wine. Then add crabmeat. Heat and serve in chafing dish as a dip, in patty shells for lunch, or as filling for crêpes.

Serves 4 entrée
25 appetizer

Clarisse Kennon Sullivan

Crabmeat Casserole

1 pound fresh lump crabmeat
Juice 1 lemon
2 hard-boiled eggs, finely grated
¼ onion, finely grated
1 cup mayonnaise
1 tablespoon Worcestershire sauce
Dash nutmeg, thyme, sage, salt and pepper
1 heaping cup bread crumbs
½ stick butter, melted

Pour gallon of ice water over crabmeat in collander and add lemon juice. Grease 6 individual shells or ramekins with butter. Mix all ingredients in order given, except bread crumbs and butter; pile in shells. Cover top with bread crumbs and pour on melted butter. Bake in 350° oven 30 minutes until bubbly and crumbs are brown.

Serves 6 — Linda Hamel Bird

Crabmeat au Gratin â la Don's

1 rib celery, finely chopped
1 medium onion, finely chopped
4 sticks margarine
½ cup flour
1 13-ounce can evaporated milk
2 egg yolks
1 teaspoon salt
½ teaspoon red pepper
¼ teaspoon black pepper
1 pound lump crabmeat
¼ pound grated American cheese

Sautē celery and onions in margarine until wilted. Blend flour in well with this mixture. Pour in milk gradually, stirring constantly. Add egg yolks, salt, red pepper and black pepper. Cook for 5 minutes. Place crabmeat in bowl and pour sauce over crab and blend well. Pour into lightly greased casserole. Top with cheese. Bake at 375° for 10-15 minutes or until brown.

Serves 6 — Chef Milton Robertson

Crayfish Pie

2 sticks margarine
½ cup flour
1 onion, chopped
2 garlic cloves
1 green pepper, chopped
2 bunches green onions, chopped, reserve tops
1 cup chopped celery
3 tablespoons tomato sauce
3 cups water
Salt, cayenne, black pepper to taste
3 pounds crayfish tails, with fat
1 bunch parsley, chopped
2 tablespoons cornstarch, if needed to thicken

Melt margarine; add flour and brown lightly. Add onion, garlic, green pepper, white part of green onions, celery and tomato sauce. Cover and simmer about 1 hour. Stir frequently. Add water and seasonings. Cook several hours. If mixture thickens too much, add more water. Mixture should be creamy and thick. Add tails and fat. Cook 15 minutes or until tails are tender. If mixture thins after above step, thicken by adding cornstarch and water (consistency of cream). Add onion tops and parsley. The mixture is now ready for the pie shell.

Flaky Pastry

4 cups flour
2 teaspoons salt
4 heaping tablespoons shortening
2 cups cold water
Extra flour and shortening

Sift flour and salt. Cut in shortening. Gradually add cold water. Flour brown paper well. Roll dough in flour. Roll out dough away from you. With a spatula, grease dough well. Sift flour lightly over this. Fold ends to center. Grease ends well. Flour lightly. Fold to center. Let stand 30 minutes. Repeat 3 times. Divide dough into 2 parts and roll out.

Pour filling over bottom crust. Cover with other layer of dough. Cut slits in top. Bake at 350° for about 15 minutes. Reduce heat to 300° and bake for another 12-15 minutes or until golden brown. May also serve filling over rice for ētouffē. *This is time consuming, but well worth the effort.*

Serves 6

Jeanne Futch Muslow

Abe's Crayfish Étouffé

30 pounds live crayfish
¼ cup oil
5 medium onions, minced
Green onion tops, chopped
¼ green pepper, chopped
Parsley
Crayfish fat or 1 stick butter
Cayenne pepper
Salt
Worchestershire sauce

Wash thoroughly and cull crayfish. To approximately 10 gallons of boiling water, add crayfish and scald for 5 minutes or until half cooked. (This is very important or they will break up and become mealy when cooking if they are not scalded long enough.) Cool and peel, separating the fat from the tails.

Heat oil in pot; add minced onions, green onion tops, green pepper and parsley. Sauté. Add crayfish fat or butter and cook over low heat until fat comes to the top, stirring constantly. Add tails, cayenne pepper, salt and Worcestershire to taste. Add a small amount of hot water until étouffé is of desired consistency. Simmer 30 minutes. Serve over steaming hot rice.

Serves 6-8

Chef Abe Ritman

Crayfish Stew

¼ cup bacon drippings
½ cup minced onion
¼ cup chopped green onion
¼ cup chopped green pepper
¼ cup chopped celery
⅓ cup flour
2 cups water
Chopped parsley, as desired
½ teaspoon Worcestershire sauce
Salt and red pepper to taste
1½-2 cups shelled crayfish
Rice

Sauté onion, green onion, green pepper and celery in bacon drippings. Add flour. Stir and cook until flour is browned. Slowly add about 2 cups of water, stirring constantly. Add remaining ingredients except crayfish and cook slowly for about 1 hour. Stir occasionally and watch for thickening. Add water when necessary. Add crayfish and simmer 10 minutes. Serve over rice.

Serves 6

Ann Keith Nauman
Baton Rouge, Louisiana

Ernest's Fried Shrimp

Jumbo shrimp
1 egg, lightly beaten
Yellow corn flour (may be purchased at fish market)
Vegetable oil
Salt and pepper

To butterfly shrimp: peel shell off, leaving tail on. Make a shallow cut down the center of the back with a sharp knife; devein and wash. Place shrimp, cut side up on a chopping surface and deepen cut to split shrimp, but not cutting completely through, leaving tail intact. Shrimp should now open almost flat. Dry between paper towels.

Dip shrimp in beaten egg, then in corn flour. Shake off excess flour. Using a deep fat fryer or heavy bottomed deep sauté pan, heat oil to 350°. Drop shrimp, a few at a time, into hot oil. Remove them immediately as soon as the shrimp come to the top of the oil. DO NOT OVERCOOK. Place shrimp on paper towels and sprinkle with salt and pepper. Serve immediately with Ernest's Sauce. *Shrimp may be breaded for frying several hours before needed and refrigerated.*

Ernest's Sauce

1 quart good mayonnaise or homemade mayonnaise
1 quart Zatarain's Creole Mustard
1 quart prepared horseradish, recently purchased
1 cup fresh celery with leaves, finely chopped
1 cup fresh parsley, finely chopped
5 pods garlic, chopped

Mix equal amounts of mayonnaise, mustard and horseradish. Add chopped ingredients to mixture. Stir well and refrigerate.

Chef Ernest Palmisano

Boiled Shrimp or Crayfish

1 sliced onion
1 tablespoon dill seed
2 bay leaves
4-6 peppercorns
24 ounces beer
3 pounds large raw shrimp in shells

Combine first 4 ingredients in water and bring to boil. Add shrimp and boil 10-15 minutes. Let cool slightly in stock. Drain. Serve hot or chilled. *Guaranteed to be odorless while cooking. You may boil onions, corn and new potatoes in the seasoned water after the shrimp is cooked.*

Serves 4 — Nell Querbes Nelson

Line a ring mold with sea shells, fill with water and freeze. Serve shrimp in it.

Jean's Barbecue Shrimp

2-3 pounds raw shrimp in shells
Accent
Salt
Ground black pepper
Cracked black pepper
Worcestershire sauce
1 teaspoon basil
5 teaspoons garlic or onion powder
3 bay leaves, crushed
½ teaspoon oregano
1½ tablespoons rosemary
2 sticks margarine
1 tablespoon liquid smoke
Juice 2 lemons
Paprika
Parsley flakes
2 lemons, sliced
Hot French bread

Place shrimp in shallow baking dish. Lightly sprinkle with Accent. Add remaining ingredients, using liberal amounts of salt, ground black pepper, cracked black pepper and Worcestershire sauce. Bake at 350° for 25-30 minutes. Serve with hot French bread; good with sauce.

Serves 4-6 — Sandra McCleary Boyd

Shrimp Imperial

2 tablespoons olive oil
2 pounds large shrimp, peeled, except tail
2 tablespoons butter
1 small clove garlic, crushed
¼ teaspoon salt or to taste
¼ teaspoon freshly ground black pepper
Juice 2 lemons
2 ounces dry vermouth

Place olive oil in large skillet. When simmering, add shrimp and allow to cook until golden brown. Reduce heat and add butter, garlic, salt and pepper. When well blended, raise heat very high. Add lemon juice and dry vermouth and cook for about 1 minute, stirring constantly. Serve as an appetizer or an entrée.

Serves 4-6 entrée
12 appetizer

Bettye "Boopie" Proctor McInnis

Succulent Shrimp Casserole

4 tablespoons butter
2 ribs celery, chopped
1 onion, chopped
3 cloves garlic
2 green peppers, chopped
2 bay leaves
3 pounds shrimp, cooked and shelled
1 cup rice, cooked
½-1 cup tomato sauce
1 cup whipping cream
½-1 teaspoon red pepper
Tabasco to taste
Salt to taste
¾-1 cup grated sharp Cheddar cheese

Sauté celery, onion, garlic and green pepper slowly in butter with bay leaves. Add cooked shrimp and remove garlic. Add rice and heat. Put in tomato sauce and cream, which has been previously combined. Add red pepper, Tabasco and salt. Put in casserole and place in refrigerator. Just before serving, top with cheese. Bake covered at 350° for 20 minutes or until cheese melts. *May need to add more tomato sauce and cream to make it moist.*

Serves 6-8

Lola Weir Herndon

Shrimp â la Mosca

- 1 cup dry white wine
- 1 cup olive oil
- 4 cloves garlic
- 1 bay leaf
- 2 teaspoons rosemary
- 2 teaspoon oregano
- 1 tablespoon salt
- ¼ teaspoon pepper
- 1 pound large raw shrimp or 2 pounds small raw shrimp in shells, washed and patted dry

Mix all ingredients except shrimp in large boiler. Bring to a boil. Add shrimp. Simmer 5 minutes. Stir several times. Transfer to broiler pan. Broil 1-2 minutes or until shells are a little brown. Serve hot. To prepare ahead, put boiled shrimp in broiler pan and refrigerate. Reheat in oven before broiling. *Shrimp are eaten shell and all. The less adventurous may peel theirs.*

Serves 2 main dish
4 appetizer

Elizabeth Posey Siskron

One pound raw shrimp yields about 2 cups of cooked, peeled shrimp.

Shrimp Patties

- 3 pounds raw shrimp, peeled and chopped
- 1½ cups evaporated milk
- ½ cup chopped green pepper
- 3 cloves garlic, finely minced
- Salt, black pepper, red pepper to taste
- Vegetable oil
- Flour

Combine shrimp, milk, green peppers and garlic. Add seasonings to taste. This can be prepared ahead and allowed to marinate in the refrigerator. When ready to cook, heat oil and add enough flour to shrimp mixture to hold the shrimp together when dropped from a spoon into hot oil. Fry until browned. *These may be made into small patties and served as an appetizer.*

Serves 6

Sharon Jenkinson Boddie

Shrimp Creole

2½ pounds raw shrimp
2 green peppers, minced
3-4 white onions, chopped
1 stalk celery, chopped
4 cloves garlic, crushed
3 1-pound cans tomatoes
1 10½-ounce can tomato paste
2 8-ounce cans tomato sauce
3 4-ounce cans mushrooms, stems and pieces
3 bay leaves
1 teaspoon thyme
2 teaspoons chili powder
Salt to taste
2 tablespoons Worcestershire sauce
1 teaspoon MSG
½ teaspoon oregano
1 teaspoon black pepper
1 teaspoon red pepper or Tabasco to taste
2 cups raw rice

Clean shrimp. Sauté in a 3-quart Dutch oven the green peppers, onions, celery and garlic in oil until onions are clear. Cook the tomatoes until they come apart. Add remaining ingredients except shrimp and rice to the vegetables and cook until vegetables are done, about 1 hour on low heat. Thicken with a few tablespoons of flour, if needed; or thin, if necessary, with a little water. Add shrimp and cook until they turn pink, about 7-8 minutes. Allow to sit for several hours to be at its best. Can be cooled and placed in refrigerator until time to heat and serve. If preparing ahead, reduce cooking time of shrimp to 4-5 minutes. Shrimp will finish cooking when Creole is reheated. Serve over any kind of hot rice. *May be prepared a day ahead. Freezes well.*

Serves 8 Lucille Long Reed

To retain freshness and protect from weevils, keep red pepper and paprika in refrigerator.

Shrimp Sauté

½	pound fresh shrimp, peeled	4	ounces warm water
3-4	chopped shallots	4	ounces milk
½	stick butter	1	tablespoon flour
6	ounces dry sauterne	1	egg yolk

Salt and pepper to taste

Sauté shrimp and shallots in butter 15-20 minutes. Add wine, salt and pepper during last 10 minutes. Add water and milk to flour and egg. Stir until well mixed. Add this mixture to cooking shrimp. Let cook until thickened and serve immediately. *May be served on toast points or over broiled fish. Also great by itself. Doubles easily.*

Serves 2 — Dixey Thornton Sanders

Shrimp Robert

1 stick butter
3 green onions, chopped
2 garlic cloves, minced
¼ pound sliced mushrooms
1½ pounds peeled raw shrimp
4-5 tablespoons flour
½ cup dry white wine
2 cups milk
½ teaspoon thyme
½ teaspoon oregano
1½ teaspoons salt
½ teaspoon pepper
1 tablespoon Worcestershire sauce
Dash Tabasco
Bread crumbs
Parmesan cheese

In a large skillet, melt butter and sauté onions, garlic and mushrooms for 5 minutes. Add shrimp and sauté 3 more minutes. Sprinkle with flour, stirring constantly until brown. Mix the wine with the milk and beat slightly. Slowly add the wine and milk to the shrimp mixture, stirring constantly until it reaches a boiling point. Add all the seasonings. Simmer over low heat for 3 minutes. Put the mixture in a casserole and top with buttered bread crumbs and Parmesan cheese. Bake 5 minutes at 475°.

Serves 6 — Lorraine Yearwood LeSage

Eggplant-Shrimp Casserole

2 eggplants, peeled and chopped
1 large onion, finely chopped
2-3 green onions, finely chopped
2 cloves garlic, finely chopped
1 rib celery, finely chopped
1 medium green pepper, chopped
4 tablespoons shortening, melted
½ cup Italian bread crumbs
½ cup regular bread crumbs
1 egg, well beaten
2 4½-ounce cans medium shrimp with juice
½ teaspoon red pepper
3 tablespoons melted butter

Cook eggplant until tender in 2 cups water. Drain. Sauté onions, garlic, celery and green pepper in shortening. Add eggplant. Mix bread crumbs together and add half to mixture. Add egg. Mix in shrimp lightly and season with red pepper. Put into 1½-quart dish. Add remaining bread crumbs and butter to top. Bake at 325-350° for 30 minutes.

Serves 6

Alice Ann Buchanan Schwendimann

Easy Shrimp Entrée

1 cup chopped green onions
2 cups chopped onions
1 cup chopped celery
1 cup chopped green pepper
¼ cup salad oil
2 tablespoons tomato paste
2 teaspoons Worcestershire sauce
¼ cup dried parsley
1 10¾-ounce can cream of mushroom soup
½ cup water
1 teaspoon seasoned pepper
½ teaspoon salt
Tabasco to taste
3 pounds shrimp, cooked and peeled

In a large heavy pot cook onions, celery and green pepper in oil until soft. Add remaining ingredients except shrimp and cook very slowly for 30 minutes. Add shrimp and cook 10 minutes more. Serve over rice.

Serves 6

Carolyn Hamel Griffen

Stir-Fried Shrimp Supreme

1 pound medium to large boiled shrimp, shelled
3 tablespoons soy sauce
2 teaspoons honey
Pinch ginger
3 cups cooked brown rice
2 tablespoons safflower oil
1 clove garlic, minced
½ cup chopped green pepper
½ cup finely chopped green onion
¾ cup diagonally sliced celery
½ small head cabbage, sliced coarsely
¼ pound snow peas, cut ends off, but leave whole
1 7-ounce can water chestnuts
12 fresh mushrooms, sliced
¼ cup chopped parsley
1 2-ounce jar chopped pimientos
2 pinches white pepper
1 tablespoon sherry
½ cup roasted cashews
1 teaspoon cornstarch
½ cup chicken broth

Marinate boiled shrimp in the honey and soy sauce with a pinch of ginger for 30 minutes. Prepare rice as directed on package, using chicken broth if desired for added flavor. Put safflower oil in a 12″ heavy skillet over medium to high heat. Stir-fry the garlic, cabbage, onions, green pepper and celery for 5 minutes. Add snow peas and fresh mushrooms to skillet and sauté for 2 more minutes. Sprinkle the vegetables with white pepper and sherry and stir well. Then add pimientos, parsley, water chestnuts, roasted cashews and the shrimp mixure. Pour chicken broth (to which 1 teaspoon of cornstarch has previously been added) over vegetable mixture and simmer over low heat for 3 minutes. Stir once more and serve immediately over beds of piping hot rice. Provide extra soy sauce at the table. *This dish must not be prepared ahead; serve immediately. It neither freezes nor doubles.*

Serves 4 generously

Johnette Querbes Barnes

Shrimp Casserole

8 eggs, hard-boiled
3 tablespoons melted butter
1 tablespoon mustard
1 teaspoon vinegar
Paprika to taste, or ½ teaspoon curry powder
2 pounds raw shrimp, peeled
2 tablespoons butter
3 tablespoons flour
Seasoned salt
1 10¾-ounce can cream of shrimp soup
1 soup can milk
½ cup grated Cheddar cheese

Make deviled eggs using the butter, mustard, vinegar and paprika or curry. Place a shrimp on each egg half and place in a shallow casserole. (Reserve 4 egg halves with shrimp to place on top of the casserole later.) Add remaining shrimp around the eggs. To prepare the sauce, melt 2 tablespoons of butter; stirring constantly, slowly add 3 tablespoons of flour. Sprinkle seasoned salt. Add shrimp soup and milk. Cook over low heat. Pour mixture over shrimp and sprinkle Cheddar cheese over the top. Place the reserved egg halves in a design over the cheese. Bake in a 325° oven about 20-25 minutes and brown on top. You may serve this over rice or in Pepperidge Farm patty shells.

Serves 6

Michele Armstrong Qvistgaard-Petersen

Shrimp 'n Rice

1 onion, chopped
2 ribs celery, chopped
1 small green pepper, chopped
1 cup cooked rice
1 cup grated sharp cheese
1 10¾-ounce can cream of mushroom soup
½ pound cooked shrimp
Lemon
Paprika

Sauté the onion, celery and green pepper. Mix with rice, cheese, soup and shrimp. Put in casserole and top with thinly sliced lemon. Sprinkle with paprika. Bake at 350° until bubbly.

Serves 4

Pam Martin Sloan

Shrimp Dejean

1 rib celery, chopped
1 green pepper, chopped
1 small white onion, chopped
1 stick butter
2 pounds raw peeled shrimp
½ cup white wine
Salt, pepper to taste
Paprika, Tabasco to taste
Flour

Sauté celery, pepper and onion in butter until golden. Add raw shrimp. Stir until shrimp are pink. Then add remaining ingredients. Simmer several minutes. Thicken with flour. This may be served in patty shells or over toast points.

Serves 4

Helen Futch Audirsch
Winnfield, Louisiana

Simple Scampi

2 tablespoons Worcestershire sauce
½ cup dry white wine
1 clove garlic, minced
2 tablespoons lemon juice
1 tablespoon sugar
1 pound raw shrimp, peeled
¼ cup parsley, minced
Rice
Parmesan cheese

Mix first 5 ingredients. Arrange shrimp in a single layer in shallow baking dish. Spoon sauce over shrimp. Broil on middle rack in oven for 8 minutes. Remove from broiler and let stand 15 minutes. Sprinkle parsley over shrimp. Broil on top rack for 3 minutes. Spoon over hot, cooked rice and sprinkle with Parmesan cheese.

Serves 2

Rebecca Strohmaier Roberts

Shrimp 'n Squash

2 pounds raw medium shrimp, peeled
Juice 2 lemons, divided
Flour
Scant ½ cup vegetable oil
4 small zucchini squash, sliced in ¼" thick rounds
4 ribs celery, sliced diagonally into 2" pieces
¼ cup parsley flakes
Seasoning salt
Cayenne pepper to taste
2 teaspoons paprika
½ cup white wine

Peel raw shrimp and pat dry. Pour half the lemon juice on shrimp just to moisten, and dust lightly with flour. In a large skillet or wok, heat oil over medium heat. Add the vegetables and seasonings. Stir-fry for 2 minutes. Add shrimp, the remaining lemon juice and white wine. Cook until the shrimp turns bright pink. *You may use a variety of different vegetables such as green peppers and yellow squash. Serve* with *rice or chinese noodles.*

Serves 4

Marilyn McGuffin Deupree

Terrebonne Jambalaya

1 pound raw shrimp, peeled
1 cup washed raw rice
1 10½-ounce can consommé
1 10½-ounce can onion soup
1 stick melted margarine
1 3-ounce can mushrooms
Parsley, chopped
Tabasco to taste
Salt to taste
Red pepper to taste
Grated Parmesan cheese

Mix all ingredients. Place in casserole. Bake at 350° for 1 hour and 15 minutes. Stir occasionally. Serve with grated Parmesan cheese.

Serves 4

Sara Hogue Herrington

Cheese-Oyster Bake

1 stick butter
2 tablespoons flour
2 cups whipping cream
2 teaspoons anchovy paste
Grated rind 1 lemon
Cayenne
Salt
2-3 tablespoons red caviar
36 large oysters
1 cup plain cracker crumbs
1 cup diced semi-soft cheese, (Muenster, Havarti)
Minced parsley, divided

Melt butter in saucepan; add flour over low heat and stir until smooth. Remove from heat and slowly stir in cream until smooth. Cook over medium heat stirring until thickened. Blend in anchovy paste, lemon rind, cayenne and salt to taste; add caviar. Place a fourth of sauce in bottom of 2-quart baking dish. Arrange oysters on top of sauce; sprinkle with crumbs, cheese and parsley. Add another fourth of sauce, oysters, etc. Add remaining sauce and top with crumbs. Bake at 375° for 20 minutes or until hot. Top with rest of parsley.

Serves 6-8

Nancy McCullough Humphrey

Sunday Night Oysters

1 pint oysters and oyster liquid
¾ stick butter
1 tablespoon minced parsley
1 tablespoon Worcestershire sauce
1 tablespoon minced green onion tops
Salt and pepper to taste
Crisp toast or buttered French bread slices
Dry vermouth (optional)

Pick through oysters and drain. Reserve liquid. Melt butter in skillet. Add parsley, Worcestershire sauce, green onion tops and oyster liquid. Simmer 2 minutes. Add oysters and simmer until edges curl. Pour over toast in large bowl. Use 2 pieces of toast per serving. A splash of vermouth may be added just before heat is turned off.

Serves 2

Rosalind Kalmbach McCullough

Oysters à la Mosca

1 stick butter
1 large onion, chopped
3 cloves garlic, chopped or
1 teaspoon garlic powder
½ teaspoon thyme
1 teaspoon oregano
2 tablespoons chopped parsley
¼ teaspoon red pepper
¼ teaspoon black pepper
1 teaspoon salt
4 dozen oysters with liquid reserved, or 4 10-ounce jars
1 cup seasoned bread crumbs
Parmesan cheese, freshly grated if possible

Sauté onion and garlic in butter until soft. Add seasonings. Add oysters. When oyster edges begin to curl, add liquid as needed from oysters. Fold in bread crumbs. Place in casserole and sprinkle with Parmesan cheese. Bake at 350° for 15-20 minutes.

Serves 6

Elizabeth Posey Siskron

Stuffed Oysters

2 tablespoons butter
2 tablespoons flour
2 cups chopped onion
2 cups chopped green pepper
2 cups chopped celery
¾ loaf French bread
Milk
3 sticks butter
1 quart oysters, drained and cut in 3 pieces
1 cup chopped green onion tops
1 cup chopped parsley
Salt, pepper to taste
20 patty shells, baked according to package directions
Bread crumbs

Combine 2 tablespoons of butter and flour to make a light brown roux, stirring constantly. Add onion, green pepper and celery to roux and cook until wilted. Soak bread in milk; squeeze out and add to the above. Add 3 sticks of butter, oysters, onion tops, parsley, salt and pepper and cook over slow fire 10 minutes. Fill patty shells and dot with butter. Bake at 325° for 20 minutes. Before serving, sprinkle with bread crumbs.

Serves 20

Jean Spurlock Schaumburg

Spinach-Oyster Supreme

2 10-ounce boxes frozen chopped spinach
2 tablespoons margarine, divided
1 medium onion, finely chopped
½ 10¾-ounce can mushroom soup, undiluted
4 ounces sharp Cheddar cheese, grated
½ cup sour cream
2-3 dozen oysters
Salt to taste
1 tablespoon garlic powder
½ cup grated Parmesan cheese
½ cup seasoned bread crumbs
1 3-ounce can French fried onion rings, chopped
2 lemons
Paprika

Cook spinach according to package directions. Drain well. Sauté onion in 1 tablespoon margarine. Heat soup and add Cheddar cheese, stirring often until melted and blended. Add sour cream. Add this sauce and sautéed onion to spinach. Sauté oysters in remaining tablespoon margarine until edges curl (about 3 minutes). Add salt, garlic powder, Parmesan cheese and bread crumbs to spinach mixture. Mix well. Put 3 large or 4 small oysters into individual baking dishes. Top with spinach. Cover with onion rings and a thin slice of lemon. Sprinkle with paprika. Bake uncovered at 300° for 30 minutes. *This makes an excellent first course. You may bake this in a tomato half and omit oysters.*

Serves 8

Charlotte Morgan Hanna

Gourmet Oysters

2 tablespoons butter or margarine
2-3 green onions with tops, chopped
2 pints oysters
Seasoned bread crumbs
Salt and pepper to taste
Worcestershire sauce to taste
Tabasco to taste

Sauté onion in butter or margarine until tender. Add oysters and cook until curled. Season to taste with salt, pepper, Worcestershire sauce and Tabasco. Add bread crumbs until mushy. Serve immediately.

Serves 4 main dish
6 appetizer

Louise Hessler King

Richard II Eggs

3 10-ounces packages frozen chopped spinach
8 strips bacon
1 cup cubed ham
1 stick butter, divided
1 cup flour
4 cups milk
2 tablespoons dried, minced onion
Seasoned salt, pepper to taste
Tabasco to taste
18 eggs
1½ cups evaporated milk
Salt and pepper to taste
½ cup canned French fried onion rings, crushed
½ cup grated Monterey Jack cheese

Cook spinach according to directions on package. Drain *very* well and chop again. Cut bacon in to ¼" pieces; fry until crisp. Remove bacon and drain on paper towel. Add ham to grease and fry 2 minutes more. Remove ham and set aside with bacon. Add ½ stick butter to grease and melt it. Add flour a little at a time, mixing well. Stir and cook until flour bubbles. Add milk a little at a time, stirring until sauce is thick and smooth. Add spinach, onion and seasonings; mix well; remove from heat. Melt ½ stick butter in another pan. Beat eggs and evaporated milk together with salt and pepper. Scramble in butter until lightly set. Butter 9" × 13" Pyrex baking dish. Spread half of eggs in bottom of pan. Layer half of bacon and ham over eggs. Cover with half of spinach mixture. Repeat these layers once more. Top with onion rings and cheese. Refrigerate overnight—*a must.* Bake at 275° for 1 hour.

Serves 12-14

Margaret Hunkin Crow

Becca's Eggs

14 1⅛-ounce packages dry McCormick's Hollandaise Sauce
36 hard-boiled eggs, chopped in large pieces
3 14½-ounce cans artichoke hearts, quartered
2 pounds ham, diced
Lemon juice to taste
2 6-ounce cans pitted ripe olives, sliced
Dash Worcestershire sauce
24-30 English muffins

Mix hollandaise sauce according to package directions. Add hard-boiled eggs, artichoke hearts, ham and lemon juice. Warm. Add ripe olives and Worcestershire sauce. Serve over English muffins (two halves per person).

Serves 24-30 — Rebecca Strohmaier Roberts

Add a teaspoon of salt and vinegar to water when boiling eggs. Should one crack, it will not drain out.

Eggs con Queso

6 English muffins
Butter
12 large eggs
18 pieces bacon
Chili con queso

Butter English muffins and toast. Keep warm. Fry bacon until crisp. Eggs may be poached or fried. To fry, place egg rings in bacon grease, and drop in the egg. Fry egg to desired texture. Place 3 slices of bacon on top of each muffin half (2 halves per person) and place egg on top of bacon. Cover with chili con queso.

Continued...

Chili con Queso Sauce

1 32-ounce package Velveeta cheese
2 10½-ounce cans Rotel tomatoes, strain and reserve liquid
½ cup finely chopped jalapeño peppers (optional)

In a double boiler melt cheese. Chop tomatoes and add to cheese. Add peppers to cheese mixture and enough tomato liquid to make a good sauce consistency, thick and not at all runny. *Great for Sunday brunch.*

Serves 6

Jon Grogan
Houston, Texas

When frying eggs, dab softened butter or margarine on yolk before turning. Prevents yolk from sticking and breaking.

Huevos Acapulco

For each serving:
1 English muffin, split
2 slices tomato
½ cup grated Monterey Jack cheese
2 poached eggs
½ cup guacamole
½ cup sour cream
2 tablespoons green chili salsa

Toast muffin lightly. Top with tomato and cheese. Run under broiler to melt cheese quickly. Top with poached eggs, guacamole and mixture of sour cream and salsa. Run quickly under broiler to warm. *Variation: Use 2 tablespoons sour cream instead of ½ cup.*

Margaret Hunkin Crow

Microwave poached eggs: 1 tablespoon of milk in the bottom of a custard cup. Drop egg in and puncture yolk with fork. Cover with paper. Cook on high 60 seconds. To do more eggs, add 60 seconds per egg and rearrange cups at 60 seconds.

Farmer's Omelet

2 tablespoons butter
Chopped fresh mushrooms
Slivered ham
Chopped green onions
Cooked potatoes, diced
3 eggs
Water, small amount
Shredded Cheddar cheese

Melt butter in omelet pan and sauté mushrooms, ham, green onions and potatoes. Beat eggs and water in bowl and pour over ham and vegetables and stir to mix. Sprinkle cheese on top as omelet begins to congeal. With forks or a flip of the wrist make a half moon of the omelet and serve on a heated plate. *Sprinkle with extra cheese if desired.*

Serves 2

Chef Joe Fertitta

Crabmeat Omelet

Filling

2 tablespoons butter, clarified
2 ounces chopped green onions
2 ounces sliced mushrooms
Salt and pepper to taste
White wine to taste
2 tablespoons butter, whole
4 ounces crabmeat

Heat clarified butter until hot. Place onions and mushrooms in butter. Sauté until onions are translucent. Add salt, pepper and wine. Sauté until reduced to one-fourth. Add 2 tablespoons whole butter and crabmeat. Reserve filling until ready for omelet.

Continued...

Omelet

2 whole eggs
Salt
½ ounce water
2 ounces butter, clarified
Crabmeat for garnish
Parsley, chopped for garnish

Mix eggs, salt and water until well beaten. Heat butter until hot but not smoking. Cook omelet and add crabmeat filling. Fold omelet into thirds and place on serving dish. Top with crabmeat and parsley.

Chef Joe Fertitta

Linguini Omelet

8 ounces linguini
1 2-ounce can anchovy fillets
6 eggs
3 tablespoons Parmesan cheese
3 tablespoons olive oil
Cayenne pepper to taste

Boil linguini according to package directions and drain in colander. Set aside. Chop anchovies. Beat eggs with anchovies and cheese. Heat olive oil in non-stick skillet; add linguini and fry bottom about 10 minutes. When bottom of linguini is very crisp, pour eggs over pasta. Let eggs begin to set. Remove from fire and place under broiler until it puffs. Slice as a quiche. *Be sure to use a non-stick skillet. Do not use salt because of the anchovies.*

Serves 4

Nancy McCullough Humphrey

Famous Dutch Baby

Pan Size	Butter	Eggs	Milk and Flour
2-3 quarts	½ stick	3	¾ cup each
3-4 quarts	⅓ cup	4	1 cup each
4-4½ quarts	1 stick	5	1¼ cup each
4½-5 quarts	1 stick	6	1½ cup each

Confectioners' sugar
Lemon juice
Peaches or strawberries
Honey, syrup or jelly

Select the recipe proportions to fit your pan. Place butter in pan and set in 425° oven; then mix batter quickly while butter melts. Put eggs in blender and whirl at high speed for 1 minute. With motor running, gradually pour in milk; then slowly add flour and continue whirling for 30 seconds. Remove pan from oven and pour batter into hot melted butter. Return to oven and bake until puffy and well browned, 20-25 minutes. Dust with confectioners' sugar and squeeze lemon juice over all. Serve with peaches, strawberries, honey, syrup or jelly.

Kimberly Wilhite

Sausage-Egg Bake

- **1 pound sausage, cooked, crumbled and drained**
- **6-8 eggs, slightly beaten**
- **2 cups milk**
- **1 cup sharp Cheddar cheese, grated**
- **6 slices white bread, cubed**
- **1 teaspoon salt**
- **1 teaspoon pepper**
- **1 teaspoon dry mustard**

Cook and crumble sausage. Mix all remaining ingredients with sausage. Pour into 9″ × 13″ casserole and refrigerate 12 hours. Bake at 350° for 40 minutes. Serve immediately.

Serves 6-8

Jane Long Hamman
Muskogee, Oklahoma

Twenty-four Hour Cheese Soufflé

8 slices bread, crusts removed, divided
1½ pounds sharp cheese, grated, divided
6-8 eggs, well beaten
1 teaspoon minced onion
½ teaspoon dry mustard
1 teaspoon brown sugar
½ teaspoon salt
¼ teaspoon paprika
½ teaspoon pepper
2½ cups half and half
1 10½-ounce can Rotel tomatoes (optional)
16 ounces Velveeta cheese (optional)

Spread bread thickly with butter and cut into cubes. Layer a 9″ × 11″ × 2″ casserole with half of bread cubes and half of cheese; repeat layers. Combine remaining ingredients and mix well. Pour over cheese layers. Refrigerate 24 hours. Remove 30 minutes before baking. Place in shallow pan of water. Bake at 350° for 30 minutes. Reduce heat to 300°. Continue baking 1 hour. Turn off heat; leave in oven until serving time. *Can be topped with cheese sauce if desired: one 10½-ounce can Rotel tomatoes heated with 16 ounces Velveeta cheese.*

Serves 8-10

Rita Elliot Wolfe
Columbus, Ohio

Chili-Cheese Soufflé

10 eggs, beat until lemon yellow
½ cup flour
1 teaspoon baking powder
½ teaspoon salt
1 16-ounce carton low-fat cottage cheese
½ cup vegetable oil
1 pound Monterey Jack cheese, grated
2 4-ounce cans chopped green chilies, seeded and drained

Beat eggs, flour, baking powder, salt, cottage cheese and vegetable oil until smooth. Add cheese and beat until smooth. Stir chilies into mixture with spoon and pour into well-greased 11½″ × 13″ casserole. Bake in upper part of a 350° oven for 25-30 minutes.

Serves 10

Louise Wheless Lee

When prebaking pie or quiche crusts, place dried rice or beans to weight crust in an oven cooking bag instead of in aluminum foil lining. When crust is baked, lift out bag, wipe and store until next time. No loose beans or rice to gather up.

Quiche Oberon

Crust

1 cup shortening
2½ cups flour
1 teaspoon salt
⅓ cup ice water
Parmesan cheese

In food processor put shortening, flour and salt. Mix until consistency of fine meal. Slowly add water until a ball is formed. Remove ball (may be sticky). Wrap in plastic wrap and refrigerate at least 1 hour. When ready to use, flour pastry board or counter; roll crust to fit a 9″×13″ dish. Crimp edges. Sprinkle a little Parmesan cheese on crust. Line muffin tins with dough for mini quiche.

Basic Filling

1 pound bacon, fried crisp and crumbled
1 pound grated sharp Cheddar cheese
½ pound grated Swiss or Gruyere cheese

Sprinkle bacon on top of Parmesan cheese and crust. Mix cheeses together and sprinkle on top of bacon.

Continued...

Custard

3 tablespoons butter, melted
1 small onion, chopped
3 ounces sliced fresh mushrooms
4 eggs, beaten
1 cup half and half
1 cup whipping cream
1 teaspoon salt
1 tablespoon Worcestershire sauce
Dash cayenne, red pepper and black pepper
Grated nutmeg (optional)

In a skillet, sauté onions and mushrooms in butter until tender. Add eggs and creams to onions, mushrooms and butter. Then add rest of custard ingredients. Mix well and pour over grated cheese. Bake at 400° for 35 minutes or until set.

Use recipe as above noting sequence below, and add 1 of the following variety:

1 cup minced ham (sprinkle on top of bacon)
1 large zucchini or 2 medium yellow squash (boil for 6-7 minutes, slice thin, layer over bacon)
1 can artichoke hearts (drained, slice, layer over bacon)
1 can asparagus (drained, layer over bacon)
2 medium tomatoes (sliced thin, layer over bacon)
1 10-ounce package frozen chopped spinach (thawed, drained, mix with custard)
3 extra ounces fresh mushrooms, or more, (butter and sauté with other mushrooms)
2 extra white onions (use a little more butter and sauté with other onions)
1 cup cooked, finely chopped broccoli (layer over bacon)
⅔ cup sliced pimientos (drain, layer over bacon)

Serves 6 main course
12-14 appetizer

Wesley Lambert Richardson

To prevent soggy pie or quiche crusts, sprinkle them lightly with fine, dry, toasted bread crumbs or cheese.

Mexican Jackpot Cheese

- 1 5-ounce can green chilies
- 2 eggs, beaten
- 6 ounces Monterey Jack cheese
- 6 ounces Cheddar cheese, grated
- ½ cup sour cream

Place chilies in bottom of 7″ X 10″ baking dish. Beat eggs lightly and mix with remaining ingredients. Pour mixture over chilies. Bake at 350° for 30 minutes. *Good with soup or salad. Good as brunch dish or hors d'oeuvre cut in small squares.*

Serves 6

Frances Payne Horner

Admiralty Crabmeat Sandwiches

- 1 7¾-ounce can crabmeat, drained and flaked
- ¼ cup finely chopped celery
- ¼ cup finely chopped sweet pickles
- ¼ cup mayonnaise
- 1 hard-boiled egg, finely chopped
- 1 scallion, finely chopped
- ½ teaspoon salt
- ¼ teaspoon pepper
- 4 English muffins, split, buttered and toasted
- 1 large tomato cut into 4 thin slices
- 4 slices Monterey Jack or Muenster cheese
- Paprika and parsley to taste

Mix first 8 ingredients together. Place a tomato slice on each muffin bottom. Top with crabmeat mixture and 1 cheese slice. Sprinkle with paprika and broil 5″ from heat source until bubbly and cheese is melted. Garnish with parsley and serve with toasted muffin top halves. *Great for brunch or supper.*

Yields 4 sandwiches

Barbara Horner Burrell
Naples, Florida

Place unsliced bread in freezer until almost hard. Remove and slice bread paper-thin or cut into fancy shapes for festive party sandwiches.

Frosted Sandwich Loaf

1 unsliced loaf bread
Butter, softened

Egg Filling

4 hard-boiled eggs
3 tablespoons mayonnaise
2 teaspoons prepared mustard
1 teaspoon grated onion
½ teaspoon salt
Dash Worcestershire sauce

Combine all ingredients in bowl and mix well.

Chicken Salad Filling

1 cup boned chopped chicken
⅓ cup mayonnaise
¼ cup finely chopped celery
2 tablespoons sweet pickle relish

Combine all ingredients in separate bowl and mix well.

Ham Salad Filling

1 cup ground cooked ham
⅓ cup mayonnaise
1 teaspoon prepared horseradish

Combine all ingredients in separate bowl and mix well.

Slice bread lengthwise in 4 equal layers. Butter slices. Spread first slice butter side up with egg salad; second slice with ham filling; and third slice with chicken salad. End with fourth slice. Wrap loaf in foil and chill.

Frosting

1 8-ounce package cream cheese
1 3-ounce package cream cheese
5 tablespoons milk

Beat cream cheese with milk until fluffy. Frost loaf. Slice and serve on lettuce leaves. Garnish on top with hard-boiled egg yolk circles and green pepper in flower shapes. *Good for luncheons.*

Serves 8-10

Vicki Longmire Hanna

Pocket Bread Sandwiches

2 pieces Pita bread, halved
1 cup cooked beef or lamb, sliced or cubed or 1 whole cooked chicken breast, sliced or cubed
4 green onions, chopped
½ cup shredded lettuce
1 medium tomato, coarsely chopped
1 2½-ounce can black olives, sliced
1 small cucumber, chopped
1 6-ounce jar marinated artichoke hearts, chopped, reserve juice, or ½ avocado, cubed

Heat Pita bread wrapped in foil in 300° oven for 10 minutes. Cut in half and fill pockets with beef or chicken filling. For beef sandwiches: layer beef, onions, lettuce, tomato, olives, cucumber and artichokes in pockets and drizzle yogurt dressing or marinade from artichokes over filling. For chicken sandwiches: layer chicken, the next 5 ingredients and avocados and drizzle yogurt dressing over all. Fillings may be varied. Each guest may make his own sandwich. *Marinated garbanzos and sesame seeds are a good addition.*

2 tablespoons mayonnaise
1 cup plain yogurt
1 0.4-ounce package ranch style salad dressing mix

Mix mayonnaise, yogurt and salad dressing mix and drizzle over sandwich filling.

Serves 4

Margaret Hunkin Crow

Monte Cristo Sandwich

3 slices bread per sandwich
Sliced turkey
Sliced Monterey Jack or Muenster cheese
Sliced ham
Beaten egg

Layer bread, turkey, cheese, bread, ham, cheese and bread. Cut into 4 triangles. Dip into egg and fry like French toast on both sides. *Sprinkle with confectioners' sugar and serve with strawberry preserves.*

Syndy Hirsch Johnson

Toasted Asparagus Sandwiches

Bread
1 10½-ounce can asparagus, drained and mashed
1 3-ounce package cream cheese
2 boiled eggs, chopped
Worcestershire sauce
Seasoned salt
Margarine
Parmesan cheese

Trim edges of bread. Mix asparagus, cream cheese and boiled eggs. Season with Worcestershire sauce and plenty of seasoned salt. Spread asparagus mixture between 2 slices of bread. Spread margarine on outside of both slices. Sprinkle top side with Parmesan cheese. Cut sandwiches in half; toast top side. Turn and toast other side.

Yields 10-12 sandwiches

Glenda Futch Farmer
Memphis, Tennessee

Cucumber Sandwiches

1 large or 2 medium unpeeled cucumbers
1 8-ounce package and one 3-ounce package cream cheese, softened
¼ cup mayonnaise
2-3 green onions, finely chopped, tops and all
2 tablespoons chopped parsley
2 dashes Tabasco
½ teaspoon seasoned pepper
1 teaspoon garlic salt (optional)
1 tablespoon chopped chives

Grate cucumber and carefully press out moisture with paper towels. Mix all ingredients well, using enough mayonnaise to moisten so filling will spread easily. Spread on very thin bread, crusts removed. Refrigerate or freeze.

Yields 20 sandwiches

Carolyn Clay Flournoy

Pimiento Cheese Sandwiches

1 7-ounce can pimientos
1 scant tablespoon sugar
½ pound sharp cheese, finely grated
1½ teaspoons onion juice
½ teaspoon Accent
Salt and pepper
2 hard-boiled eggs, finely chopped
½ cup chopped pecans
Mayonnaise

Place pimientos in large mixing bowl. Mash pimientos; add sugar and mix well. Add cheese, onion juice, Accent, salt, pepper, hard-boiled eggs, chopped pecans and mix well. Add enough mayonnaise to make a nice spreading consistency.

Yields 4-6 sandwiches
Serves 20 dip

Gerda Roth Crow

Stromboli

Mayonnaise
Pizza dough—enough for nine 10″ pizzas
1 pound Monterey Jack cheese
1 pound ham or corned beef, thinly sliced
1 pound salami, thinly sliced
Durkee Sauce
½ head lettuce, shredded
1 pound Monterey Jack cheese with jalapeño peppers

Divide dough into 9 pieces and roll out 10″ circles. Spread mayonnaise on pizza dough. On half of dough circle, start building your sandwich. Put Monterey Jack first, 3 slices corned beef, 4 slices salami (or more if you like), and Durkee's on top of salami.

Add shredded lettuce and Monterey Jack with jalapeño peppers. Fold dough over. Crimp edges so melted cheese will not come out. Bake on cookie sheet at 325° for 20-30 minutes or until browned. *May use rye bread, granola, or pumpernickel. Wrap sandwiches in foil to heat.*

Yields 9 sandwiches

Virginia Ferguson Chastain

Stuff a Bun

12 rolls, French or hot dog
2 6½-ounce cans tuna
2 hard-boiled eggs, chopped
2 tablespoons India relish
Lemon juice
Onion juice
Worcestershire sauce
1 large rib celery, finely chopped
1 small green pepper, finely chopped
Mayonnaise (enough for correct consistency)
Pinch horseradish (optional)
Pinch basil and thyme

Slice rolls. Scoop out inside, leaving crust. Mix all ingredients and stuff buns. With soft butter, grease roll tops. Wrap 2 in foil or arrange several in a pan and cover with foil. This recipe will stuff 12 four-inch rolls. Heat about 10 minutes; remove foil and leave in oven about 2 minutes longer.

Yields 12 sandwiches

Eleanor Johnson Colquitt

Spanish Rolls

1 pound ground beef
2 ounces olive oil
Salt and pepper to taste
1 clove garlic, chopped
6 green onions, finely chopped
6 or less jalapeño peppers, chopped
1 2¼-ounce can black olives, finely chopped
4 ounces tomato sauce
2 tablespoons taco sauce
1 pound American cheese, grated
3 dozen French or sourdough rolls

Brown meat with olive oil, salt and pepper. Add garlic. Cool. Mix all other ingredients with meat. Scoop out rolls; fill with mixture. Wrap in foil. Heat at 350° for 20-30 minutes.

Yields 36 rolls

Susan Sigler Updegraff

Sunday Sandwiches

- 2 tablespoons butter
- 2 tablespoons flour
- 7 ounces clear beef broth
- 8 medium fresh mushrooms, sliced
- 2 dashes garlic salt
- 12 thin slices tenderloin of beef
- 4 Kaiser rolls, sliced and buttered

In large skillet over low heat, make a roux with butter and flour. Add broth, mushrooms and garlic salt. If sauce is lumpy, add additional broth. Increase to medium heat for 5 minutes. Add thinly sliced tenderloin and cook for 3-5 minutes. Serve open or closed face on toasted and buttered Kaiser rolls (preferably grilled). *A good way to use leftover roast beef.*

Serves 4

James D. Boyd, M.D.

Béchamel Sauce

- 1 stick butter
- ½ cup flour
- 1 cup chicken stock
- 1 cup half and half
- 1 teaspoon salt
- ½ teaspoon red pepper

Melt butter and stir in flour. Stir constantly while cooking 8-10 minutes over very low heat. Do not brown. Gradually stir in stock and cream until smoothly blended. Add salt and pepper. Continue cooking until thickened.

Yields 2½ cups

Georgia Adams Cook

Cashew Butter Sauce

- ½ stick butter
- 2 teaspoons lemon juice
- ¼ teaspoon marjoram
- ¼ cup salted cashews in lengthwise halves

In small saucepan melt butter; add lemon juice, marjoram and cashews. Serve over fresh green vegetables.

Yields ½ cup

Leone Guthrie Reeder

Cheese Sauce

4 tablespoons butter
3 tablespoons flour
⅛ teaspoon pepper
¼ teaspoon dry mustard
¼ teaspoon salt
1 cup milk
¾ cup grated sharp cheese

Melt butter and add flour. Add seasonings, making a paste. Slowly add milk and stir until thick. Add cheese and stir until melted.

Yields 2 cups — Rosemarie Wimer Gerhardt

Hollandaise Sauce

3 egg yolks
1 stick butter
2 tablespoons lemon juice
1 tablespoon boiling water
Red pepper
Salt

Beat egg yolks and place in a *glass* double boiler over warm (not boiling) water. Cut butter into pats. Slowly add butter a pat at a time, alternating with lemon juice and stirring constantly. Remove from fire when mixture is thick. Stir in boiling water. Season to taste with red pepper and salt. *Sauce may be made days ahead and stored in refrigerator in a glass jar. Reheat by placing jar in pan of hot water.*

Serves 4 — Stewart Lee Nelson Mead

Sour Cream Horseradish Sauce

1 8-ounce carton sour cream
1½ tablespoons horseradish
1 teaspoon fresh lemon juice
1 teaspoon seasoned pepper

Mix all ingredients well. *This is good served with corned beef and keeps at least 1 week in the refrigerator.*

Yields 1 cup — Carolyn Clay Flournoy

Horseradish Sauce

1 stick margarine
1-1½ cups mayonnaise
2 heaping tablespoons horseradish
1 small onion, grated
½ teaspoon dry mustard
¼ teaspoon salt
¼ teaspoon pepper

Melt margarine in small saucepan. Add other ingredients and mix well. May be kept several weeks. *Serve with green vegetables or over rare beef.*

Yields 1 pint

Corinne Kelly Calder
Dallas, Texas

Quick Rémoulade

2 cups mayonnaise
Juice 1½ lemons
1 tablespoon Worcestershire sauce
¼ teaspoon garlic powder or garlic salt
½ cup Creole mustard
¼ teaspoon Tabasco
1 bunch finely chopped green onions

Mix all ingredients and chill for several hours.

Yields enough for 5 pounds shrimp

Susan Stewart Hall

Tartar Sauce

1 pint mayonnaise
2 small or 1 large bunch green onions, finely chopped
½ bunch parsley, finely chopped
1 large dill pickle, finely chopped
1 tablespoon capers
¼ teaspoon red pepper
¼ teaspoon sugar
2 tablespoons lemon juice

Add onions, parsley and pickles to mayonnaise along with seasonings. Mix well and refrigerate. Better if refrigerated 24 hours.

Yields 1½ pints

Fannie Mae Robinson

Shrimp Sauce

2 large onions, chopped
1 2-ounce jar capers, reserve juice
6 cloves garlic
5-6 ribs celery, chopped, strings removed
1 quart salad dressing
1 24-ounce bottle catsup
4 tablespoons Worcestershire sauce
Juice 1 lemon
¾ cup sherry
1 tablespoon sweet basil
3 tablespoons mustard
1 pint horseradish, or to taste

Blend first 4 ingredients in blender for 2 minutes. Pour into large mixing bowl and slowly add remaining ingredients mixing well after each addition. Refrigerate. *Keeps well in refrigerator for weeks.*

Yields 2½ quarts

Sandra Boddie Hoffman

Rockefeller Sauce

2 10-ounce packages frozen chopped spinach, thawed
4-5 green onions with tops, finely chopped
Small bunch parsley, finely chopped
1 rib celery, finely chopped
12-15 lettuce leaves, preferably romaine
¼ cup mint, finely chopped (optional)
2 sticks butter
½ cup bread crumbs
2 dashes Tabasco
1½ tablespoons Worcestershire sauce
2 tablespoons lemon juice
1 ounce Pernod
1 tablespoon anchovy paste
1½ ounces clam juice
Freshly grated Parmesan cheese

In food processor, combine all ingredients except Parmesan cheese. Process well. For Oysters Rockefeller, wash oysters and shells; then replace oysters in shells. Cover the oysters with the sauce, sprinkle with cheese and place shells on pie tins filled with rock salt. Bake in a 450° oven for 15 minutes. Serve hot. *Sauce may also be spread over tomato halves and broiled for a delicious vegetable dish.*

Yields approximately 1 quart

Carolyn Clay Flournoy

Barbecue Sauce

1 stick butter
5 ounces A-1 Sauce
2½ ounces Worcestershire sauce
Juice 2 lemons
2 medium onions, chopped
½ cup chili sauce
1 tablespoon salt
1 tablespoon pepper
4 whole cloves garlic, resting in sauce while heating

Put garlic cloves on toothpicks so they can be removed later. Heat all ingredients. Baste chickens or meat frequently while cooking. *This is a very spicy, delicious sauce.*

Yields 1 quart — Louise Wheless Lee

Use celery tops as a basting brush. Eliminates brush washing, and may even impart extra flavor to grilled meats, fish and fowl.

Steak Sauce

4 tablespoons butter or margarine, divided
2 tablespoons flour
1 10½-ounce can beef bouillon
Fresh cracked pepper
2-3 tablespoons dry red wine
2 tablespoons fresh lemon juice
3 drops Worcestershire sauce
½-1 pound fresh mushrooms, sliced
3 green onions and tops, chopped

Make a dark roux by stirring flour into 2 tablespoons butter or margarine over medium heat in a heavy skillet until the roux is a chocolate color. Add bouillon and continue cooking until reduced to about half of original volume. Add pepper, wine, lemon juice and Worcestershire sauce. Sauté mushrooms and green onions in 2 tablespoons butter or margarine. Set aside. Just before serving, add mushrooms and onions to sauce. Heat thoroughly and serve in sauce boat or atop steaks.

Serves 4-6 — Margaret Roberts Evans

Marchand de Vin Sauce

¼ cup butter
½ cup finely minced, cooked ham
½ cup finely chopped onion
⅓ cup finely chopped mushrooms
⅓ cup finely chopped shallots
1 tablespoon minced garlic
2 tablespoons flour
½ teaspoon salt
⅛ teaspoon pepper
Dash cayenne pepper
¾ cup beef broth
½ cup dry red wine

Melt butter and sauté ham, onion, mushrooms, shallots and garlic until onion begins to brown. Blend in flour, salt, pepper and cayenne. Cook stirring constantly until flour browns, about 7 minutes. Blend in beef broth and wine. Heat sauce until boiling. Reduce heat and simmer 35 minutes to blend flavors. *This sauce can be made several days ahead, stored in the refrigerator and reheated when ready to serve.*

Yields 2 cups

Anne Krison Mitchell

When a recipe calls for both garlic and salt, cut or mash the garlic on a cutting board sprinkled with salt. The salt will absorb the juices and minimize the garlic odor on the board.

Raisin Sauce

1 tablespoon butter
3 tablespoons brown sugar
3 tablespoons flour
2 teaspoons prepared mustard
1 teaspoon cinnamon
1 teaspoon cloves
Paprika
1 teaspoon salt
2 tablespoons dark molasses
2 cups water
¼ cup sugar
5 tablespoons vinegar
1 cup seedless raisins

Cream butter, brown sugar, flour, mustard, spices, paprika, salt and molasses. Combine water, sugar and vinegar and bring to a boil. Pour over cream mixture. Add raisins and cook 10 minutes over low heat. *Good served over baked ham, sweet potatoes or apples.*

Yields 3 cups

Antoinette Burt Sentell

Beef Marinade Supreme

Salt, pepper, and Accent to taste
1 cup Worcestershire sauce
1 cup cane syrup
3 tablespoons soy sauce
3 tablespoons brown sugar
Dash red pepper
Dash garlic powder

Salt, pepper and Accent the meat. Combine remaining ingredients and heat until warm. Pour over meat and refrigerate for 24 hours. Remove meat from marinade before cooking. *This appears to be a very sweet marinade, but it is delicious. Good on any cut of beef.*

Bryson D. Jones, M.D.

Beef Marinade

¼ cup Worcestershire sauce
½ cup vinegar
¼ cup soy sauce
Seasoning salt

Mix ingredients and marinate meat about 10 hours. *This is enough to marinate 2 large steaks or a large roast.*

Yields 1 cup

Alice Ann Buchanan Schwendimann

Dewberry-Crabapple Jelly

3½ cups dewberry juice
3½ cups crabapple juice
8½ cups sugar
1 1¾-ounce box Sure-Jell
1 teaspoon citric acid

Use above ingredients and follow exact cooking instructions in Sure-Jell box for cooked jellies. *Crabapple may be substituted with mayhaws or use all 3 together.*

Yields 9 ½-pint jars

Kay Kern Ziegenbein

Mayhaw Jelly

Mayhaw berries
Water
Sugar
Paraffin

Wash berries thoroughly. Do not remove green berries as they provide the pectin. Place washed berries in a large pan with enough water to cover. Bring to a boil and cook until juice turns bright pink. Line a large colander with a clean towel. Being careful not to mash berries, drain juice into container. If you have good fresh berries, you can boil again, then drain and mash berries thoroughly for extra juice. The juice will not be as clear or as pretty but will taste the same. To make the jelly, use 3 cups juice to 2 cups sugar. Do not double. Cook to 220° on a candy thermometer. Pour immediately into jelly glasses. Seal with hot paraffin. Both berries and juice freeze well.

Maggie Belle Atkins Hodges

Ripe Fig Jam

14 cups ripe figs
1 30-ounce can crushed pineapple
Juice 3 lemons
4½ pounds sugar (11½ cups)
1 tablespoon cinnamon
1 tablespoon cloves
1 tablespoon allspice

Mash figs to a fine pulp and mix with other ingredients. Cook until thick, stirring often. Seal in sterile jars while hot.

Yields 7 pints

Sue Holladay Bradbeer
Mexico City, Mexico

Dilled Carrot Sticks

4½ cups water
1½ cups white vinegar
½ cup salt
4-5 pounds carrots

Per jar:
1 garlic clove, chopped
½ teaspoon red pepper
1 teaspoon pickling spice
1 teaspoon dill seed

Boil water, vinegar and salt in covered pot. Let cool. Thoroughly scrape, wash, and quarter carrots lengthwise. Cut ½" shorter than jar. Pack carrots tightly in hot sterile jars. To each jar, add 1 chopped garlic clove, ½ teaspoon red pepper and 1 teaspoon each of dill seed and pickling spice. Pour in cool juice and seal. Chill at least 24 hours before serving. Jars *must* be stored in refrigerator. *If hotter carrot sticks are desired the next time they are prepared, use more red pepper.*

Yields approximately 10 half-pint jars

Sandra MacCleary Boyd

Pickled Eggs

12 peppercorns, crushed
2 teaspoons pickling spice
2 teaspoons ground ginger
2 cups malt vinegar

12 hard-boiled eggs, peeled
2 medium onions, thinly sliced
½ teaspoon dill weed
3 cloves garlic

Combine peppercorns, pickling spice, ground ginger and vinegar in a medium saucepan. Bring to boil; reduce heat and simmer 5 minutes. Put eggs in a glass jar or crock with cover. Pour hot liquid over eggs so they are covered. (Water may be added if more liquid is needed.) Add onion, garlic and dill weed. Cover and refrigerate at least 4 days, turning occasionally. Eggs may be stored in refrigerator in pickling liquid for several months. Serve in wedges as appetizer or on salad. *These should be prepared at least 4 days ahead.*

Yields 1 dozen

Betty Garrett Vogel

Pickled Peaches

12 pounds peaches, peeled
6 pounds sugar
2 pints cider vinegar
4 tablespoons cloves
4 cinnamon sticks
2 pieces ginger root (optional)

Boil sugar, vinegar and spices that have been tied in a bag 12 minutes or until clear. Add peaches; cook until fruit can be easily pierced with a straw. Take peaches out of syrup and put in hot jars. Keep jars covered to keep hot. Cook syrup until thick. Put a few whole cloves and a piece of cinnamon in each jar and fill with hot syrup and seal.

Margaret Scott Burks

Place pared fresh ginger root in a glass jar with sherry to cover. It will keep indefinitely, and the flavor of the ginger will not be altered. The ginger-tinged sherry can be used in marinades.

Dill Green Tomatoes

6 1-pint canning jars, sterilized
1 gallon water
1 gallon white vinegar
½ pound salt
Small, firm whole green tomatoes
18-24 garlic cloves, divided
18-24 1½" green or red hot peppers, divided
6 sprigs fresh dill
¾ teaspoon black pepper, divided
6-18 drops Tabasco, divided

Boil water, vinegar and salt. While boiling, fill jars with green tomatoes. Into each jar, put 3-4 garlic cloves, 3-4 green or red peppers, 1 sprig of dill, ⅛ teaspoon pepper and 1-3 drops Tabasco. Fill jars with water mixture. Seal jars tightly and store upside down for 6-8 weeks.

Yields 6 pints

Mary Virginia Saunders Quinn

Pickled Tomatoes

1 gallon green tomatoes, quartered
1 quart diced onions
½ cup hot green peppers, sliced across
5 cups distilled vinegar
3 cups sugar
½ cup salt (scant)
2 teaspoons pepper (optional)

Mix and bring to a quick boil. Pack in sterile jars.

Yields 4 quarts

Martha Turner Schober

Dill Pickles

2 quarts vinegar
1¼ quarts water
¾ cup salt

For each jar:
6-8 peppercorns
1 heaping teaspoon dill seed
1 clove garlic, halved
1-2 whole cloves
32-40 small cucumbers, 1″ diameter

Bring vinegar, water and salt to a boil. In each quart jar add peppercorns, dill seed, garlic and cloves. Then add cucumbers and pour vinegar solution over all and seal. Let pickles stand for 1 week.

Yields 4 quarts

Ivy Hedgcock Frierson

Sweet-Hot Pickles

1 48-ounce jar crinkle cut, hamburger dill pickles
3 cups sugar
1½ ounces Tabasco
3 cloves garlic, sliced

Drain pickles, discarding juice. Put all ingredients in large bowl. Stir as sugar dissolves. Let mixture sit 45 minutes, stirring occasionally. Put mixture back in pickle jar. Turn upside down one day, right side up next day, etc., for 5 days. These will keep indefinitely. *Good for gift giving.*

Yields 6 cups

Dixey Thornton Sanders

Bread and Butter Pickles

1 gallon medium cucumbers, thinly sliced
8 small white onions, sliced
1 green pepper, cut in thin strips
1 sweet red pepper, cut in thin strips
½ cup coarse medium salt
Cracked ice
5 cups sugar
1½ teaspoons turmeric
½ teaspoon ground cloves
2 tablespoons mustard seed
2 teaspoons celery seed
5 cups vinegar

Mix cucumbers, onion and peppers. Add salt; cover with ice and mix thoroughly. Let stand 3 hours. Drain. Combine remaining ingredients. Pour over cucumber mixture. Bring to a boil. Seal in sterilized jars. *Chill in refrigerator before serving.*

Yields 8 pints

Cynthia Johnson Nowery

Squash Relish

8 cups chopped yellow squash
3 quarts water
⅔ cup non-iodized salt
3 cups sugar
2 cups vinegar
2 tablespoons mustard seed
2 tablespoons celery seed
2 cups chopped onions
3 green onions with tops, chopped
2 cups chopped green peppers
1 4-ounce jar chopped pimientos, drained

Soak squash 1 hour in brine made with water and salt. Drain in colander. For syrup, bring sugar, vinegar, mustard and celery seed to boil. Drop all vegetables in boiling syrup. Turn out fire. Put in sterile jars while hot. Seal.

Yields 8 ½-pint jars

Mabel Smith Overton

Hot Tomato Relish

1 28-ounce can tomatoes or 10-12 fresh tomatoes
2 small onions, minced
½ cup white vinegar
½ cup brown sugar
1 teaspoon salt
½ teaspoon black pepper
¼ teaspoon ground cinnamon
¼ teaspoon allspice
¼ teaspoon ground cloves
4 small hot green peppers, seeded and chopped

If using fresh tomatoes, remove skins by plunging them into boiling water about 10 seconds. Skin will slip right off. Combine all ingredients in large saucepan and bring to a boil. Boil uncovered until barely soupy. It will be a dark, rich sauce. Seal in sterile jars or keep in refrigerator until needed. *This is a very hot relish. This certainly perks up a winter meal when summer tomatoes are only a pleasant memory.*

Yields 5 10-ounce jars

Ione Dowdy Roberts

Sombrero Hot Sauce

8 cups fresh tomatoes, peeled and cut up
8-10 jalapeño peppers, chopped
2 large onions, chopped
2 cups apple cider vinegar
¼ cup oil
4 tablespoons salt
1½ tablespoons garlic powder

Put all ingredients together and boil until as thick as desired. It usually takes around 2½-3 hours. Pour into sterilized jars and seal while hot.

Yields 2 quarts

Betsy Chandler Peatross

To peel tomatoes or peaches plunge in boiling water for 10 seconds.

Charoses

6 fresh apples
½ cup sugar
2 tablespoons cinnamon
½ cup raisins
1 cup chopped pecans

Chop apples; sprinkle with mixed sugar and cinnamon. Add raisins and pecans and mix well. Serve in a bowl surrounded by matzo crackers. *Must be tasted to be understood. Rather like a fresh mincemeat.*

Marion Wiener Weiss

Sweet-Hot Mustard

1 cup Colman's Dry Mustard
1 cup tarragon vinegar
3 eggs, beaten
1 cup sugar

Mix mustard and vinegar. Let soak several hours. Mix eggs, sugar and mustard mixture in double boiler. Cook until thick.

Yields 1-1½ pints

Sue Goldstein Rubenstein

Mustard Spread

¼ cup dry mustard
1 teaspoon turmeric
1 teaspoon seasoned salt
3 tablespoons sugar
1½ tablespoons cornstarch
⅔ cup water
⅓ cup plus 1 tablespoon cider vinegar
1 teaspoon salad herbs (mixture savory, basil and tarragon)

Mix first 5 ingredients. Add half the water and stir until smooth. Add remaining water and cider vinegar. Cook stirring constantly over low heat or in a double boiler until thick. Remove from heat; add salad herbs and blend. Place in a glass jar and refrigerate overnight until flavors blend. *Good for ham or any kind of sandwich.*

Yields 1 cup

Linda Tharpe Cann

Pepper Jelly

½ cup ground green pepper
¼-½ cup ground hot peppers (1½" long)
6½ cups sugar
1½ cups vinegar
2 3-ounce packages Certo
Green food coloring (optional)
Paraffin

Grind peppers in meat grinder. Stir sugar and vinegar together with peppers. Bring to a fast hard boil. Boil 1 minute. Add Certo and boil 1 more minute. Add as much food coloring as desired. Strain into jelly glasses and add 1 heaping teaspoon of pepper mixture to each glass. Cover with hot paraffin. *Good on top of cream cheese as an hors d'oeuvre with crackers. Red sweet peppers may be mixed with green peppers for added color.*

Yields 6 ½-pint jars

Mary Gannon Friend

Pepper Sauce

Pint jar packed with cayenne peppers
⅔ cup vinegar
⅓ scant cup water
1 teaspoon sugar
½ teaspoon salt
1 clove garlic

Boil vinegar, water, sugar and salt. Pour over peppers and garlic in jar or cruet. Seal. Let stand for 3 weeks.

Yields 1 pint

Mimi Moss Winterton

Miss Olivia's Bread

- 1 cup milk, scalded
- 2 tablespoons butter
- 1 tablespoon shortening
- 1 cake yeast or 1 package dry yeast
- ¼ cup lukewarm water
- 1 egg
- 1½ teaspoons salt
- 3 tablespoons sugar
- 3½-4 cups unbleached flour

Scald 1 cup milk. Remove from fire to cool. While still warm, add butter and shortening; let this get lukewarm. Dissolve yeast in water in large mixing bowl. Add milk mixture. Add unbeaten egg and stir well. Gradually add salt, sugar and flour, using 3½ cups flour. If dough is still quite sticky, add more flour. Knead well with hands. Grease sides of bowl and top of dough; cover with cloth. Put in warm place to rise until doubled, about 45 minutes to 1 hour. Grease hands with shortening. Work dough down and knead on floured board. It may take ½ cup more flour to keep dough from being sticky. To make 1 pan of rolls and 1 loaf of bread, divide dough into 2 balls.

Rolls

Roll dough on floured board to slightly less than ½". Cut with biscuit cutter; fold in half; put in buttered 9" baking pan. Butter tops. Let rise to double, covered. Bake at 400° for about 20 minutes until lightly browned.

Bread

After kneading down, fold several times, side to side, end to end, finally making a smooth oval. Place in greased bread pan. Grease top of dough; put in warm place to double. Cover with cloth. When ready, put in 350° oven for 30 minutes or until hollow sound occurs when you thump the top. Remove to cool on wire rack.

Yields 2½ dozen rolls, or 2 loaves, or 1 dozen rolls and 1 loaf

Olivia Quattlebaum Lambert

Refrigerator Rolls

4 sticks margarine
2 cups milk
2 packages dry yeast
2 teaspoons sugar
4 eggs, beaten
½ cup sugar
8 cups sifted flour
½ teaspoon salt

Melt margarine and add milk gradually. Dissolve yeast and 2 teaspoons sugar in ¼ cup water. Add beaten eggs. Add yeast mix to butter. Add flour, salt and ½ cup sugar. Dust top of dough with flour and place in bowl, tightly covered. Place in refrigerator overnight. Next day, divide dough into 6 wedges while still in bowl. Each wedge makes 1 dozen rolls. Roll each piece out in a 10″ circle (size of plate). Cut each circle in 12 pieces, like a pie. Roll each piece, starting at the large end. Place on greased cookie sheet and let rise 2½-3 hours. Bake at 425° about 8 minutes. *May be made ahead of time and frozen in plastic bags.*

Yields 6 dozen — Susan Metcalf James

Sourdough Rolls

1 yeast cake
1 cup water
2 cups buttermilk
6 cups flour
1 teaspoon salt
½ cup sugar
4 teaspoons baking powder
¼ teaspoon baking soda
½ cup oil

Dissolve yeast in water and buttermilk. Sift dry ingredients. Add oil and milk mixture. Mix well. Store tightly covered in refrigerator and use as desired. Roll out desired amount of dough on floured surface. Cut out rolls. Pour oil on cookie sheet to cover. Dip both sides of cut rolls in oil on sheet. Fold in half and position on sheet. Bake at 400-425° for 20 minutes.

Yields 2-3 dozen — Lucretia Taylor Miller

Whole Wheat Rolls

1 package yeast or yeast cake
2 tablespoons lukewarm water
2 eggs, beaten
1 cup milk, scalded
½ stick butter or margarine
⅓ cup honey
1½ teaspoons salt
4-4½ cups whole wheat flour, or unbleached flour

Dissolve yeast in water. Beat eggs; scald milk and melt butter in the milk. Add honey and salt to the milk. Let cool to lukewarm. Then add eggs and yeast. Whisk to blend. Then add flour. Let rise until double in bulk. Knead a little on floured board. Roll out and cut. Place on greased cookie sheet, or close together in pans, and let rise 1 hour. Bake at 450° until lightly browned, about 10-12 minutes. *These freeze well.*

Yields 36-40 2" rolls

Frances Hodges Smitherman

Proofing yeast is a very important step in bread making. To proof means to test to see if the yeast is still active. This is done by dissolving the yeast in warm (100°-110°) water with ½ teaspoon of sugar. The bubbling of the mixture is proof that the yeast is active.

Whole Wheat Biscuits

1½ cups whole wheat flour
½ cup white flour
1 teaspoon salt
1 tablespoon sugar
3 teaspoons baking powder
⅓ cup shortening
¾ cup milk
1 egg

Sift dry ingredients into mixing bowl. Cut in shortening with fork. Beat egg into milk and gradually add to dry ingredients, mixing well until the consistency of a soft dough.

Toss on a floured board and knead lightly. Roll to ½" thickness, fold and roll to ½" thickness, again. Cut and place on oiled baking sheet. Bake at 450° for 12-15 minutes. *Can be made ahead and refrigerated several hours, and baked just before serving.*

Yields 2 dozen

Camp Waldemar
Hunt, Texas

Buttermilk Biscuits

2 cups flour
3 teaspoons baking powder
½ teaspoon salt
¼ teaspoon sugar
½ cup cold chicken fat or shortening
½ teaspoon soda
¾ cup buttermilk

Sift first 4 ingredients. Cut in fat. You may substitute shortening, but chicken fat is especially good. Put soda in cup. Add buttermilk. Stir into dry ingredients. Knead gently. Do not roll out; pat with hands on lightly floured wax paper. Lightly grease 2 round cake pans. Cut out biscuits. Bake at 450° for 10-15 minutes. If serving later, bake until set. Remove from oven; cover when cool. Reheat to golden brown. For sausage biscuits, divide dough into 2 parts. Pat out 1 portion. Sprinkle generously with cooked crumbled sausage. Pat out remaining dough on wax paper. Invert over sausage layer. Press lightly. Cut out biscuits and bake as above.

Yields 20 biscuits

Eleanor Johnson Colquitt

Crusty Biscuits

2 scant cups flour
1 teaspoon salt
2 teaspoons sugar
4 teaspoons baking powder
½ cup shortening
¾ cup milk

Sift flour, salt, sugar and baking powder together. Add shortening and work in with pastry blender or in food processor until consistency of coarse corn meal is attained. Add milk all at once; blend and place dough on lightly floured board. Knead lightly 15 times; then roll out to thickness of about ⅓". Cut with standard biscuit cutter. Place on greased baking sheet and bake at 450° for 15 minutes or until lightly browned. *These biscuits are rather crisp (tender on inside) and less than 1" in height. Recipe may be doubled and kept several days in refrigerator.*

Yields 30

Continued...

Bran Biscuits

Substitute 1 cup 100% bran cereal for 1 cup of flour, but a little extra flour must be used to handle the dough. Use party-size cutter for these.

Cheese Biscuits

Add ¾ cup grated Cheddar cheese to regular ingredients and cut with small cutter.

Sausage Biscuits

Cook crumbled bulk sausage thoroughly and drain. Roll dough as thin as possible, not over ¼ ", and spread sausage thickly over half the dough. Fold uncovered half over sausage-covered dough. Cut with small biscuit cutter.

Herb Biscuits

Add ½ teaspoon of mixed dried herbs for each cup of flour. For cocktail biscuits, try poultry seasoning, sage or Italian seasoning.

Onion Biscuits

Add ½ cup canned French fried onions, finely chopped, to recipe. For hors d'oeuvres, center with ham slice.

Cinnamon Pinwheels

Roll dough in oblong sheet. Brush with melted butter and sprinkle heavily with cinnamon mixture composed of 1 cup sugar and 1½ tablespoons cinnamon. Roll tightly like a jelly roll; wrap in plastic wrap and chill. Can be done day or two ahead and sliced day of baking. Slice thinly and bake at 350° until brown. *May add chopped pecans sprinkled with cinnamon sugar.*

Marilee Davis Harter

Choctaw Cornbread (Old Choctaw Recipe)

2 cups fresh corn, grated (scrape the cob)
2 tablespoons flour
1 teaspoon salt
1 tablespoon sugar
2 tablespoons melted bacon drippings
1 egg
⅔ cup sweet or sour milk
2 teaspoons baking powder
2 tablespoons corn meal
½ teaspoon soda

Mix all ingredients. Grease cornstick irons well with small amount of bacon grease. Bake the batter in sizzling hot cornstick irons at 450° for 15 minutes. They should be golden brown and crisp. This batter is heavy and does not rise quite as much as ordinary meal bread, so the irons may be filled deeper than usual. The batter will keep in refrigerator for a few days. *You have to be part Indian really to make this one; but if you're not... Good Luck!*

Yields 18 sticks

John N. Paschall
Natchitoches, Louisiana

Mexican Cornbread

1½ cups stone-ground corn meal
3 tablespoons baking powder
1½ teaspoons salt
2 eggs, well beaten
1 cup creamed corn
1 cup sharp grated cheese
1 cup sour cream
4 chopped jalapeño peppers

Mix all ingredients. Bake in greased hot iron skillet at 375° until brown for 20-30 minutes.

Serves 8-10

Irene Klein Hermer

Virginia Spoon Bread

2 cups milk
¾ cup white corn meal
4 eggs, separated
¼ teaspoon salt
1 teaspoon sugar

Cook corn meal and milk in double boiler to form mush, stirring constantly. Remove from heat and let cool slightly. Add beaten yolks, salt and sugar. Beat egg whites and fold into other mixture. Pour into a greased hot 2-quart baking dish. Bake at 350° for 30 minutes, or a little longer, until set and brown.

Serves 6

Sara Scott Hargrove

Hot Herb Bread

1 loaf Italian bread
1 stick butter
1 teaspoon parsley flakes
¼ teaspoon oregano
1 clove garlic, minced
¼ teaspoon dried dill weed
Grated Parmesan cheese

Cut bread diagonally into 1″ slices (not all the way through). Combine next 5 ingredients and spread on bread. Shape foil around loaf leaving top open and twisting ends. Sprinkle loaf top liberally with cheese and extra parsley flakes. Heat at 400° for 10 minutes.

Serves 6

Janell Maeder Falter

Flour tortillas cut in strips are a quick, easy substitute for rolled dumplings.

Viennese Bread

2 sticks butter
½ teaspoon crumbled rosemary
½ teaspoon crushed thyme
½ teaspoon crushed marjoram
½ teaspoon crushed parsley
½ teaspoon celery salt

Combine all ingredients. Brush on sliced French bread and bake to desired crispness.

Louise Jackson

Whole Wheat Bread

2½ cups milk, scalded
2 cups cold water
¼ cup sugar
⅓ cup melted butter or salad oil
3 tablespoons salt
2 cakes yeast or 2 packages active dry yeast
½ cup lukewarm water
2 pounds or 7 cups pre-sifted flour
2 pounds or 7 cups whole wheat flour

Scald milk and pour into bowl. Add cold water, sugar, butter and salt. Dissolve yeast in lukewarm water. Add to mixture. Add flours and mix. Knead until spongy in texture. Put in warm place and let rise 2 hours. Knead down. Divide dough into 4 loaves. Place in greased loaf pans. Let rise 1 hour. Put in 400° oven 15 minutes. Reduce heat to 350° and bake 45 minutes more or until golden brown. Remove to racks and let cool.

Yields 4 loaves

Eleanor Long Simmons

Boston Brown Bread

- **1 cup white flour**
- **1 cup whole wheat flour**
- **1 cup yellow corn meal**
- **¾ cup molasses or syrup**
- **1 teaspoon salt**
- **2 teaspoons soda**
- **2 cups buttermilk**
- **1 cup raisins**
- **1 cup chopped dates**
- **1 cup chopped pecans**

Mix ingredients and pour batter into 2 greased 1-pound coffee cans. Seal tops of cans with wax paper, then a piece of foil, and tie with string. Put cans on rack in pot with water. Place cover on pot and steam 2½ hours. Cool 15 minutes in can. Remove. *Serve with ice cream as a dessert or cream cheese as a sandwich. Freezes well.*

Yields 2 loaves

Lurene Owens

Six-Weeks Bran Muffins

- **4 eggs**
- **1 quart buttermilk**
- **1 cup vegetable oil**
- **1 15-ounce box raisin bran**
- **3 cups sugar**
- **5 cups flour**
- **5 teaspoons soda**
- **2 teaspoons salt**

Mix eggs, buttermilk and oil. Add to the remaining ingredients and mix well. Fill muffin tins greased or lined with cupcake papers ⅔ full and bake at 400° for 15 minutes. This may be stored covered in refrigerator for 6 weeks. Use as desired.

Yields 3 dozen

Roslyn Papa Cotter

Cherry Muffins

- ½ cup finely ground nuts
- 4 tablespoons butter
- ½ cup sugar
- ½ cup brown sugar
- 1 cup sifted flour
- 2 egg yolks, well beaten
- ¼ teaspoon baking powder
- 2 tablespoons maraschino cherry juice
- ¼ teaspoon salt
- 2 eggs whites, well beaten
- Maraschino cherries
- Confectioners' sugar

Put ½ teaspoon nuts into each greased miniature muffin tin. Mix butter, sugar, brown sugar, flour, egg yolks, baking powder, cherry juice and salt together. Gently fold in egg whites. Spoon 1 teaspoon of batter into tins and place cherry on top of batter. Add 1 teaspoon of batter and sprinkle with nuts. Bake at 400° for 10-12 minutes. While warm roll in confectioners' sugar. *These are nice for the holidays.*

Yields 30-36 muffins — Zee Cox Cunningham

If muffins get done before they are needed, take a fork and flip them over in the tins to keep them crisp on bottom.

Danish Puffs

First Dough

- 1 stick margarine or butter
- 1 cup flour
- 2 tablespoons cold water

Cut margarine or butter into flour until it looks like coarse meal. Add cold water; mix until soft dough. Divide into 2 parts. Press each half into 3″×12″ oblong shape on an ungreased baking sheet.

Continued...

Second Dough

- 1 cup water
- 1 stick butter
- 1 teaspoon almond flavoring
- 1 cup flour
- 3 eggs

Place water and butter in a saucepan and bring to a boil. Remove from heat; add almond flavoring; stir in flour. Add eggs, one at a time, beating well after each addition, using electric beater. Spread this mixture over the 3″×12″ oblongs. Bake at 400° for 50 minutes. Watch carefully as may be done sooner. Frost hot cakes with thin confectioners' sugar frosting. Cut in squares for 40. Can be reheated if made day ahead. *To make 3″×12″ oblongs, roll like a pencil and then flatten on heavy cookie sheet.*

Yields 40 squares

Isabelle Phipps Chapman

Fig Coffee Cake

- 1 egg
- 2 tablespoons sugar
- 1 teaspoon vanilla
- ½ cup vegetable oil
- 1 cup + 3 tablespoons flour
- ½ teaspoon baking soda
- ½ teaspoon salt
- 1 teaspoon baking powder
- 1 pint fig preserves, cut into small pieces
- ½ cup chopped pecans

Beat egg, sugar and vanilla in a large mixing bowl until well blended. Add cooking oil and beat again. Add dry ingredients and blend until smooth. Add fig preserves and pecans. Bake in a lightly greased 8″ square pan at 350° for 35-40 minutes. *May add confectioners' sugar or whipped cream as topping.*

Serves 6-9

Ann Dunbar Davis
Austin Texas

Oatmeal Cinnamon Bread

- **1 package active dry yeast**
- **⅓ cup warm water**
- **1½ cups scalded milk**
- **½ cup sugar**
- **2 teaspoons salt**
- **⅓ cup shortening**
- **5-5½ cups all-purpose flour**
- **2 eggs, beaten**
- **1½ cups rolled oats**
- **⅓ cup sugar**
- **2 teaspoons cinnamon**
- **3 tablespoons butter or margarine, melted**

Sprinkle yeast over warm water to soften. In a large bowl, pour scalded milk over ½ cup of sugar, salt and shortening. Stir until shortening melts. Cool to lukewarm. Into lukewarm milk mixture, stir 1 cup flour and beaten eggs, then yeast and rolled oats. Mix until blended. Stir in enough flour to make a soft dough. Turn dough onto floured board and knead about 10 minutes or until smooth and satiny. Place dough in large greased bowl; grease top of dough lightly. Cover and let rise in a warm place until doubled. Punch down dough; place on a floured cloth-covered board. Cover with bowl and let rest 10 minutes. In small bowl combine ⅓ cup sugar and cinnamon. Stir until completely blended. Divide dough in half. Roll 1 half into 8″×15″ rectangle. Brush with 1½ tablespoons melted butter and sprinkle with half of sugar-cinnamon mixture. Roll up dough, jelly-roll fashion, starting at short end. Place seam side down in well greased 5″×9″×3″ loaf pan. Repeat with other half of dough. Cover bread; let rise in warm place until nearly doubled. Bake at 375° for 30-35 minutes or until it gives a hollow sound when tapped. Brush tops of loaves with melted butter and let cool in pans on side for 15 minutes. Remove from pans to wire racks and finish cooling on side.

Yields 2 loaves

Rosemary Pate LaFargue

Whole Wheat Banana Bread

1 stick margarine, softened
1½ cups firmly packed brown sugar
2 eggs, slightly beaten
1 cup mashed bananas
1 teaspoon vanilla
1½ cups whole wheat flour
½ teaspoon soda
½ teaspoon salt
½ cup milk
½ cup chopped pecans

Cream margarine and sugar until light and fluffy. Add eggs, bananas and vanilla, beating well. Combine dry ingredients into another bowl, blending well. Stir this into banana mixture. Stir in milk and pecans. Spoon batter into a greased 5¼ "×9¼ "×2¾ " loaf pan. Bake at 350° for 60-75 minutes. *Very moist. Good sliced, buttered and toasted for breakfast, or good sliced and served with spread of cream cheese mixed with finely chopped dates and honey.*

Yields 1 loaf

Sissy Masters Harper

Strawberry Bread-Sandwiches

2 sticks butter
1½ cups sugar
4 eggs
1 cup strawberry jam
1 cup sour cream
3 cups flour
½ teaspoon soda
¾ teaspoon cream of tartar
1 teaspoon lemon extract
1 teaspoon vanilla

In a bowl, cream butter and sugar and add lightly beaten eggs. In another bowl, fold sour cream into jam. Sift the flour, soda and cream of tartar. Add to the butter mixture alternately with the jam mixture. Fold in the lemon extract and the vanilla. Line 2 loaf pans with wax paper. Add mixture and bake at 325° for 1 hour. *Slice very thin and spread with softened cream cheese for tea sandwiches.*

Yields 2 loaves

Jeannie Hamel Marston

Apricot Bread-Sandwiches

- ⅔ cup dried apricots
- 1⅓ cups milk, scalded
- ⅔ cup grape nuts cereal
- 1 egg, well beaten
- 3 tablespoons shortening, melted and cooled
- 2 cups sifted all-purpose flour
- 2½ teaspoons baking powder
- 1 teaspoon salt
- ⅔ cup firmly packed light brown sugar
- 1 8-ounce package Neufchâtel cheese, softened
- 1 cup nuts (pecans or walnuts)
- 1 cup apricot preserves
- 1 9-ounce carton non-dairy whipped topping

Prepare apricots as directed on package, but cook only half the time indicated. (This prevents apricots from being too soft in bread.) Drain; cool and cut into pieces. Pour scalded milk over cereal in mixing bowl; stir in apricots; let cool. Add egg and shortening; mix well. Combine sifted flour, baking powder, salt and sugar; add to cereal mixture. Stir just until moistened. Pour into greased 4″ × 8″ loaf pan. Bake at 350° for 1 hour or until cake tester inserted into center comes out clean. Cool in pan for 10 minutes; remove from pan and finish cooling on rack. Wrap in wax paper, plastic wrap or foil. You may serve as plain sliced bread or, *for a real culinary delight, mix softened cheese, nuts, preserves and non-dairy whipped topping until smooth. Spread between thin slices of bread.*

Yields 1 loaf — Caroline Jones Ellison

Rice Pancakes

- 1 cup cooked rice
- 2 whole eggs
- 1 tablespoon sugar
- ½ teaspoon vanilla

Mix all ingredients and cook as you would pancakes. These freeze well and can be heated in microwave. *Serve topped with jelly, syrup, confectioners' sugar, cinnamon sugar or mix whipped butter and strawberry jam together for the best topping of all.*

Yields 4 pancakes — Scott Wilhite

Cottage Cheese Pancakes

6 eggs, separated
1½ cups cottage cheese
½ teaspoon salt
½ cup flour
¼ teaspoon baking powder
Bits of meat (optional)

Beat egg whites until stiff and set aside. Beat yolks and cottage cheese. Add rest of ingredients, folding in whites last. Add a little milk if batter too thick. Bits of meat may be added. Drop by tablespoonful onto lightly greased griddle and cook until browned. *Serve immediately with syrup or crushed fresh berries.*

Yields about 2 dozen 3″ pancakes

Laura Lane Breaux

Layer unfilled crêpes between wax paper; roll entire stack into tube shape and freeze. Stored in this space-saving way, crêpes will not crack and are ready to thaw and fill.

Basic Crêpe Batter

2 eggs
¾ cup flour, sifted
1 teaspoon sugar
Pinch salt
¾-1 cup milk

Mix eggs with flour, sugar and salt. Add milk to batter until it is the consistency of condensed milk. Beat until smooth and refrigerate for 30 minutes. Batter can be kept in refrigerator for 2-3 days. Heat a 6″ skillet and oil lightly. Pour approximately 2 tablespoons batter into pan. Tilt quickly to distribute batter evenly. Cook about 1 minute until edges are lightly browned. Flip over with a spatula. The second side will cook more quickly. Use the browned side for the outside.

Serves 4-6

Chef Joe Fertitta

Cornbread Dressing

- **3 cups white corn meal**
- **6 tablespoons flour**
- **2 teaspoons baking powder**
- **2 teaspoons salt**
- **½ teaspoon baking soda**
- **4 tablespoons shortening**
- **4 cups buttermilk**
- **2 eggs, beaten**
- **3 cups chopped celery (use some leaves)**
- **1 bunch green onions, chopped**
- **1 medium onion, chopped**
- **½ cup chopped green pepper**
- **1 stick margarine**
- **4-5 slices white bread**
- **1 teaspoon poultry seasoning**
- **4 eggs, beaten**
- **Turkey neck and gizzard**

Sift corn meal, flour, baking powder, salt and soda. Melt shortening in deep 10″ iron skillet in 450° oven. Add milk and eggs to dry ingredients. Add melted shortening. Mix and pour batter into very hot skillet. Bake in skillet at 450° for 20-25 minutes. Sautê vegetables in margarine very slowly. Toast bread on a cookie sheet at 250° for 1 hour. Cut brown crust off cornbread and crumble cornbread and toast. Mix with sautêed vegetables. Boil turkey neck and gizzard. This will be broth for dressing. Add poultry seasoning and eggs. Mix enough broth with all these ingredients so it will be moist throughout. Steam in colander over boiling water for 1 hour.

Yields dressing for 12-pound turkey

Diane Gilbert Lawhon

Pine Nut Dressing

2 pounds hot sausage
1 pound ground steak
3 tablespoons butter
2 large onions, finely chopped
3 cups raw rice
6-8 eggs, boiled, shelled and grated on large end of grater
¼ cup pine nuts
1 tablespoon sage
Poultry seasoning to taste
Salt and pepper to taste
Chicken broth, enough to make moist before baking

Brown ground steak and sausage in large skillet until finely crumbled. Drain well. Mix onion with meat while rice is cooking. Then mix remaining ingredients in a large container. Season to taste and add enough broth to make juicy. You may put chicken, turkey, duck or game birds on top of dressing and bake at 350° for 1½ hours. *Pine nuts may be found in gourmet food shops or grocery shops. You may substitute pecans for pine nuts.*

Serves 10-12

Lydia McGlathary Ehrhardt

Rice Dressing

Giblets of 5 fryers
6 cups water
4 teaspoons Kitchen Bouquet
1 teaspoon black pepper
2 teaspoons salt
Dash red pepper
1 bunch green onions, chopped
2 medium yellow onions, chopped
5 ribs celery, chopped
⅔ cup oil
2 cups rice, uncooked

Cook giblets in water with seasonings and Kitchen Bouquet. Chop finely when tender. Reserve stock. If using processor, chop gizzards and livers separately. Chop vegetables in processor. Sauté vegetables in 4-cup container in oil in microwave oven or on top of stove until glazed. Measure 4 cups of stock and add vegetables and giblets to stock. Use large Dutch oven. Add 2 cups of rice and bring to boil. Cover; simmer over low heat 30 minutes or until rice is tender. Serve immediately or add more chicken stock to reheat and keep moist.

Yields dressing for 12-pound turkey

Ann Olene Covington Querbes

Fettuccine

- 12 ounces white or green fettuccine, cooked
- 1 stick butter
- 1 cup whipping cream
- ⅓ cup grated Parmesan cheese
- 1 cup sliced mushrooms
- 3 tablespoons butter
- Parmesan cheese for garnish
- Salt and cracked black pepper to taste

Prepare fettuccine according to package directions. Rinse and drain. While fettuccine is cooking, prepare sauce. Place butter, cream and ⅓ cup Parmesan cheese in a skillet and heat slowly over low heat until warm. Do not boil. Stir in fettuccine. Sauté mushrooms in 3 tablespoons butter very quickly. Drain and toss with fettuccine. Serve immediately. Garnish with Parmesan cheese, cracked pepper and salt to taste.

Serves 4-6

Wesley Lambert Richardson

Fettuccine with Prosciutto

- 6 ounces white fettuccine
- 6 ounces green fettuccine
- 1 cup LeSueur small, early peas, drained
- 1 tablespoon basil
- 4 tablespoons butter, divided
- 1 cup sliced mushrooms
- 4 slices prosciutto ham, julienned
- ⅓ cup grated Parmesan cheese, plus more for garnish
- Salt and cracked pepper to taste

Prepare fettuccine, green and white, as packages direct and keep hot. In a small pan heat peas and 1 tablespoon butter with basil and keep hot. Sauté mushrooms in 3 tablespoons butter for 5 or 10 minutes. Remove mushrooms and add to peas. Place ham in mushroom butter and let sizzle just a few minutes. Drain butter from peas and mushrooms; toss with ham. Add ⅓ cup Parmesan cheese and hot fettuccine. Garnish with extra Parmesan, cracked pepper and salt to taste. Serve immediately.

Serves 6

Wesley Lambert Richardson

Fettuccine a la Giavanni

1 pound fettuccine
1 egg yolk
⅔ cup half and half
1 stick butter
Fresh garlic crushed or garlic powder to taste
½ cup grated Romano cheese, divided

Cook noodles. While noodles are cooking, beat egg yolk lightly with fork and add half and half. Melt butter and add garlic. Place drained hot noodles in bowl. Pour egg and cream mixture with melted butter over noodles. Add half of cheese and toss with fork until mixed well. Then add rest of cheese and serve. Add chopped parsley if desired.

Serves 4

Chef John LaBue

For perfect pasta the water should be brought to a rolling boil, lightly salted. A teaspoon of cooking oil in the pot stops the stickiness. Put the pasta in a bit at a time so the water keeps boiling; stir with a wooden spoon (a metal one lowers the temperature). As a rule of thumb, cook a little less time than that recommended by commercial pasta manufacturers.

Cheese Manicotti

14 manicotti shells
1 28-ounce jar Ragú sauce
1 pound Mozzarella cheese, diced
2 eggs
½ cup chopped parsley
1 pound Ricotta cheese
½ cup grated Parmesan cheese
1 teaspoon salt
1 teaspoon pepper
Parmesan cheese

Boil manicotti shells until tender and drain well. Pour half of Ragú sauce into a large flat casserole. Reserve other half for last step. Mix remaining ingredients well and stuff the pasta shells. Pour the remaining Ragú sauce over the shells and sprinkle with additional Parmesan cheese. Cover with foil and bake at 350° for 40 minutes; or you may freeze and bake 1 hour and 10 minutes.

Serves 6

Margaret Downs Hargrove

Pasta Casserole

- 4 slices bacon cut in 1″ pieces
- 4 tablespoons butter or margarine
- ½ cup chopped green onions, tops and bottoms
- 1 pound fresh mushrooms, sliced
- 1 pound spaghetti
- ½ cup dry white wine or chicken broth
- ½ cup finely chopped fresh parsley
- ¼ teaspoon salt
- ¼ teaspoon pepper
- ½ cup whipping cream or half and half, warmed
- ½ cup grated Parmesan cheese

In a large skillet, cook bacon until it begins to brown. Pour off all but 1 tablespoon fat. Leave in bacon. Add butter and cook green onions until soft. Add mushrooms and cook until soft (about 5 minutes). Cook spaghetti in boiling water 7 - 8 minutes until done, but still firm. Add wine or broth, parsley and seasonings. Simmer 5 minutes. Drain spaghetti and turn into a warm bowl. Stir warm cream into bacon and mushroom mixture. Pour this over the spaghetti. Toss gently. Add cheese and toss again. Serve immediately. You may serve with extra cheese if desired. *Four ounces of ham, cut in strips, may be used in place of bacon. Brown in 2 tablespoons of butter. Bacon may be cooked crisper if desired.*

Serves 8 — Jean Pressburg Gruber

Chop fresh parsley and put it into a sectional ice cube tray; then fill with water and freeze. Just drop the cubes into soups, stews, etc., when needed.

Armenian Rice

1 cup raw rice
2-2½ cups chicken broth
1 stick butter
4 cloves garlic, halved
1 cup nested vermicelli, broken up (or regular spaghetti or vermicelli, broken in thirds)
1 large green pepper, chopped
1 6-ounce can mushrooms, stems and pieces with juice
1 6-ounce can ripe olives, cut in halves

Place rice in casserole. Cover with chicken broth. Melt butter in skillet. Add garlic and cook slowly until golden brown. Remove garlic. Add vermicelli and cook until dark brown, stirring frequently. Add vermicelli with pan drippings, green pepper, mushrooms with liquid and olives to rice mixture. Stir until well mixed. Cover and bake at 350° for 45 minutes.

Serves 8-10 Adelaide Murdock Hunt

Baked Louisiana Rice

1½ cups Uncle Ben's Rice
½ cup chopped green pepper
4-5 green onions, chopped
2 green onion tops, chopped
1 cup chopped parsley
1 pound Velveeta cheese, grated
½ cup milk
2 eggs, beaten
½ cup vegetable oil
1 teaspoon basil
½ teaspoon thyme
Salt and pepper to taste

Cook rice until almost done. Set aside chopped vegetables. Mix remaining ingredients well. Add vegetables and rice and mix slowly. Bake at 325° in a greased 2-quart casserole for 45 minutes to 1 hour. Add milk if necessary to thin. *This is a hearty dish and doubles well.*

Serves 8 Lola Weir Herndon

Chinese Fried Rice

1⅓ cups rice, cooked, chilled
2 tablespoons bacon grease
1 6-ounce can mushrooms, drained
¼ cup finely chopped green onions
1 tablespoon soy sauce
8 or more slices bacon, cooked crisp and crumbled
1 egg, beaten

Prepare rice according to directions. Chill. Heat bacon grease in skillet, add rice, mushrooms, onions and soy sauce. Cook over low heat 10 minutes, stirring occasionally. Add bacon and egg. Cook, stirring, 5 minutes longer. Serve hot.

Serves 4

Gail Kelley Shell

Wild Rice Amandine

1 stick butter
1 cup raw wild rice
½ cup slivered almonds
1 tablespoon chopped green pepper
1 tablespoon chopped chives or onions
½ pound sliced mushrooms
3 cups chicken broth

Put all ingredients, except chicken broth, in heavy frying pan. Cook until rice turns yellow, stirring constantly. Put in buttered casserole with broth. Cover tightly and bake at 350° for 1 hour.

Serves 8-10

Rubye Adkisson Couch

Wild Rice and Apples

- 1½ cups wild rice
- 3 cups hot beef or chicken consommé
- 1½ cups dry white wine
- 3 Delicious apples, peeled, cored and sliced
- ⅓ cup butter

Wash wild rice well. Put in small sieve and run water through. Put 3 cups hot beef or chicken consommé and 1½ cups dry white wine in a buttered casserole; cover, and bake at 400° for 1 hour or until rice is tender. Sauté apples in butter until soft. Fork stir apples into rice.

Serves 6-8

Garland Houck Guth

Wild Rice Casserole

- 1 cup raw wild rice, cooked
- 2 tablespoons butter
- 1 small onion, chopped
- ½ green pepper, chopped
- 2 ribs celery, chopped
- 1 4-ounce can sliced mushrooms, reserve juice
- ½ pound American cheese, diced
- ¾ teaspoon salt
- ½ teaspoon pepper
- ½ cup half and half

Sauté onion, green pepper and celery in butter. Combine with rice and add mushrooms, cheese, salt and pepper. Mix well and put in buttered casserole. Mix half and half and mushroom juice together and pour over rice. Bake at 350° for 30 minutes.

Serves 6

Linda Hamel Bird

Calabasitas

- 2 tablespoons butter
- 2 medium green peppers, cut in thin strips
- 4 small zucchini, sliced
- ¼ pound fresh mushrooms, sliced
- ¾ teaspoon salt
- 4 green onions, chopped
- 2 avocados, diced
- 1 teaspoon chili powder
- 3 cups grated Swiss cheese, divided

Fry peppers, zucchini and mushrooms quickly in butter and add salt. This may be done 2-3 hours ahead and reheated just before serving. Mix green onions, avocados, chili powder and 2 cups of cheese in separate bowl. Stir in hot vegetables and top with remaining cup of cheese. *Serve as a salad-vegetable combination with Mexican dinner.*

Serves 6-8

Jean Freeman Echterhoff

Artichoke Casserole

- 1 14½-ounce can artichoke hearts, rinsed, drained, sliced in half
- 3 hard-boiled eggs, sliced
- ½ cup sliced stuffed olives
- ¼ cup sliced water chestnuts
- 1 10¾-ounce can cream of mushroom soup, diluted with ¼ cup milk
- ½ cup coarsely grated sharp Cheddar cheese
- ½ cup buttered bread crumbs

Arrange artichoke hearts in 1-quart casserole. Layer eggs, olives and water chestnuts. Cover with soup. Top with grated cheese and buttered crumbs. Bake at 350° for 30 minutes until bubbly hot and crumbs are brown. *Add cooked chicken breasts which have been cut in chunks for a delicious party casserole.*

Serves 4-6

Marion Sailor Attaway

Ritz cracker crumbs are a nice substitute for bread crumbs.

Chinese Asparagus

1½-2 pounds young fresh asparagus, each stalk no more than ½" in diameter
4 tablespoons soy sauce
1 tablespoon sugar
2 tablespoons sesame oil

Discard tough root end of asparagus. Slice remaining stalks in 1½" lengths, making about 3 cups of asparagus pieces. Wash under cold running water and parboil the pieces by dropping them into 2 quarts of rapidly boiling water for 1 minute. Drain at once and run cold water over the asparagus. Spread them on paper towels and pat dry. To assemble, combine soy sauce, sugar and sesame oil in small bowl and mix until the sugar is completely dissolved. Pour dressing over asparagus in shallow bowl and toss to coat each asparagus piece thoroughly. Chill before serving, no longer than 2 hours.

Serves 4 — Nancy Kate Green Hargrove

For cooking fresh asparagus so that it is bright green and crunchy, all you need is a deep heavy iron skillet or similar heavy pan. Snap off bottom third of stalks or where they snap easily. Arrange the thoroughly washed stalks in 2 or 3 layers (bigger stalks on the bottom). Cover with cold water until it stands ½" above the asparagus. Add a tablespoon each of salt and sugar. Bring UNCOVERED to a rolling boil; let boil from 2-4 minutes depending upon the thickness of the asparagus and whether you like it very crisp of not quite so chewy. Remove from the heat and let stand, still uncovered, in the water at least 8 minutes or until ready to serve. If the wait to serve is too long and the asparagus gets cold, simply bring to a boil once more, drain and serve immediately. Frozen asparagus may be cooked the same way. Start with frozen, cover with cold water, bring to a boil separating stalks; boil 1 minute; take off the heat and let stand for 4 minutes. Broccoli, after splitting stalks, may be cooked the same way.

Asparagus Vin Blanc

1½ pounds fresh asparagus
2 tablespoons butter
3 ounces white wine
Salt
Seasoned pepper
½ cup grated Parmesan cheese

Cook asparagus and place in a baking dish. Pour melted butter and white wine over the asparagus. Salt and pepper lightly and sprinkle with grated Parmesan cheese. Place in 425° oven for about 10 minutes, or until cheese lightly browns. Can run it under the broiler if preferred.

Serves 6

Carolyn Clay Flournoy

Baked Broccoli and Onions

2 10-ounce packages frozen broccoli spears
1 cup chopped onions
½ stick butter
⅓ cup flour
1 cup milk
½ cup chicken bouillon
½ cup white wine
Salt and pepper
⅓ cup slivered almonds
½ cup grated sharp cheese

Cook broccoli according to package directions. Drain and place in shallow baking dish. Chop onions and add to broccoli. Melt butter; stir in flour and add milk and chicken stock gradually. Cook over low heat, stirring constantly, until sauce bubbles. Remove from heat and add wine, salt and pepper. Pour over vegetables and top with almonds and cheese. Bake at 375° for 30 minutes.

Serves 4-6

Michele Armstrong
Qvistgaard-Petersen

An average-size onion, chopped, equals 1 cup chopped onion.

Blindehuhn (Westphalian Green Beans and Carrots)

- 1 cup sliced carrots
- 1 9-ounce package frozen cut green beans
- 2 slices bacon
- 1 medium onion, sliced
- 1 apple, peeled, cored and sliced
- 2 tablespoons vinegar
- 1 tablespoon sugar
- ½ teaspoon salt
- ½ teaspoon summer savory

In saucepan cook sliced carrots, covered, in small amount boiling, salted water until nearly tender, about 10 minutes. Add cut green beans and return to boiling. Cover and cook until the vegetables are tender, about 5 minutes more. Drain well. In a skillet cook bacon until crisp; drain, reserving 1 tablespoon drippings. Crumble bacon and set aside. Cook sliced onion in reserved drippings until golden. Add sliced apple, vinegar, sugar, salt and summer savory. Cover and cook until apples are just tender, about 3-4 minutes. Add cooked beans and carrots; heat thoroughly. Sprinkle with bacon.

Serves 6 — Carolyn Clay Flournoy

Pennsylvania Dutch Green Beans

- 3 strips bacon, cooked, reserve drippings
- 1 small onion, sliced
- 1 8½-ounce can water chestnuts, sliced
- 1 16-ounce can green beans
- 2 teaspoons cornstarch
- ¼ teaspoon salt
- ¼ teaspoon dry mustard
- 1 tablespoon brown sugar
- 1 tablespoon vinegar

Brown onion and chestnuts slightly in hot bacon drippings. Drain beans, saving ½ cup liquid. Mix liquid with remaining ingredients and add to onions in skillet. Cook stirring constantly until mixture boils. Add beans and heat thoroughly. Serve garnished with crumbled bacon. *Better on second day!*

Serves 4 — Judy Lind Chidlow

Husband Pleasin' Baked Beans

1 pound ground beef
2 medium onions, chopped
½ stick margarine
3 15-ounce cans ranch style beans
2 16-ounce cans pork and beans
¼ cup prepared mustard
¼ cup maple syrup
½ cup brown sugar
1 cup catsup

Brown beef and onions in margarine and combine with remaining ingredients. Refrigerate overnight. Bake at 300° for 1½ hours. *For a delicious one-dish meal, increase beef to 2 pounds. Great for a barbecue dinner.*

Serves 12 generously

Edie Broyles Williams

Red Beans and Rice

1 pound dried red beans
1 meaty ham bone
2 large onions, chopped
1 green pepper, chopped
1 rib celery with leaves, chopped
½ cup chopped parsley
2 cloves garlic, finely minced
¼ teaspoon thyme
Red or black pepper to taste
½ teaspoon salt
1 teaspoon Tabasco
½ teaspoon sugar
1 bay leaf (optional)
1 tablespoon Worcestershire sauce
½ cup catsup or tomato sauce
Water to cover
2 pounds spicy, smoked sausage, cut in 1" pieces
Cooked rice

Soak beans in water to cover overnight. Rinse. Cover with water in heavy pot, such as a Dutch oven. Add ham bone (fat trimmed off) and remaining ingredients, except sausage and rice. Bring to a boil and simmer 2 hours, stirring occasionally. Add sausage (which has been steamed in a skillet, drained, and fried). Just before serving remove bay leaf and add a little more fresh parsley. For added thickness, remove about a cup of beans from pot, mash thoroughly and return to mixture. Serve the beans with fluffy boiled rice; garnish with chopped scallions. *Do not forget the vinegar and Tabasco bottles on the side.*

Serves 8

Carolyn Clay Flournoy

Black Beans and Rice El Carmelo Habana

2 pounds dried black beans
1 onion, chopped
3 cloves garlic, minced
3 tablespoons olive oil
3 tablespoons vinegar or red wine
3 tablespoons sugar
1 teaspoon oregano
1 teaspoon crushed bay leaves
Salt and pepper to taste
Ham hock or chopped ham
Cooked rice
8 slices baked or grilled ham
Chopped green onions and tops

Wash beans well and soak overnight. In large heavy-bottomed pot, fry onion and garlic in olive oil until just brown. Add beans and the water in which they have been soaking. This will make a rich, dark bean gravy. Add the rest of the seasonings with the hock or chopped ham. Cook until very soft, 2-3 hours, or longer if desired. Add more water as necessary. Just before serving, reduce liquid until thick. Serve over rice with a slice of baked or grilled ham on the side. Serve with a bowl of chopped green onions and tops. *Serve as a soup by putting cooked beans in blender and diluting with chicken broth if too thick.*

Serves 6-8

Carl Wiley Jones

Sweet and Sour Beets

½ cup sugar
¼ cup water
1½ teaspoons cornstarch
1 medium onion, thinly sliced (optional)
½ cup vinegar
1 16-ounce can sliced beets, drained

Boil all ingredients, except beets, for 5 minutes or until mixture thickens. Pour over beets and serve. Good cold or hot. *A cold accompaniment for cooked summer vegetables can be prepared using the same boiled ingredients except onion and cornstarch. Pour over 2 thinly sliced cucumbers and 1 thinly sliced onion. Keeps indefinitely in refrigerator.*

Serves 4-6

Martha Tomlinson Atkins

Granny Wile's Carrot Fritters

5-6 carrots
1 egg
1 tablespoon butter, melted
½ teaspoon salt
1 tablespoon sugar
½ cup flour
1 scant teaspoon baking powder
Oil for browning

Peel and boil carrots until very tender. Remove from water and mash until smooth. Beat egg lightly; add melted butter, salt, sugar, flour and baking powder. Add mashed carrots. This should make a nice batter. If it is too thick, thin with a little milk. Drop the batter from a spoon and fry in hot oil. Brown lightly on 1 side; turn to other side and brown lightly. *A small eggplant may be done the same way. Squeeze water from eggplant after boiling.*

Serves 8 Mimi Wile Hussey

Carrots Vichy

½ stick butter
2 tablespoons finely chopped onion
8 small carrots, thinly sliced
1 teaspoon salt
4 tablespoons sugar
½ cup water
1 tablespoon finely chopped fresh parsley

Sauté onion in butter. Add carrots, salt, sugar and water. Cover and cook on medium heat for approximately 10 minutes. Serve garnished with fresh chopped parsley.

Serves 4 Chef Dietmar H. Molitar

Carrot Soufflé

1 16-ounce can carrots
1 stick margarine
1 cup sugar
3 eggs
1 teaspoon baking powder
3 tablespoons flour
1 teaspoon vanilla

Drain carrots. Melt margarine; add carrots and blend. Add rest of ingredients and mix. Pour in greased casserole. Bake at 350° for 45 minutes.

Serves 4-6

Lynn Snyder Roos

Carrots aux Herbes

2 pounds carrots, peeled and sliced in strips
1 medium onion, chopped
4-4½ tablespoons butter
Salt and pepper
½ teaspoon sweet basil
½ teaspoon rosemary
½ teaspoon dill
¼ teaspoon nutmeg
2-2¼ teaspoons lemon juice
Minced parsley

Boil sliced carrots until tender; drain. In a large skillet sauté onion in butter until clear. Add carrots and remaining ingredients except parsley. Simmer 3-5 minutes until hot and well mixed. Top with parsley to serve.

Serves 6-8

Wesley Lambert Richardson

Cabbage or Celery Sauté

3-4 ribs celery per person, sliced very thin and cut in half or 2 cups shredded cabbage per person
1-2 sticks butter
1-2 tablespoons vinegar
1 teaspoon lemon juice
Salt and pepper to taste

In a large skillet, melt 1 stick of butter for celery and 2 sticks for cabbage. Add 1 tablespoon vinegar for celery and 2 for cabbage and 1 teaspoon lemon juice. Cover and simmer over low heat until just tender. When you uncover skillet, it should smell very spicy; if not add a little vinegar. This can be reheated very easily if prepared earlier in day. *This is a very easy vegetable recipe to prepare and is delicious with almost any meat, fish or poultry. Doubles well.*

Serves 4 — Wesley Lambert Richardson

Cauliflower Soufflé

1 head cauliflower
4 tablespoons butter
4 tablespoons flour
1 teaspoon salt
Black pepper to taste
1 cup milk
1 cup grated Cheddar cheese
4 eggs, separated

Cook cauliflower in boiling water until tender and drain. Purée in blender or food processor. Melt butter; mix in flour, salt and pepper, making a smooth paste. Add milk and cook until thick. Remove from fire and add grated cheese and cauliflower. Add beaten egg yolks to mixture and let cool about 15 minutes. Beat egg whites until stiff and fold into mixture. Put into a buttered 2-quart casserole or soufflé dish. Place this dish in a pan of water 1″ deep and bake at 325° for 50 minutes. *Broccoli may be substituted for cauliflower, and add 1 onion chopped and sauteed in cooking oil.*

Serves 6-8 — Ruth Elgin Nordyke

Celery Amandine

- **1 stalk celery, sliced in ½" slices**
- **½ cup grated Cheddar cheese**
- **1 cup sliced almonds**
- **2 10¾-ounce cans cream of celery soup**
- **Pepperidge Farm Stuffing Mix**

Butter casserole dish. Layer celery, cheese, almonds and 1 can of soup. Repeat for second layer. Sprinkle stuffing mix on top. Cook uncovered at 375° for 45 minutes.

Serves 6 — Nancy Hudson Ketner

Cushaw

- **1 medium to large cushaw**
- **½ teaspoon salt**
- **2 sticks butter**
- **10-12 eggs**
- **3-4 cups sugar**
- **1 5.33-ounce can evaporated milk**
- **1 tablespoon vanilla**
- **1 teaspoon nutmeg**

Cut up cushaw in large pieces and boil in salted water until tender; drain. Peel; put pieces through a ricer. Mix butter with warm cushaw. Mix eggs one at a time into cushaw. Add sugar and mix; add milk and mix. Add vanilla and nutmeg and mix. Butter two 2-quart casseroles and put in cushaw mixture. Bake at 350° for 1½ hours or until golden brown. *Most of the meat of a cushaw comes from the neck. So, it is much better to get a cushaw with a big neck.*

Serves 16-20 — Mimi Wile Hussey

Eggplant Casserole

2 eggplants, peeled, diced, soaked in salt water for 30 minutes and drained
½ cup chicken broth
2 slices whole wheat bread, processed into soft crumbs
2 eggs, beaten
½ cup grated American cheese
2 slices bacon
1 small onion, chopped
Salt, pepper and Tabasco to taste
½ cup grated Parmesan cheese

Cook soaked eggplant in salted water until tender. Drain well. Add chicken broth, bread crumbs, eggs and American cheese. Fry bacon until crisp; then crumble. Reserve drippings. Sauté onion in bacon grease. Add onion and bacon to eggplant mixture. Season to taste. Pour in a greased casserole and top with Parmesan cheese. Bake at 350° for 45 minutes. *This can be frozen.*

Serves 10

Mary Graham Pate

Fried Eggplant

1 egg beaten
1 tablespoon milk
1 cup Italian seasoned bread crumbs
Salt and pepper to taste
2 tablespoons grated Romano cheese
1 eggplant, sliced

Beat egg and milk until well blended. Mix bread crumbs, salt, pepper and cheese together. Dip eggplant into bread crumbs, into egg and milk mixture, then back into bread crumbs. Fry to a golden brown in deep hot oil. Drain on paper towel and serve hot. *Squash, cauliflower, broccoli or any vegetable may be done the same way.*

Serves 4

Isabel Wile Goldman

Frijoles

3 cups cooked and mashed pinto beans
1 clove garlic, pressed
1 onion, grated
1 teaspoon soy sauce
Pinch basil
Pinch oregano
½ cup grated Cheddar cheese

Mix all ingredients. Heat in double boiler until the cheese is melted and blended. *Serve as a vegetable or as bean dip with corn chips.*

Serves 4

Candy Carroll Bond

Mushrooms Aspen

½ medium onion, chopped
½ stick butter
1 pound fresh mushrooms, sliced
Salt and pepper to taste
1 teaspoon dill weed
1 tablespoon parsley flakes
½ cup milk
¾ cup sour milk (stir in vinegar until milk tastes sour)
1-2 tablespoons flour, if necessary
Dash dry white wine

Sauté onion until limp in butter. Add mushrooms, salt and pepper. Sauté 5 minutes. Add dill, parsley and milks. Simmer for 5 minutes. At this point, thicken with flour if necessary. (Pour a little liquid mixture in a cup, add flour, dissolve, and then add all to original mixture.) Add a dash of wine, if desired, and heat 5 minutes longer. *Serve over noodles or rice.*

Serves 4-6

Dixey Thornton Sanders

Savory Onions

4 large onions
2 tablespoons brown sugar
1 cup chili sauce
½ teaspoon prepared mustard
2 tablespoons butter, melted
Buttered bread crumbs

Cut onions in half. Cook slowly in frying pan in salted water until almost done. Be careful to keep intact. Place in baking dish, keeping cut side up, and top with mixture of sugar, chili sauce and mustard. Top with buttered crumbs. Bake at 350° until topping melts and crumbs are brown.

Serves 8 — Gladys Bozarth Lincoln

Delicious Black-Eyed Peas

1 pound dried black-eyed peas
1 tablespoon salt
1 clove garlic, cut in half
2 ham hocks
3 cloves garlic, crushed
3 medium onions, chopped
3 green peppers, chopped
2 bay leaves
2 tablespoons bacon grease
1 teaspoon salt
Black pepper to taste

Wash peas; cover with water overnight in heavy saucepan. Drain peas and cover with fresh water. Add 1 tablespoon salt, garlic halves and ham hocks. Cover and simmer 2 hours, adding water as needed. In skillet, cook crushed garlic, green pepper, onion and bay leaves in bacon grease until soft. Add to peas with 1 teaspoon salt and black pepper. Simmer 1 hour.

Serves 10 — Martha Turner Schober

Pickled Black-Eyed Peas

- 4 1-pound cans black-eyed peas, drained
- 1 cup vegetable oil
- ¼ cup vinegar
- 1 cup garlic cloves
- 1 bunch chopped green onions, using half of tops
- ¼ cup wine vinegar
- ½ teaspoon salt
- Freshly ground pepper

Put peas in collander; rinse and drain well. Mix all ingredients. Store in a covered container in refrigerator. Remove garlic after 1 day. May be kept as long as 2 weeks in refrigerator.

Serves 12-14

Lola Weir Herndon

Black-Eyed Peas and Sausage

- 1 8-ounce piece smoked bacon, cubed
- 2 cups chopped celery
- 1 green pepper, chopped
- 1 cup chopped onion
- 1 clove garlic, finely chopped
- 3 15-ounce cans black-eyed peas and liquid
- 1 can warm water
- ½ teaspoon salt
- ¼ teaspoon cayenne pepper (omit if using hot sausage)
- 1 tomato, peeled and diced
- 1 pound smoked sausage (hot or regular), thinly sliced

Fry bacon 5-7 minutes. Drain grease, leaving 2 tablespoons in pan. Add celery, green pepper, onion and garlic to bacon and drippings. Sauté until onions are clear. Transfer to Dutch oven. Add black-eyed peas, water, salt, pepper and tomato. While bringing peas to a boil, fry sausage in same skillet and drain well. Add sausage to peas and simmer 40 minutes, or longer if thicker broth is desired. *Extra cans of peas and more sausage can be added without changing the basics.*

Serves 6-8

Margaret Roberts Evans

Peas Anglaise

4 slices bacon, cut in pieces
½ large onion, chopped
1 tablespoon flour
1 cup whipping cream
1 cup canned or fresh mushrooms, cut in pieces, if large
½ teaspoon salt
½ teaspoon black pepper
1 teaspoon Worcestershire sauce
Dash Accent
¼ cup sherry
2½ cups canned tiny English peas

Sauté bacon pieces with chopped onion until brown. If fresh mushrooms are used, these may be sautéed at the same time. Add flour and cream, stirring constantly over low flame. After sauce has thickened and is smooth, add canned mushrooms, seasonings and sherry. Add peas last and fold gently into mixture.

Serves 8 — Florence Hendrick Wray

Sautéed Snow Peas and Celery

2 beef bouillon cubes
½ cup boiling water
⅓ cup thinly sliced almonds
2 tablespoons butter or margarine
1 cup celery, cut in 1″ diagonal pieces
1 6-ounce package frozen snow peas or ¼ pound fresh snow peas
1 cup fresh mushrooms, sliced

Dissolve bouillon cubes in boiling water. Set aside. Sauté almonds, slightly, in butter. Remove almonds from butter and set aside. Sauté celery and snow peas in same butter about 3 minutes. Add mushrooms and sauté 3 minutes more. Pour bouillon mixture over vegetable mixture and simmer about 4 minutes. Vegetables should be crunchy. Sprinkle almonds over vegetables just before serving. *Toast almonds at 350° for 8 minutes for a variation.*

Serves 4 — Betty Gunn Arceneaux

Potatoes Alexandre

8 large Idaho potatoes
2 tablespoons butter
1 cup sour cream
2 tablespoons chopped fresh chives or scallions
¼ teaspoon nutmeg (optional)
Salt and freshly ground pepper to taste
1 2-ounce jar caviar (optional)

Bake potatoes by favorite method. (Without foil is better for stuffing shells.) When potatoes are done and still hot, cut a slice from the top; scoop out pulp and leave shell for stuffing. Spoon pulp into saucepan. Turn off oven heat and place shells in oven to keep warm. Place saucepan over low heat and immediately add butter, sour cream, chives, nutmeg, salt and pepper. Stir rapidly. Add more butter or sour cream, if desired. Stuff shells with mixture. Can be made ahead to this point and refrigerated. When heated thoroughly and ready to serve, add a teaspoon of caviar on top. *Serve with green salad and shish kabobs.*

Serves 8

Phyllis Hinchin Selber

Scalloped Potatoes

1 cup diced onions
½ cup celery leaves
¼ cup parsley
3 tablespoons flour
3 tablespoons butter
1½ teaspoons salt
2 teaspoons pepper
1½ cups milk
4 large potatoes, peeled, boiled 30 minutes, sliced
1½ cups grated sharp Cheddar cheese

Mix first 8 ingredients in blender. (This may be done early in day and refrigerated.) Place potato slices in buttered casserole. Pour mixture over potatoes. Top with cheese. Bake at 350° for 1 hour.

Serves 8

Nancy Kate Green Hargrove

Bavarian Potato Dumplings

- 2 large potatoes, peeled and quartered
- ⅔ cup all-purpose flour
- 2 eggs, slightly beaten
- 1 teaspoon salt
- ½ teaspoon pepper
- 4 tablespoons plain croutons (24-32 count)
- 1½ cups fresh bread crumbs, (2 slices bread)
- 3 tablespoons butter, melted
- 2 tablespoons parsley

Cook potatoes in boiling salted water to cover until tender, 20-25 minutes. Drain; put potatoes through a ricer. In large mixing bowl combine potatoes, flour, slightly beaten eggs, salt and pepper; mix thoroughly. Allow to cool. Divide potato mixture into eighths; flatten each portion. Place 3 or 4 plain croutons in center of each flattened cake; shape potato dough around croutons to make a ball. Drop balls into boiling salted water to cover. Simmer for 8-10 minutes; remove with slotted spoon. Combine fresh bread crumbs with parsley and melted butter. Roll dumplings in crumb mixture. Serve hot.

Serves 8 — Carolyn Clay Flournoy

Sweet Potato Soufflé

- 3 cups mashed sweet potatoes (about 4 medium potatoes)
- 3 eggs
- ¼ cup milk
- 1 stick butter
- ½ teaspoon vanilla

Mix all of the above ingredients and place in a 2-quart baking dish.

Continued...

Topping

1 cup brown sugar
½ cup flour
½ stick butter
1 cup chopped pecans

Mix well and place on top of potato mixture. Bake at 350° for approximately 40 minutes (or until light, fluffy and brown.) *This recipe may also be cooked over a gas grill. Bake indirectly on a medium flame setting approximately 30 minutes.*

Serves 6

Betsy Harwood Willard
Baton Rouge, Louisiana

Broccoli and Rice Supreme

½ cup margarine
2 ribs celery, chopped
½ cup chopped onion
2 10-ounce packages frozen chopped broccoli
1 4-ounce can mushrooms, sliced
1 10¾-ounce can cream of mushroom soup
1 6-ounce roll garlic cheese or 1 8-ounce jar Cheese Whiz
2 cups cooked rice
½ cup bread crumbs

Melt margarine in skillet. Sauté celery, onion, frozen broccoli and mushrooms. Add soup, cheese and rice. Remove from heat and place in casserole. Top with bread crumbs. Bake at 350° for 30 minutes or until bubbly.

Serves 6-8

LuAnn Alford Browder

Mix leftover sugar-free cereals in blender or food processor. Sprinkle crumbs on casseroles, or use in breading chicken and chops. Adds flavor and crunch.

Spanakopita
(Spinach-Feta Cheese Pie)

2 10-ounce packages frozen chopped spinach or 2 10-ounce packages fresh spinach, chopped
1 medium onion
¼ cup olive oil
½ teaspoon ground nutmeg
½ pound Feta cheese, rinsed and drained
1 8-ounce package cream cheese
3 eggs, beaten
½ cup pine nuts, chopped
¼ cup parsley, chopped
Salt and pepper
2 sticks butter, melted
½-¾ pound Filo pastry*

Thaw frozen spinach and squeeze out as much moisture as possible. Sauté onion in oil until golden. Add spinach and nutmeg and cook for several minutes. In a mixing bowl, beat cream cheese until smooth. Add beaten eggs, crumbled Feta cheese, the spinach mixture, pine nuts, parsley, salt and pepper. Brush a 10" pie pan with melted butter and line with 5 sheets of Filo, brushing each with butter and letting the ends fall over the sides of the pan. Add filling and place 3 more sheets of buttered pastry on top. Fold overhanging edges toward the middle. Brush with butter and bake at 350° for 45 minutes or until golden brown.

**To thaw frozen Filo, wrap in a moistened tea towel and refrigerate for at least 8 hours. Sheets tend to stick together if refrozen.*

Serves 10-12

Carolyn Clay Flournoy

Spinach-Artichoke Casserole

- 2 4-ounce cans sliced mushrooms
- 6 tablespoons butter
- 1 tablespoon flour
- ½ cup milk
- 2 10-ounce packages frozen chopped spinach, cooked and drained well
- 1 8½-ounce can artichoke hearts, halved
- ½ cup mayonnaise
- 2 tablespoons lemon juice

Sauté mushrooms in butter and set aside. Add flour to butter and stir until bubbly. Add milk slowly and stir until smooth and thick. Add spinach that has been mixed with mushrooms. Place artichoke hearts around bottom of casserole. Pour in spinach mixture. Combine mayonnaise and lemon juice. Spread on top of casserole. Bake at 350° for 30 minutes. *This doubles easily.*

Serves 4-6

Mary Louise Block Levy

Italian Spinach Pie

- 1 unbaked pie shell
- 2 10-ounce packages frozen spinach, cooked and drained
- ½ stick margarine
- 1 egg, beaten
- 1 cup grated Parmesan cheese
- 1 cup Hidden Valley Creamy Italian Salad Dressing prepared according package directions
- 1 clove garlic, minced or ⅛ teaspoon garlic powder

Sprinkle pie shell with a little extra Parmesan cheese. Mix remaining ingredients, and pour into pie shell. Bake at 350° for 30 minutes. *This can be prepared without pie shell for those counting calories.*

Serves 6

Glenda Futch Farmer
Memphis, Tennessee

Spinach Priscilla

3 tablespoons flour
½ stick butter, melted
1 10-ounce package frozen chopped spinach, thawed
3 eggs, slightly beaten
½ pint cottage cheese
¼ cup grated sharp cheese

Mix flour and butter and add all ingredients except the sharp cheese. Sprinkle with cheese and bake at 350° for 45 minutes. *Doubles well.*

Serves 6

Mary Graham Pate

Best Squash Casserole

1½-2 pounds yellow or white squash
1 carrot, grated
1 large onion, finely chopped
3 tablespoons chopped green pepper
1 10¾-ounce can cream of chicken soup
½ pint sour cream
1 4-ounce jar pimientos, drained and sliced
1 8½-ounce can water chestnuts, thinly sliced
1½ cups Pepperidge Farm Herb Stuffing Mix
¾ stick butter
8 ounces grated Cheddar cheese
Seasoned pepper
Worcestershire sauce
Cayenne pepper
Salt
Parsley

Cook squash until tender, about 12 minutes, in salted water. Drain well and mash with spoon. In large bowl mix squash, carrot, onion, green pepper, soup, sour cream, pimientos and water chestnuts. Add 1 cup of buttered dressing mix. (Melt butter and mix well with all of stuffing mix.) Add half of grated cheese. Add seasoned pepper, Worcestershire sauce, cayenne pepper, salt and parsley to taste. Pour into a 2-quart greased baking dish and cover with remaining cheese and stuffing mixture. Bake at 350° for 30 minutes. *Freezes well before or after baking. This is delicious with brisket, broiled chicken or fish.*

Serves 8

Gwen Buhler Talbot

Squash Sauté

12 medium tender yellow squash
1 medium onion
1 stick butter
1-1½ teaspoons salt
1 teaspoon oregano
Pepper to taste
Juice ½ lemon
½ cup seasoned bread crumbs

Slice squash and onion fairly thin. Melt butter in skillet and sauté vegetables over medium-low heat, stirring until cooked but still crisp. Add salt, oregano, pepper and lemon juice and cook 10 minutes for flavors to blend. Add just enough bread crumbs to absorb the juice. Keep warm on the stove or heat in 350° oven for 20 minutes. *For diet, omit bread crumbs and use a diet margarine.*

Serves 6-8

Susan Stewart Hall

Scalloped Tomatoes

½ stick butter
1 small onion, chopped
2 cups fresh bread crumbs
1 teaspoon salt
½ teaspoon basil
¼ teaspoon black pepper
2 14½-ounce cans sliced baby tomatoes
4 teaspoons sugar

About 40 minutes before serving melt butter in a medium saucepan over medium heat. Cook onion in butter until tender, about 5 minutes. Stir in bread crumbs, salt, basil and pepper. In a 1½-quart casserole, place one-fourth of the tomato slices and their liquid. Sprinkle with 1 teaspoon of the sugar and one-fourth of the onion mixture. Repeat, layering 3 more times, ending with onion mixture. Bake at 375° for 30 minutes.

Serves 4-6

Anne Krison Mitchell

Broiled Tomato Topping

½ cup sour cream
½ cup mayonnaise
2 tablespoons grated onion
1 heaping teaspoon fresh dill weed, chopped, or ½ teaspoon dried dill
¼ teaspoon salt
2 dashes white pepper
Paprika
4-6 tomatoes, halved

Thoroughly mix all ingredients except paprika. May be kept in refrigerator until needed. Broil tomatoes. Just before done, put a big dollop of sauce on top and sprinkle with paprika. Place under broiler until sauce is lightly browned. If too much topping is used it will run over.

Serves 8-12

Francais Glassell Lambert

Green Tomato Pie

1 9″ pie shell, baked at 450° for 8 minutes
2 large green tomatoes
¼ cup flour
½ teaspoon salt
⅛ teaspoon pepper
2 tablespoons salad oil
½ cup sliced ripe olives
1 cup minced scallions
2 eggs, slightly beaten
1 cup grated Cheddar cheese
1 cup half and half

Cut tomatoes into 6 slices. Salt and pepper lightly. Dip each slice in a mixture of the flour, salt and pepper. Sauté quickly in oil until brown. In bottom of cooked pie shell, arrange olives and scallions. Add tomatoes. Stir together slightly beaten eggs, cheese and cream. Pour over pie. Bake at 375° for 40-45 minutes.

Serves 6

Corinne Kelly Calder
Dallas, Texas

Fresh Turnip and Mustard Greens

¼ pound dry salt meat, wash and cut several slits in rind
1 quart cold water
1 tablespoon bacon grease
2 bunches turnip greens with small turnips
1 bunch mustard greens
½ teaspoon sugar
2 turnips, washed, peeled and coarsely chopped

In large heavy pot, cover salt meat with the quart of water. Boil slowly, covered, until water is reduced by half and meat is tender (about 45 minutes-1 hour). Wash greens very well. Pick out stems. Reserve turnips from turnip greens. When salt meat has cooked sufficiently, add bacon grease, sugar and greens to seasoned water, leaving in the meat. Do not stir. Cover again and boil gently for about 30 minutes, stirring occasionally. Greens should be tender at this point. Add the reserved turnips and the 2 extra turnips. Cover; lower heat and cook for about 30 minutes, until turnips are tender, but not mushy. *Serve with hot pepper vinegar.*

Serves 8 — Alice Collins

One tablespoon of vinegar with 1 quart of water when washing green or any leafy vegetable will guarantee clean vegetables in half the washing time.

Cooking in a covered casserole: because the lid of a covered casserole dish gets as hot as the sides of the dish, steam rising from the cooking surface escapes rather than condensing. The escaping steam can change the consistency of a sauce or cooking liquid, often undesirably. To maintain the consistency, cover the casserole with buttered foil before putting the lid on. The dead air space between the foil and the lid will then insulate the lid, making it cool enough to condense the steam.

Emmie Lou's Creamed Turnips

- 3 pounds fresh turnips
- Salt and pepper to taste
- 1 stick butter
- 1 4-ounce package slivered almonds

Peel, slice and boil turnips until tender. Drain. Cream immediately with hand mixer. Add salt, pepper and butter. You can leave this in the pot on the stove to be reheated very slowly. Toast slivered almonds in small amount of butter. When ready to serve, put in dish and sprinkle top with almonds. *Delicious with game, beef or lamb.*

Serves 6-8

Pauline Huddleston Ilgenfritz

Green Vegetable Casserole

- 2 14½-ounce cans green asparagus
- 2 14½-ounce cans LeSueur peas
- 1 14½-ounce can French style green beans
- 1 10-ounce can button mushrooms
- 1 8-ounce can water chestnuts, sliced
- 1 10-ounce bag frozen English peas, or 1 17-ounce can English peas
- Buttered bread crumbs

Drain canned vegetables, reserving liquid. Do not cook frozen vegetables; just thaw before adding. Layer each vegetable in casserole and pour a small amount of cream sauce between the layers. Top with bread crumbs or more Swiss cheese. Cook until bubbly at 350°-375° for 40 minutes. *Brussel sprouts and frozen broccoli may be added.*

Continued...

Cream Sauce

1 stick butter
¾ cup sifted flour
1 teaspoon Worcestershire sauce
½ teaspoon seasoned salt
¼ teaspoon Accent
½ teaspoon white pepper
1 cup liquid from vegetables
¼ cup milk
6 ounces Swiss cheese, grated

Melt butter; add flour and seasonings. Cook over low heat, stirring until mixture is smooth and bubbly. Remove from heat. Stir in vegetable liquid and milk. Bring to boil, stirring constantly. Boil 1 minute. Add cheese and stir until melted.

Serves 10-12

Knox McGuffin Goodman

Baked Zucchini

8-10 medium zucchini
1 stick butter
1 cup Cheddar cheese, grated
1 cup sour cream
½ teaspoon salt
Paprika
¼ cup fresh chopped chives
1 cup bread crumbs
Grated Parmesan cheese

Wash zucchini and boil whole for about 10 minutes. Cut ends off and cut in half lengthwise. Arrange in buttered casserole. Melt butter and mix in cheese and sour cream, salt, paprika and chives. Pour mixture over zucchini and sprinkle crumbs on top. Dot with butter and sprinkle with Parmesan cheese. Bake at 350° for 45 minutes.

Serves 8

Susan Sigler Updegraff

Zucchini-Corn Casserole

- 1½ pounds zucchini or yellow crookneck squash
- 1 medium onion, finely chopped
- ½ green pepper, finely chopped
- 2 tablespoons vegetable oil
- 2 eggs, beaten
- ½ cup grated Cheddar cheese
- 1 16-ounce can cream style white shoe peg corn
- ½ teaspoon salt
- ½ teaspoon garlic salt
- ¼ teaspoon pepper
- ¼ teaspoon dried rosemary

Slice zucchini and steam until just tender. Let cool. Sauté onion and pepper in oil until limp. Add eggs, cheese and seasonings to corn. Fold into zucchini along with sautéed onion and pepper. Pour into buttered casserole and place in pan of hot water. Bake at 350° for 45 minutes or until firm. *Crumbled bacon or cubed ham makes a nice addition.*

Serves 6-8

Margaret Hunkin Crow

Zucchini Frittata

- 1 stick butter
- 2 medium yellow onions, diced
- 3 bunches green onions, sliced with tops
- 5 small zucchini, cut in bite-size pieces
- 5 eggs, beaten
- 3 ounces Parmesan cheese, grated
- 10 ounces Monterey Jack cheese, grated
- Salt and pepper to taste

Sauté onions in butter until limp in a large skillet or soup pan. Add cut up zucchini. Cook until softens (5-10 minutes). Add grated cheeses, beaten eggs, salt and pepper to taste. Pour in buttered 9″ × 13″ Pyrex dish. Bake at 325° for 1 hour.

Serves 10-12

Lecie Roos Resnick

Cranberry Apples

1 cup cranberry juice cocktail
¾ cup port wine
1½ cups sugar
1 tablespoon lemon juice
1 cinnamon stick
½ teaspoon red food coloring
8 small whole apples, pared and cored

Combine first 6 ingredients in saucepan; cover and simmer for 5 minutes. Add apples to boiling syrup; cover and cook over very low heat for 10 minutes. Turn apples often and baste regularly. Uncover and cook 5-10 minutes longer, until apples are tender. Cool in syrup.

Serves 8 — Sara Scott Hargrove

Baked Apricots

2 1-pound 13-ounce cans apricot halves, drained
1 16-ounce box light brown sugar
1 12-ounce box Ritz crackers, crumbled
1-2 sticks butter

In a greased 9″×13″ baking dish layer apricot halves, brown sugar, crumbled crackers and pats of butter. Bake at 300° for 1½ hours. Recipe may be halved in small square pan. *This may be served as an accompaniment to the main course or with whipped cream on top for dessert.*

Serves 10-12 — Susan Metcalf James

Black Forest Cake

Meringue Discs

1 cup egg whites
1 small pinch cream of tartar
2 cups sugar + 2 tablespoons
1 teaspoon vanilla
4½ ounces slivered almonds, finely chopped

Cut four 9″ parchment paper discs. Place on cookie sheets and grease discs. (The same paper discs may be used many times; just be sure to grease them each time.) Whip egg whites until foamy and add cream of tartar. Continue whipping egg whites until stiff enough to follow the beater around. With mixer on low speed, blend sugar and vanilla in whites. Add sugar about ⅓ cup at a time. If you stir it too much, the sugar will melt the whites. Fold in almonds with a wooden spoon. Use rubber spatula and gently spread meringue on discs. Be sure the meringue is not higher in the center. Cook for 2½ hours at 225°; then turn off the ovens and leave inside at least 6 hours with the doors closed so that the discs can dry thoroughly.

Chocolate Filling

3 egg whites
¾ cup sugar
3 tablespoons cocoa
3 ounces German sweet chocolate, melted
3 sticks butter, very soft

Whip egg whites over hot, but not boiling water. Add sugar and whip until stiff. Add cocoa. Take off fire. Add German chocolate; then fold in butter. Let chocolate mixture get cold enough to spread. Then use a rubber spatula and smooth it right on top of each disc and set in the refrigerator to chill.

Continued...

Whipped Cream Icing

3 cups whipping cream
1/3 cup sugar
2 tablespoons vanilla
3 ounces German sweet chocolate, grated

Whip cream very stiff. Add sugar and vanilla. Remove meringue and chocolate discs from refrigerator. To build the cake, simply ice the first disc with whipped cream, place the second on top of this and ice it, and so on until all 4 layers are arranged. Then ice the sides and top with remainder of whipped cream and sprinkle grated German chocolate on top. Store in refrigerator or freezer.

Suggestions: start the cake in the early evening. First, break off six 1″ squares from a 4-ounce package of the chocolate to grate later for top of cake. Rewrap the rest and save to melt in top of double boiler when making chocolate filling later. Remove butter from refrigerator so it will soften. Preheat ovens. Make meringue; put each one on a cookie sheet and bake one above the other in double ovens. If you have only 1 oven, it might be necessary to mix and bake just 2 at a time. (There *must* be room for the heat to circulate, or the meringues will melt.) After they are baked, turn off the ovens and leave them in there overnight. After putting the meringues in the ovens, mix the chocolate filling and leave it at room temperature. It will be the right consistency to spread the next morning.

Lynne Crutcher Gill

Confectioners' sugar blends with whipping cream better than granulated sugar.

When you run out of confectioners' sugar, blend 1 cup granulated sugar and 1 tablespoon cornstarch in blender on medium-high or in food processor for 2 minutes.

Carrot Cake in Muffin Tins

2 cups sugar
2 cups flour
1 teaspoon salt
2 teaspoons soda
3 teaspoons cinnamon
1½ cups oil
4 eggs, slightly beaten
3 cups shredded carrots

Blend first 5 ingredients. Add oil, eggs and carrots, mixing well after adding each ingredient. Pour into ungreased 9″×13″×2″ pan or divide evenly into three 9″ cake pans, or muffin tins for individual cakes. Bake at 350° for 35 minutes for cake or 25 minutes for muffins. Cool before frosting.

Frosting

1 8-ounce package cream cheese
1 stick margarine
1 1-pound box confectioners' sugar
2 teaspoons vanilla

Cream margarine and cream cheese together. Add sugar; beat until smooth. Add vanilla. Spread on cooled cake.

Serves 10-12 — Nancy Brock Johnston

When preparing cupcakes for a picnic basket or lunch boxes, split them in half and spread the icing inside.

Chocolate Cheesecake

Crust

1½ cups finely crushed chocolate wafers
⅓ cup margarine, melted

Combine crumbs and margarine. Press onto bottom of 10″ spring form pan. Bake at 325° for 10 minutes.

Continued...

Filling

- **2 8-ounce packages cream cheese**
- **1 cup sugar, divided**
- **2 teaspoons vanilla**
- **4 eggs, separated**
- **2 6-ounce packages semi-sweet chocolate morsels, melted**
- **3 cups whipping cream, whipped, divided**
- **1½ cups chopped pecans**

Combine softened cream cheese, ½ cup sugar and vanilla. Mix until well blended. Stir in beaten egg yolks and melted chocolate. Beat egg whites until soft peaks form. Gradually beat in remaining ½ cup sugar. Fold into chocolate mixture. Fold in whipped cream and nuts. Pour over crumb crust and freeze. Before serving, garnish with whipped cream and grated chocolate. Place in refrigerator, not freezer, for 1 hour before serving.

Corinne Lengsfield Roos

Sprinkle cake plate with granulated sugar to prevent cake from sticking when serving.

Boo's Chocolate Icebox Cake

- **1 6-ounce package semi-sweet chocolate morsels**
- **4 tablespoons sugar**
- **4 eggs, separated**
- **½ cup hot water**
- **1 teaspoon vanilla**
- **2 3-ounce packages ladyfingers or sponge cake cut in strips**

Melt chocolate morsels in top of double boiler and add sugar. Beat egg yolks; stir hot water into yolks and add to chocolate. Cook mixture slowly in top of double boiler until thickened and smooth, stirring constantly. Cool to lukewarm. Beat egg whites until stiff but not dry. Add vanilla. Fold gently into chocolate mixture. Put layer of ladyfingers in bottom and side of a serving bowl. Pour ⅓ of chocolate sauce over this. Repeat layers twice, ending with chocolate. Refrigerate overnight.

Serves 4

Louise Jackson

Black-Bottom Cupcakes

- 1 8-ounce package cream cheese, softened
- 1 egg, beaten
- ⅓ cup sugar
- ⅛ teaspoon salt
- 1 6-ounce package semi-sweet chocolate morsels

Combine cream cheese, egg, sugar and salt. Beat until blended. Add chocolate morsels and set aside.

Cupcake Batter

- 3 cups flour
- ½ cup cocoa
- 2 cups sugar
- 2 teaspoons soda
- 1 teaspoon salt
- 2 cups water
- ⅔ cup oil
- 1 tablespoon vinegar
- 2 teaspoons vanilla

Combine first 5 ingredients. Slowly add water, oil, vinegar and vanilla. Mix well. Fill cupcake liners ⅔ full of batter; then drop a heaping teaspoonful of cream cheese mixture on top. Bake at 350° for 30-35 minutes.

Yields 2 dozen

Nancy Hudson Ketner

Dust pans for chocolate cake with cocoa instead of flour to keep the outside of the cake from being white when it is removed from the pan.

Chocolate Ice Cream Meringue Cake

6 egg whites
1½ cups sugar
1½ cups graham cracker crumbs
1 cup lightly toasted pecans, chopped

Beat egg whites until stiff; add sugar ½ cup at a time. Fold in crumbs and pecans. Grease bottoms of three 9″ cake pans. Divide meringue evenly into pans. Spread well to the sides. Bake at 350° for 30 minutes. Cool slightly. Lift from pans onto foil and freeze.

Filling

1½ cups semi-sweet chocolate morsels
1½ cups evaporated milk
1½ cups miniature marshmallows
½ gallon chocolate chip ice cream, softened

Combine first 3 ingredients and cook over low heat until marshmallows are melted and sauce is smooth, stirring frequently. Cool. Spread on top of meringue layers. Return layers to freezer to chill. Divide ice cream into thirds and spoon onto layers. Stack layers.

Frosting

½ pint whipping cream, whipped
1 9-ounce carton non-dairy whipped topping
Grated chocolate

Fold cream into non-dairy whipped topping and frost top and sides well. Decorate top with grated chocolate.

Doris Pratt Box

Put a vanilla bean in sugar to give it a heavenly taste.

Chocolate Torta

2 eggs
2 cups buttermilk
2 teaspoons vanilla
2½ cups flour
½ teaspoon salt
2 cups sugar
2 teaspoons soda
4 squares unsweetened chocolate
1 stick butter

Beat eggs with buttermilk and add vanilla. Sift the dry ingredients and add to the egg mixture. Melt chocolate and butter in double boiler and add to egg mixture. Beat thoroughly. Pour into 3 greased 8″ cake pans. Bake at 350° for 30 minutes. Cool completely before icing.

Icing

4 squares unsweetened chocolate
1 stick butter
1 pound confectioners' sugar
2 teaspoons vanilla
Milk

Melt chocolate and butter. Add sugar and vanilla. Add enough milk for good spreading consistency.

Marie Rountree Rosenfield

Cream Cheese Pound Cake

3 sticks butter
8 ounces cream cheese
3 cups sugar
3 cups cake flour, sifted
6 eggs
2 teaspoons vanilla

Cream butter and cream cheese. Add sugar. Sift cake flour 3 times. Alternate adding eggs and flour to butter mixture. *Beat well* after adding each. Add vanilla. Cook in well greased and floured tube pan. Cook at 325° for 1 hour and 45 minutes. *Can be made easily in processor.*

Becca Fraser Drummond

Sour Cream Chocolate Pound Cake

3 cups sugar, divided
2 sticks butter
6 eggs, separated
⅔ teaspoon almond or vanilla extract
¼ teaspoon soda
1 cup sour cream
3 cups cake flour
4 tablespoons cocoa

Cream 2 cups of sugar with butter. Add beaten egg yolks. Mix extract and soda with sour cream and add alternately with dry ingredients to creamed mixture.

Beat egg whites with remaining cup of sugar and fold into batter. Grease and flour bundt pan and pour in batter. Bake at 300° for 1¼-1½ hours.

Icing

1 stick butter
2 squares unsweetened chocolate
1 1-pound box confectioners' sugar
1 teaspoon vanilla
Half and half

Melt butter and chocolate. Add sugar, vanilla and half and half for desired consistency.

Rosemary Cherry Futch

Use large eggs in recipes to assure accuracy and extra-large for frying and hard boiling.

For a delicous, low-calorie whipped-topping substitute, beat a sliced, very ripe banana and an egg white with egg beater until stiff and banana completely dissolves, about 4 minutes.

Holiday Cake

1 cup sugar
2 sticks butter
2 eggs, added separately
1 cup buttermilk
1 teaspoon soda (dissolved in buttermilk)
1 8-ounce package dates, finely chopped
4 ounces walnuts, finely chopped
Grated rind 2 oranges
2½ cups cake flour
1 teaspoon baking powder
1½ teaspoons vanilla

Cream butter and sugar. Add remaining ingredients and blend. Bake in greased and floured bundt or tube pan at 300° for 1 hour. When done, leave in pan until cool.

Icing

Juice 2 oranges
1 cup sugar

Make icing from the juice of 2 oranges and sugar. Boil 3 minutes. Pour over cake. Do not cut until completely cold.

Bettie Wilson Hastings

Spray knife with nonstick vegetable spray for sticky cutting jobs.

Oatmeal Cake

1¼ cups boiling water
1 cup quick oats
1 stick butter
1 cup sugar
2 eggs
1⅓ cups flour
1 cup brown sugar
1 teaspoon soda
½ teaspoon cinnamon

In a large mixing bowl combine the boiling water, oats and butter. Let sit 20 minutes. Add the remaining ingredients and stir until smooth. Pour into a greased 9″×12″ pan. Bake at 350° for 35 minutes.

Continued...

Topping

1 stick butter
¼ cup evaporated milk
½ cup sugar
1 teaspoon vanilla
1 cup coconut
1 cup chopped pecans

Combine all the above and spoon over cake while still warm. Put under broiler for 2 minutes.

Yields 24 squares

Michele Armstrong Qvistgaard-Petersen

Fresh Apple Cake with Cream Cheese Icing

2 eggs
2 cups sugar
½ cup vegetable oil
1 teaspoon vanilla
2 cups flour
½ teaspoon salt
1 teaspoon soda
2 teaspoons cinnamon
¼ teaspoon nutmeg
4 cups peeled, diced apples
1 cup chopped pecans

Grease a 9″ × 13″ pan or bundt pan. Beat eggs until light and fluffy. Gradually add sugar, oil and vanilla. Sift next 5 ingredients and add to first mixture. Stir in apples and pecans. Batter will be very stiff. Bake at 350° for 45 minutes for 9″ × 13″ pan or 60-65 minutes for bundt pan. Let cool in pan 10-15 minutes on a rack; then spread with cream cheese icing in the pan. If using bundt pan, remove from pan and ice.

Cream Cheese Icing

1 3-ounce package cream cheese at room temperature
3 tablespoons margarine or butter, softened
Pinch salt
½ teaspoon vanilla
1½ cups confectioners' sugar

Mix all ingredients together until smooth.

Susie Tucker Overdyke

Super Cream Cheesecake

Graham Cracker Crust

2 cups coarse graham cracker crumbs
¼ cup sugar
1 stick butter or margarine, melted
Dash cinnamon

Combine graham crumbs, sugar and butter. Mix well. Press firmly into greased 10″ pie plate. Save a few crumbs to toast and sprinkle on top of cream, just before serving. Bake crust at 375° for 8-10 minutes.

Filling

4 3-ounce packages cream cheese
1 cup sugar
2 eggs, separated
1 teaspoon vanilla
Juice 1 lemon

Blend cream cheese and add sugar slowly. Add 2 egg yolks, vanilla and lemon juice. Beat 2 egg whites until stiff and fold into batter. Pour into pie shell and bake at 300° for 45 minutes. Cool.

Topping

½ pint whipping cream
½ pint sour cream
¼ cup sugar
2 teaspoons vanilla

Beat whipping cream. Add sour cream, sugar and vanilla. Blend well.

After cheesecake has cooled, add topping and toasted graham cracker crumbs. Refrigerate. Good several days if refrigerated.

Serves 10-12

Shirley Parker Wilhite

Pumpkin Cake

4 eggs
2 cups sugar
1 cup oil
2 cups flour
2 teaspoons soda
2 teaspoons cinnamon
2 teaspoons salt
2 cups canned pumpkin

Beat eggs with sugar until light and well blended. Add oil and continue to beat. Sift dry ingredients together and beat into egg mixture. Add pumpkin and mix well. Pour into greased and floured 9″ tube pan or two loaf pans. Bake at 350° for 55 minutes. Cool in pan 10 minutes before removing.

Icing

1 3-ounce package cream cheese, softened
1 stick butter, softened
1 1-pound box confectioners' sugar
1 teaspoon vanilla
1 cup chopped pecans

Combine cream cheese and butter. Add sugar and vanilla and beat until smooth. Stir in pecans and spread on the cake when cool.

Martha Harris Mellett

Blueberry Cake

1 box Duncan Hines Butter Cake Mix
1 8-ounce package cream cheese, softened
⅓ cup oil
1 cup fresh or frozen blueberries

Prepare cake mix as directed, but do not add the water. Add cream cheese and mix well. Add oil and blueberries. Bake in greased 9″ × 13″ pan at 350° for 25-30 minutes. Cake should be very moist.

Serves 10-12

Sissy Masters Harper

Thirty-Dollar Cake

2½ cups sugar
2 sticks butter
5 egg yolks
1 cup buttermilk
3 cups cake flour
1 teaspoon soda
1 teaspoon cocoa
5 teaspoons liquid coffee
1 teaspoon lemon extract
1 teaspoon vanilla
5 egg whites, beaten

Cream sugar and butter. Add 5 egg yolks; beat. Add other ingredients alternately with buttermilk. Beat well. Fold in beaten egg whites. Bake in 3 well greased and floured cake pans at 350° for 30 minutes.

Icing

1 stick butter
2 teaspoons cocoa
1 1- pound box confectioners' sugar
3 teaspoons liquid coffee
1 teaspoon vanilla
2-4 teaspoons sour cream
1 egg yolk

Mix all ingredients in mixer until creamy. If too thick, add more sour cream. Ice cake. *This makes a large cake, but it is very light.*

Gail Kelley Shell

Rum Cake

1 box Duncan Hines Butter Yellow Cake Mix
1 3-ounce package vanilla pudding (non-instant)
4 eggs, added 1 at a time
⅓ cup rum
½ cup vegetable oil
½ cup water

Blend all ingredients and pour into greased and floured tube pan. Bake at 325° for 1 hour.

Continued...

Glaze

1 stick butter
1 cup confectioners' sugar
¼ cup rum
½ cup water
½ cup chopped pecans

Mix all ingredients except pecans and boil 2 - 3 minutes. Reserve approximately ⅓ cup glaze, and pour remainder over cake while in pan. Let soak up glaze. Add pecans to reserved glaze; invert cake and pour remaining glaze on top.

Georgia Harmon Chandler

Coconut Sour Cream Cake

1 box white cake mix
¼ cup oil
3 eggs
1 8-ounce carton sour cream
1 8½-ounce can Coco Lopez (cream of coconut)

Mix cake mix with eggs and oil. Add sour cream and Coco Lopez. Bake in greased and floured 9″×12″ pan at 350° for 30 minutes.

Frosting

1 8-ounce package cream cheese
1 1-pound box confectioners' sugar
2 tablespoons milk
1 teaspoon vanilla
1 3½-ounce can Angel Flake Coconut

Soften cream cheese. Add sugar and beat until well mixed. Add milk and vanilla. Frost cake; then sprinkle with coconut.

Elizabeth Posey Siskron

Mandarin Orange Cake

1 box Duncan Hines Yellow Butter Cake Mix
½ cup oil
4 eggs
1 11-ounce can mandarin oranges

Mix cake mix, oil and eggs. Add can of oranges, including juice. Divide batter into three 8″ greased and floured pans. Bake at 350° for 18-20 minutes.

Filling

1 3-ounce box instant vanilla pudding
1 20-ounce can crushed pineapple
1 9-ounce carton non-dairy whipped topping

Mix vanilla pudding and pineapple (including juice) in mixer. Add non-dairy whipped topping and mix well. Ice layers and cake after they have cooled. Chill in refrigerator before serving. *This is a very light dessert and will keep for a week in the refrigerator.*

Mamie Lee Beltz

Lemon Filling

4 egg yolks
½ cup sugar
Juice and grated rind 1 lemon
2-3 tablespoons butter

Beat egg yolks well. Add sugar, lemon juice and rind. Cook over low heat, stirring frequently until thickened. Add butter and spread on cooled cake layers.

Yields filling for 2 round layers

Bertha Harrison Campbell

To grate orange rind or lemon rind, add a little sugar to food processor and grind with steel blade.

Pineapple Icing

1 8-ounce can crushed pineapple
¾ cup sugar
¼ cup flour
⅓ stick margarine

Combine all ingredients in saucepan and cook until thickened. Pour over 9″×13″ cake.

Martha Nunn Hitchcock

Fill a ziplock plastic bag with icing, meringue or whipped cream; then seal the bag and clip off 1 bottom corner to the right size for cake and cookie decorating. When pastry decorating is finished, just toss out the bag—no messy cleanup.

Best-Ever Chocolate Fudge Icing

2 squares unsweetened chocolate
2 cups sugar
⅔ cup milk
1 stick butter
1 heaping tablespoon light corn syrup
2 teaspoons vanilla

Mix first 5 ingredients. Put in heavy pot and bring to a rolling boil; boil 3 minutes, stirring constantly. Add vanilla. Cool and beat until it reaches spreading consistency.

Yields icing for a 2-layer cake or a bundt cake

Lynda Bethea Borden

Freeze small mounds of whipped cream on a cookie sheet and store in freezer bag for quick toppings.

Food-for-the-Gods Pie

Crust

1½ cups sifted flour
2 teaspoons cocoa
½ teaspoon salt
½ cup shortening, minus 1 tablespoon
3 scant tablespoons boiling water
1 teaspoon milk
4 tablespoons thinly sliced almonds, chopped

Sift flour, cocoa and salt in mixing bowl. Add shortening, water and milk. Mix well. Roll out between wax paper. Place in 10″ pie pan. Sprinkle chopped almonds over dough in bottom of pan and press nuts into dough. Bake at 400° for 15 minutes. Cool.

Filling

1 cup milk
3 egg yolks
¾ cup sugar
1 envelope unflavored gelatin
¼ cup cold water
½ teaspoon salt
1 teaspoon vanilla
½ teaspoon almond extract
3 egg whites, beaten
1¾ cups whipping cream, whipped and divided
⅔ cup grated semi-sweet chocolate
1 teaspoon vanilla
Sugar
Whole toasted almonds
Shaved chocolate

Combine and cook milk, egg yolks and sugar in double boiler to make custard. Remove from heat. Add gelatin which has been dissolved in cold water. Add salt, vanilla and almond extract. When cool, fold in egg whites. Place in refrigerator. When mixture begins to thicken, fold in ¾ cup of whipped cream and chocolate. Refrigerate until mixture holds shape when dropped from spoon. Pour into pie shell and return to refrigerator until firm. Top with 1 cup whipped cream which has been flavored with vanilla and a little sugar. Sprinkle with almonds and shaved chocolate.

Serves 8

Brandon Taylor Stephens

Chocolate Pie

1 baked 9″ pie crust
3 egg yolks
3 cups milk, divided
1½ cups sugar
½ cup cocoa
½ cup cornstarch
Pinch salt
3 tablespoons butter
1 teaspoon vanilla

In a double boiler over low heat, beat egg yolks with about ¼ cup of milk. Add rest of milk. Mix dry ingredients separately; add to milk and eggs in boiler. Stir constantly until thick. Add butter and vanilla when finished cooking. Pour into pie shell and top with meringue below.

Meringue

3 egg whites
¼ teaspoon cream of tartar
6 tablespoons sugar

Beat egg whites after adding cream of tartar. Gradually add sugar. Spread on top of pie. Bake at 350° for 10 minutes.

Serves 6

Carolyn Vaughn Hamilton

Chocolate Pecan Pie

2 squares unsweetened chocolate
3 tablespoons butter
1 cup light corn syrup
¾ cup sugar
½ teaspoon salt
3 eggs, slightly beaten
1 teaspoon vanilla
1 cup chopped pecans
Whipped cream
1 unbaked 9″ pie shell

In double boiler, melt chocolate and butter together. In separate pan combine corn syrup and sugar and simmer 2 minutes. Add chocolate mixture and cool. Add salt to eggs. Slowly dribble syrup mixture into eggs, stirring constantly. Blend in vanilla and nuts. Pour into shell. Bake at 375° for 35 minutes. Serve with whipped cream.

Serves 8

Regina Levinson Wren

Chocolate Chess Pie

1½ cups sugar
3 tablespoons cocoa
3 eggs, well beaten
1 tablespoon white vinegar
1 tablespoon vanilla
½ stick butter, melted
5 tablespoons evaporated milk
1 unbaked 9″ pie shell

Mix sugar and cocoa and set aside. Beat eggs and add vinegar, vanilla, butter and milk. Mix well. Add egg mixture to sugar and cocoa mixture and mix well. Pour into crust and bake at 325° for 35-40 minutes. Do not overbake.

Whipped Topping

1 cup whipping cream
¼ cup sugar
1 teaspoon vanilla

Whip cream and add sugar and vanilla while beating. Put dollop of topping on each slice of pie.

Serves 6-8

Laura Stevens Boyd

Forty-Karat Gold Brick Pie

2½ sticks margarine or butter
1⅓ cups sugar
4 1-ounce squares unsweetened chocolate, melted
6 large eggs
1 tablespoon vanilla
2 cups chopped pecans
2 8″ graham cracker crumb pie crusts
Whipping cream
Semi-sweet chocolate shavings

Cream margarine and sugar. Add chocolate and mix. Add eggs 1 at a time and beat 3 minutes after adding each egg. Then stir in vanilla and nuts. Pour into crusts and top with sweetened whipped cream and chocolate shavings before serving. Chill 3 hours before serving. *Freezes well.*

Yields 2 pies

Mary Brown Giddens

French Silk Pie

1 stick margarine, melted
1 cup finely grated pecans
1 cup crushed vanilla wafers

Combine ingredients and press into 9″ pie pan. Bake at 300° for 25 minutes. Cool before adding filling.

2 squares unsweetened chocolate
2 sticks butter or margarine
1½ cups sugar
2 teaspoons vanilla
4 eggs

Melt chocolate. Cream butter and sugar. Add vanilla to chocolate and add to creamed butter and sugar mixture. Add 2 eggs and beat 5 minutes. Add 2 more eggs and beat 5 more minutes. It is important that filling has been beaten a complete 5 minutes after adding the eggs each time. Pour filling into crust.

1 cup whipping cream
5 tablespoons sugar

Whip cream and add sugar gradually. Put atop pie. Chill 2-4 hours before serving.

Serves 6-8

Mary Turner Harris

Chess Pie

4 eggs
1½ cups sugar
2 teaspoons corn meal
Pinch salt
¼ cup melted butter
4 tablespoons cream
1 teaspoon vanilla extract
1 unbaked 10″ pie shell

Combine all ingredients. Blend well before pouring into pie shell. Bake at 350° for 30-35 minutes. *Gets firmer as it cools.*

Serves 6

Clare McIntyre Wheless

Old South Buttermilk Pie

1½ cups sugar
3 tablespoons flour
2 eggs, well beaten
1 stick butter, melted
1 cup buttermilk
1 tablespoon lemon juice
1 teaspoon vanilla
Nutmeg
1 unbaked 9" pie shell, chilled

Combine flour and sugar in a large mixing bowl. Add the beaten eggs; stir in butter and buttermilk, mixing well. Add the lemon juice and vanilla. Pour into the pie shell and grate nutmeg over top.

Place pie in center of a 425° oven for 10 minutes. Lower heat to 350° and continue to bake for 35 minutes. Serve at room temperature. *May top with whipped cream and a fresh strawberry on each slice.*

Serves 6-8

Carolyn Clay Flournoy

Hollywood Black-Bottom Pie

Crust

2 cups sugar
½ cup butter, melted
2 cups cookie crumbs (vanilla or graham)

Mix sugar, butter and crumbs. Pat into two 9" pie pans. Bake at 350° for 10 minutes. Set aside to cool.

Continued...

Filling

- 2 cups milk
- 4 egg yolks
- 1 cup sugar
- 2 tablespoons cornstarch
- 1½ squares unsweetened chocolate
- 1 teaspoon vanilla
- 1 cup chopped pecans (optional)
- 1 envelope unflavored gelatin
- ½ cup milk
- 4 egg whites, stiffly beaten
- ½ pint whipping cream, whipped
- Chocolate shavings

To the milk, add the egg yolks and beat with rotary beater until smooth. Mix sugar and cornstarch in pan; add milk and egg mixture. Cook until thick, stirring constantly. Add chocolate, which has been melted over hot water, vanilla and nuts. Add gelatin that has been soaked in milk to custard. When cool, fold in egg whites. Fill pie crusts and place in refrigerator until ready to serve. Before serving, top with whipped cream and sprinkle with shaved chocolate.

Yields 2 pies

Nita Calhoun Smith
Mansfield, Louisiana

Custard Pie

- 1 baked 10″ graham cracker crust
- 1 4½-ounce package egg custard mix
- 1½ teaspoons unflavored gelatin
- 2¼ cups milk
- ¼ teaspoon ground nutmeg
- 2 tablespoons dark rum
- 2 cups non-dairy whipped topping
- Strawberries (optional)

Combine custard mix and gelatin in saucepan and blend in milk. Bring quickly to a boil stirring constantly. Chill until thickened. Beat until smooth. Add nutmeg and rum. Blend in 1½ cups whipped topping; pour into pie shell and chill. Garnish with remaining whipped topping. Place strawberries on top or sprinkle with nutmeg.

Serves 6-8

Sandra Boddie Hoffman

Coconut Cream Pie

- 1 baked 9″ pie crust
- 1 cup sugar
- ⅓ cup flour
- ½ teaspoon salt
- 2 egg yolks (3 if small), reserve whites
- 2 cups milk
- 1 tablespoon butter
- 1 teaspoon vanilla or coconut extract
- ¾ cup shredded coconut
- Whipped cream, whipped topping or meringue

Combine sugar, flour and salt. Beat egg yolks and add milk, butter and extract. Mix all ingredients about 2 minutes. Bring to a boil in a saucepan and stir continuously. Never leave the pan unattended or mixture will stick. Let boil for 1 minute. Take off heat and fold in coconut. Let cool. Top with whipped cream, whipped topping or meringue.

- 2 large egg whites
- 4 tablespoons sugar

Beat egg whites and sugar until stiff. Bake at 350° for 15 minutes to brown peaks. *If whipped cream topping is used, the pie will be good for only 1 day. If meringue is used, it will keep in refrigertor for several days.*

Serves 8

Shirley Willman Skipworth

Coffee Ice Cream Pie

- 1½ cups chocolate cookie crumbs
- 2 tablespoons sugar
- ¼ teaspoon cinnamon
- 6 tablespoons margarine, melted
- ½ cup toasted, slivered almonds
- 1 quart coffee ice cream, softened

Combine all ingredients except ice cream. Press into 9″ pie pan and freeze. When frozen well, fill with softened coffee ice cream.

Continued...

Topping

- 2 **eggs, separated**
- ⅔ **cup sugar**
- ⅓ **cup water**
- 3 **teaspoons cocoa**
- 1 **cup whipping cream**

Beat egg whites until stiff. Cook sugar and water until it spins a thread. Pour over egg whites while beating like divinity. Cool. Blend cocoa with whipping cream and whip. Fold cream mixture into egg white mixture and top pie. Freeze. *Sprinkle more almonds and shaved chocolate on top if desired.*

Serves 8

Frances Carolyn Wood Pavletitch
Jacksonville, Texas

Two Ice Cream Pies

- 1 **cup flour**
- ½ **cup soft margarine**
- ¼ **cup brown sugar**
- ½ **cup finely chopped pecans**
- 1 **jar Kraft's Choc-Caramel topping (or ½ jar chocolate and ½ jar caramel mixed)**
- ½ **gallon vanilla ice cream, softened**

Mix flour, margarine, brown sugar and pecans. Place this mixture on a cookie sheet and brown in a 400° oven for about 15 minutes. Watch carefully and stir often. In two 8″ pie pans or one 10″ pie pan, spread the mixture with a fork, reserving some for topping. Mash any large lumps. Dribble chocolate-caramel topping over the crust, reserving some for topping; then fill with ice cream, slightly softened. Dribble remaining chocolate-caramel mixture and remaining crumb mixture on top. Place foil over pies and place in freezer.

Serves 8 per pie

Ruth Grey Knighton Jackson

Crême de Menthe Ice Cream Pie

5½ tablespoons butter
1 8½-ounce box Nabisco Famous Chocolate Wafers

Melt butter and crush chocolate wafers (blender works great). Mix butter and crumbs and press into a 9″ spring-form pan on bottom and up sides about 1½″. Put into freezer.

Filling

½ gallon vanilla ice cream, divided
5 tablespoons green crême de menthe

Let ice cream soften to foldable stage. In a large bowl swirl the crême de menthe with 6 cups ice cream. Pour into crust and spread evenly. Return to freezer. Whip 2 cups ice cream in blender and pour over crême de menthe mixture to form a smooth white layer. Return to freezer.

Fudge Sauce

1 1-ounce square unsweetened chocolate
2½ tablespoons water
¼ cup sugar
1½ tablespoons butter
Dash salt
¼ teaspoon vanilla

Over low heat melt chocolate in water. Add sugar and salt, cooking and stirring until sugar is melted and mixture is thickened. Remove from heat and add butter and vanilla. Cool slightly. Drizzle fudge sauce over top of pie and return to freezer for at least 3 hours.

Serves 10

Janell Maeder Falter

Lemon Sour Cream Pie

1 baked 9″ pie crust
1 cup sugar
3 tablespoons cornstarch
1 cup milk
3 egg yolks, beaten
¼ cup lemon juice
1 tablespoon grated lemon rind
¼ cup butter
1 cup sour cream
½ pint whipping cream, whipped and sweetened with 1-2 tablespoons sugar

Combine sugar and cornstarch. Add milk, egg yolks, lemon juice, rind and butter. Cook until thick. Cool. When cool, add sour cream and pour into baked pie shell. Top with whipped cream. *Refrigerate for several hours.*

Serves 6 Karen Willis Burns

A lemon heated in hot water for 2 minutes or microwaved for 30 seconds will yield 2 tablespoons more juice than an unheated one. This applies to all citrus fruits.

La Tapatia Lemon Pie

⅔ cup vanilla wafer crumbs
⅓ cup coconut bar cookie crumbs
5 tablespoons margarine or butter, melted

Mix crumbs and butter well and press into 9″ pie plate. Cook at 300° for 8-10 minutes. Cool thoroughly.

Filling

24½ ounces condensed milk
¾ cup fresh lemon juice (4-5 lemons)
½ pint whipping cream, whipped and divided

Pour condensed milk in a bowl and add a small amount of lemon juice at a time, beating 5-8 minutes until well mixed. Add a little more than half of the whipped cream to the lemon mixture and pour into crust. Top the pie with remaining whipped cream. Refrigerate until firm.

Serves 8 Lola Weir Herndon

Frozen Pumpkin Pie with Butterscotch Sauce

Gingersnap Crust

20 gingersnaps, crushed
6 tablespoons margarine, melted

Mix and put in 9″ cake pan. Bake at 375° for 8 minutes. Let cool.

Filling

1 cup pumpkin
½ cup dark brown sugar
½ teaspoon cinnamon
¼ teaspoon nutmeg
1 quart vanilla ice cream slightly softened

Mix pumpkin, brown sugar, cinnamon and nutmeg in electric mixer. Add ice cream to this mixture. Pour into crust. Freeze.

Butterscotch Sauce

½ cup + 2 tablespoons dark brown sugar
⅓ cup light corn syrup
2 tablespoons margarine
¼ cup half and half
½ pint whipping cream, whipped, for garnish

Prepare any time from 1 week to 1 day before serving pie. Cook brown sugar, corn syrup, and margarine until it boils. Cook 2-3 minutes longer, stirring constantly. When cool, add half and half. Refrigerate. Serve pie topped with whipped cream and sauce drizzled on top.

Serves 6-8

Diane Gilbert Lawhon

Substitute crushed granola in pie crust recipes calling for graham cracker crumbs for a sweet and healthful crust.

Sweet Potato-Pecan Pie

1½ cups mashed sweet potatoes
½ cup brown sugar
1 teaspoon cinnamon
1 teaspoon ginger
¼ teaspoon salt
1½ cups scalded milk
2 well beaten eggs
1 unbaked 9″ pie crust

Combine first 7 ingredients in order given. Let cool. Put in unbaked pie shell. Bake at 350° until nearly set, about 30 minutes. Sprinkle with topping. Continue cooking until done.

Topping

¼ cup butter
½ cup brown sugar
¾ cup chopped pecans

Mix and reserve for top of pie.

Serves 8

Neal Campbell Siskron

Pennsylvania Apple or Pear Pie

4 medium apples, or pears peeled and thinly sliced
Sugar to taste
1 tablespoon Wondra Instant Flour
1 tablespoon lemon juice
¼ teaspoon cinnamon
¼ stick butter, melted
½ cup water
½ teaspoon vanilla
1 double 8″ pie crust, unbaked

Heat all ingredients, except crust; do not boil. Remove fruit from syrup and place in pie crust. Pour syrup over fruit. Sprinkle more sugar over fruit, if desired. Mix a small amount of sugar and cinnamon to sprinkle on top of crust and dot with butter. Bake at 400° for 10 minutes; reduce heat to 350° and continue baking for 35 minutes.

Serves 8

Elizabeth Smith Meadows

Millionaire Pie

1 8-ounce package cream cheese
1 13½-ounce container non-dairy whipped topping
¾ cup sugar
1 cup chopped pecans, divided
1 8¼-ounce can crushed pineapple, drained
1 9″ graham cracker crust

Mix first 3 ingredients and beat until thick and smooth. Add nuts and pineapple, reserving 1 tablespoon of nuts. Mix well. Pour into crust and sprinkle reserved nuts on top. Refrigerate until ready to serve. *This is a very rich but delicious dessert.*

Serves 8 — Vicki Longmire Hanna

To prevent crumbling when cutting graham cracker crust pies, dip pie pan (except for springform pans) in warm water for a few seconds before slicing.

Fresh Dewberry Pie

1 baked 9″ pie crust
2 pints fresh dewberries, divided
¾ cup sugar
2 tablespoons cornstarch
1 pint whipping cream, whipped
¼ cup sugar
1 teaspoon vanilla

Wash and drain berries. Set aside 1 pint of berries. Mash the remaining berries. Combine mashed berries, sugar and cornstarch in a saucepan. Cook over moderate heat until mixture has thickened, stirring continually. Set aside to cool. Place drained berries in the cooked pastry shell; pour the cooled mixture over them. Top with whipped cream which has been sweetened with sugar and vanilla. Place in the refrigerator for 2-3 hours before serving. *Strawberries may be substituted for dewberries.*

Serves 8 — Fay Chandler Musgrave

Blueberry Bavarian Cream Pie

1 9″ graham cracker crust
1 banana
1 cup whipping cream, whipped
1 cup sugar
1 8-ounce package cream cheese, softened
1 21-ounce can blueberry pie filling

Line bottom of pie crust with sliced banana. Whip cream and add sugar gradually. Add cream cheese to whipped cream and blend with electric mixer. Pour mixture over banana slices and top with blueberry pie filling. Chill.

Serves 8

Nancy Hudson Ketner

Always add lemon juice or lemon rind to any berry pie to enhance fruit flavor.

Centenary Strawberry Pie

1 baked 9″ pie crust
¾ cup sugar
3 tablespoons cornstarch
Pinch salt
1 cup + 2 tablespoons water
1 tablespoon lemon juice
½ teaspoon red food coloring
1½ pints fresh strawberries
1 pint whipping cream, whipped
1-2 tablespoons sugar

Combine ¾ cup sugar, cornstarch and salt. Mix into a paste with 2 tablespoons of water. Place the remaining 1 cup water over fire and bring to a boil. Stir in sugar mixture and cook until thick and clear. Remove from heat and add lemon juice and coloring. When cool, fold in berries. Spoon into crust and top with whipped cream sweetened with sugar.

Serves 6

Helen Robinson Rasberry

Magic Window Cookies

¾ cup shortening (part butter or margarine)
1 cup sugar
2 eggs
1 teaspoon vanilla
2½ cups flour
1 teaspoon baking powder
1 teaspoon salt
6 packages of Life Savers (use clear bright colors)
Cookie cutters of 2 sizes (smaller cutter should be ¼"-½" smaller than the larger)

Mix first 4 ingredients well. Blend in flour, baking powder and salt. Divide in half and wrap in wax paper and refrigerate at least 1 hour. Roll dough ⅛" thick on floured board and cut out cookies with larger cutter. Place cookies on baking sheet lined with foil. Use small cutter to cut out section from middle of cookie. Crush candy into small pieces and fill in cutout areas, making sure there is enough to spread into corners. You may leave candy whole or halve it to put into cutout area. (Half of a Life Saver when baked in cookie comes out about the size of a dime. A whole Life Saver covers the size of a quarter.) This will depend on what size cutter you use. If to be used as a tree ornament, make a hole in the top of the unbaked cookie with a plastic straw. Bake at 375° for 7-9 minutes or until dough is light brown and candy is melted. Watch carefully. When done, if candy does not completely cover center of cookie, spread candy out quickly while still soft with metal spatula. Cool completely on baking sheet and remove gently. When hanging on Christmas tree, string with ribbon, and place cookie in front of lights for stained-glass effect. *Heart-shaped cookies make cute Valentines.*

Yields about 70 cookies

Karen McCulloh Dorsey

Easy Graham Cracker House

Frosting - 2 egg whites beaten stiff with 2½ cups confectioners' sugar and ⅛ teaspoon cream of tartar
½ pint milk carton
Graham crackers
Tube white decorating gel
Assorted small candies

Frost all sides of the milk carton and cover with graham crackers. Nibbling is the best way to cut the crackers to fit! Frost roof, using enough frosting to fill in recesses. Cover with graham crackers, letting them slightly overlap sides of house. Outline the "door," "windows," and a scalloped "pebble roof" with decorating gel. Decorate "to taste" with candies. Use a caramel for the chimney. *Red licorice twists may be used to make a little red schoolhouse with thin peppermint sticks pressed into the frosting for roof. To make a log cabin, use pretzels or Tootsie Rolls and adhere with clear-drying glue.*

Cookbook Committee

Gingerbread People

2 sticks butter or margarine
1½ cups sugar
1 egg
4 teaspoons grated orange peel
2 tablespoons dark corn syrup
3 cups flour
2 teaspoons baking soda
2 teaspoons ground cinnamon
1 teaspoon ground ginger
½ teaspoon salt
½ teaspoon ground cloves

Thoroughly cream butter and sugar. Add egg; beat until light and fluffy. Add orange peel and corn syrup. Mix well. Combine dry ingredients and spices with creamed mixture. Mix well. Chill dough thoroughly. Roll to ¼" thickness on a lightly floured surface. (Pastry cloth facilitates lifting the arms and legs without stretching them.) Cut with appropriate cookie cutter. Place 1" apart on ungreased cookie sheet. Bake at 375° for 8-10 minutes. Cool 1 minute; remove from pan and decorate. *Remove small amount of dough at a time from refrigerator so it will stay cold during cutting.*

Yields 2 dozen

Cynthia George Wood

Fruitcake Cookies

½ stick butter
1 cup brown sugar
1½ teaspoons soda
1½ teaspoons milk
1½ cups sifted flour
Pinch salt
2 eggs
¾ teaspoon cinnamon
¾ teaspoon nutmeg
⅓ cup bourbon
1 pound chopped pecans
½ pound glazed pineapple, chopped
½ pound chopped cherries
1 pound chopped white raisins

Cream butter and sugar. Dissolve soda in the milk and mix with the flour and salt. Add eggs to flour mixture and then add to butter and sugar mixture. Add cinnamon, nutmeg, liquid, fruits and nuts; mix and drop 1 teaspoon at a time on a greased cookie sheet. Bake at 275° for 20 minutes. *These may be made year-round without the fruit, and are just as good.*

Yields 3 dozen

Lel Goodwin Allen

Almond Wafers

⅔ cup blanched almonds
½ cup sugar
1 stick butter
1 tablespoon flour
2 tablespoons milk

Grind almonds in blender or food processor to a fine powder and mix with remaining ingredients in a skillet. Stir over low heat until the butter melts. It will appear lumpy and not well mixed. Drop 1 teaspoon at a time of this mixture on a well greased and floured cookie sheet about 2″ apart. Bake at 375° until light brown, about 7 minutes. Watch them closely and take out of the oven as soon as they are golden. Let cool 1 minute before removing—longer and they will stick forever.

Yields 4 dozen

Lecie Roos Resneck

Brown-Eyed Susans

- 1 stick margarine, softened
- 1 stick butter, softened
- 4 tablespoons confectioners' sugar
- 2 cups flour
- 1½ teaspoons baking powder
- ½ teaspoon salt
- 1 tablespoon vanilla
- 1 cup finely chopped pecans

Cream margarine, butter and confectioners' sugar until very light and fluffy. Sift flour, baking powder and salt. Gradually add flour mixture to creamed mixture. *Do not overbeat.* Add vanilla and nuts. Drop in ½″-1″ balls onto greased cookie sheets. Make a thumbprint indentation to flatten cookies slightly. Bake at 400° for 10-12 minutes until very lightly browned. Cool slightly and frost the center of each cookie.

- 1½ cups confectioners' sugar
- 2 tablespoons cocoa
- 2-3 tablespoons hot water
- ½ teaspoon vanilla

Combine sugar and cocoa; add hot water and vanilla. Stir until smooth. Let icing drizzle from knife tip to make a nice round center in each cookie. If necessary, add a little more water to thin icing.

Yields 5-6 dozen

Susie Tucker Overdyke

Orange Balls

- 1 12-ounce box vanilla wafers, crushed
- 1 6-ounce can orange juice concentrate, thawed
- 1 1-pound box confectioners' sugar
- 1 stick butter or margarine, melted

Mix all ingredients and roll in small balls. *The orange balls can be rolled in extra confectioners' sugar, chopped pecans or coconut. This recipe doubles easily and freezes well.*

Yields 6 dozen

Carolyn Bewley Gray

Butter Nut Cookies

- 2 sticks butter, softened
- ½ cup confectioners' sugar
- ½ teaspoon salt
- 2 teaspoons vanilla
- 2 cups sifted flour
- 1½ cups chopped pecans
- Confectioners' sugar

Beat butter and sugar until creamy. Add salt, vanilla, flour and pecans. Mix well. Shape dough into 1″ balls. Place on greased baking sheet. Bake at 350° for 12-14 minutes, until golden brown. Roll in confectioners' sugar while still warm. Let cool; roll in confectioners' sugar again. *Good for parties, teas or as a snack.*

Yields 2½ dozen

Dee Jackson Bustillo

When baking large batches of cookies—especially for holidays—use a refrigerator shelf or extra oven rack as an oversize cooling rack.

Molasses Cookies

- ¾ cup shortening or margarine
- 1 cup sugar
- ¼ cup molasses
- 1 egg
- 1 teaspoon cinnamon
- ½ teaspoon salt
- 2 teaspoons soda
- 2 cups sifted flour
- ½-1 teaspoon cloves
- 1 teaspoon ginger

Melt shortening in 2-quart saucepan over low heat. Remove and cool. Add sugar, molasses and egg. Beat well. Sift together other ingredients. Add to first mixture. Mix well and chill. Form in 1″ balls. Roll in granulated sugar. Cook 2″ apart on greased cookie sheet at 375° for 8-10 minutes. *Store in airtight container to keep crisp.*

Yields 120 small cookies

Ellen Daniel Brown

Sugar Cookies

2 sticks butter
1 cup vegetable oil
2 cups sugar
½ teaspoon salt
2 eggs
2 teaspoons baking soda
2 teaspoons cream of tartar
2 teaspoons vanilla
1 teaspoon lemon extract
4½ cups flour

In mixer beat butter, vegetable oil, sugar and salt. Add eggs, soda, cream of tartar, vanilla, lemon extract and finally flour. Mix well. Chill. Make into small balls and press down on an ungreased cookie sheet with fork or small glass dipped in sugar. Bake at 350° for 10 minutes or until *light* brown. *Do not overbake. Dough keeps well in freezer.*

Yields 6 dozen

Nan Smith Stewart

Use sifted confectioners' sugar instead of flour on your work surface when rolling out sweet cookie dough.

Pecan Crispies

2 sticks butter
1 cup sugar
1 cup brown sugar
1 egg
3 cups flour (sift once before measuring)
½ teaspoon baking powder
½ teaspoon soda
2 teaspoons vanilla
1 cup chopped pecans

Cream butter and both sugars together. Add the egg. Sift the flour, baking powder and soda. Add to the butter and sugar mixture and mix well. Add the vanilla and pecans. Divide into 4 rolls and wrap in wax paper. Refrigerate overnight. Cut into thin slices and bake at 350° for 8-10 minutes. The rolls of dough freeze well, and thawing is not necessary before slicing and baking. For variation sprinkle a little confectioners' sugar on the wax paper before you roll the dough.

Yields approximately 4 dozen

Katherine Leopard Bicknell

Koulouria (Easter Twist Cookies)

4 sticks unsalted butter
1¼ cups sugar
4 eggs
1 cup whipping cream
2 teaspoons vanilla
3 heaping teaspoons baking powder
8-10 cups flour
2 eggs + 2 tablespoons water
2 cups sesame seeds

Cream butter. Add sugar. Cream until smooth. Beat 4 eggs until frothy. Beat into creamed mixture until smooth. Beat in whipping cream. Stir in vanilla and baking powder. Beat to thoroughly blend ingredients. Gradually stir in flour, 2 cups at a time, until dough is soft and pliable. Knead on lightly floured surface for 10 minutes until smooth. To test for right consistency for shaping, tear off a bit of dough about 1½" in diameter. Using fingers like a rolling pin, roll into a strip ½" × 8". Fold strip in half and braid. Dough is ready for shaping if it does not crack during process. If it does crack, continue kneading a little longer. When ready, shape dough as in test. Keep unused dough covered as you work to prevent its drying out. Place twists 1" apart on buttered baking sheets. Beat 2 eggs with 2 tablespoons water. Brush over cookies. Sprinkle with generous amounts of sesame seeds. Bake in 350° oven 10-15 minutes or until cookies are light golden.

Yields 12-14 dozen

Nancy Pfeiffer Cosse

Honey that has turned grainy will reliquefy if the jar is placed in a pan of warm water.

Keflies (Scandinavian Cookies)

2 sticks butter or margarine
½ pound cream cheese
2 cups flour
½ teaspoon salt

Mix all ingredients with hands. Form into large ball. Divide dough into fourths and flatten between wax paper sheets. Chill 4 hours or overnight.

Continued...

Filling

1 cup finely ground nuts
¾ cup sugar
¼ cup milk
1 tablespoon honey
½ lemon rind, grated
Confectioners' sugar

Mix all ingredients. Take 1 piece of dough at a time and roll out on floured and sugared surface. Roll to ¼" thickness and cut into 2" squares. Put small amount of filling on each square; fold over and seal with fingers. Place close together on ungreased cookie sheet. Bake at 450° for 7-8 minutes until golden brown. Remove immediately and sprinkle with confectioners' sugar. *The dough and filling may be prepared several days ahead if kept covered in refrigerator.*

Yields 4 dozen — Judy Stout McCarthy

Brownies

4 eggs
2 cups sugar
2 sticks margarine or butter, melted
2 squares bittersweet chocolate, melted
1 cup flour
1 teaspoon vanilla
1 cup chopped pecans

Beat eggs 3 minutes. Add sugar and beat 1 more minute. Add butter and chocolate to mixture. Add remaining ingredients. Bake in greased 9" × 13" pan at 300° for 1 hour, or longer if not done.

Icing

1 stick margarine or butter
1 cup sugar
¼ cup milk
2 teaspoons cocoa
1 teaspoon vanilla
½ cup (or more) chopped pecans

Mix ingredients except vanilla and pecans and bring to a boil. Boil 2 minutes. Cool and beat until not sugary. Add vanilla. Pour over brownie cake. Sprinkle with chopped pecans.

Yields 20-24 large squares — Mary Graham Pate

German Cream Cheese Brownies

Chocolate Batter

1 4-ounce package German's sweet chocolate
3 tablespoons butter
2 eggs, beaten
¾ cup sugar
½ teaspoon baking powder
¼ teaspoon salt
½ cup flour
½ cup coarsely chopped nuts
¼ teaspoon almond extract
1 teaspoon vanilla

Melt chocolate and butter over very low heat, stirring constantly. Cool. In separate bowl, beat eggs until thick and light in color. Gradually add sugar and beat until thickened. Add baking powder, salt and flour. Blend in nuts, almond extract, vanilla and cooled chocolate. Measure 1 cup chocolate batter and set aside. Spread remaining chocolate batter in greased 9″ square pan.

Cheese Batter

2 tablespoons butter
3 ounces cream cheese
¼ cup sugar
1 egg
1 tablespoon flour
½ teaspoon vanilla

In separate bowl, cream butter and cream cheese until softened. Gradually add sugar, creaming until light and fluffy. Blend in egg, flour and vanilla. Pour over chocolate batter in pan. Drop measured chocolate batter from tablespoon onto cheese mixture; swirl with spatula to marble. Bake at 350° for 45-50 minutes. Cool. Cut in squares. Store in refrigerator.

Yields 16 squares

Vicki Longmire Hanna

Oatmeal Carmelitas

- **1 cup flour**
- **1 cup quick cooking rolled oats**
- **¾ cup firmly packed brown sugar**
- **½ teaspoon soda**
- **¼ teaspoon salt**
- **¾ cup margarine, melted**
- **1 cup semi-sweet chocolate morsels**
- **½ cup chopped nuts**
- **¾ cup caramel ice cream topping**
- **3 tablespoons flour**

Combine first 6 ingredients in large bowl to form crumbs. Press half of crumbs into bottom of well greased 9″ square pan. Bake at 350° for 20-30 minutes until brown. Sprinkle chips and nuts over baked crust. Mix caramel topping and flour well. Drizzle over chocolate and nuts. Sprinkle remaining crumbs over topping. Bake 20-30 minutes at 350° until brown. Chill for easy cutting. *These are very rich.*

Yields 24 bars

Sissy Masters Harper

Toll House Pan Cookies

- **2¼ cups unsifted flour**
- **1 teaspoon baking soda**
- **½ teaspoon salt**
- **2 sticks butter or margarine**
- **¾ cup sugar**
- **¾ cup brown sugar, firmly packed**
- **1 teaspoon vanilla**
- **2 eggs**
- **1 12-ounce package semi-sweet chocolate morsels**
- **1 cup coarsely chopped nuts**

In small bowl combine flour, baking soda and salt. Set aside. In large bowl combine butter, sugar, brown sugar and vanilla. Beat with mixer until creamy. Beat in eggs. Gradually add flour mixture, mixing well. Stir in chocolate and nuts. Spread in greased 10″ × 15″ × 1″ jelly roll pan. Bake at 375° for 20 minutes. Cool before cutting.

Yields 35 2″ squares

Betty Gunn Arceneaux

Carrot Bars

1½ cups vegetable oil
2 cups flour
2 cups sugar
3 cups grated carrots
½ cup chopped nuts
1 teaspoon salt
4 eggs
2 teaspoons baking soda
1½ teaspoons cinnamon

Mix and bake in 10″ x 15″ x 1″ jelly roll pan at 300° for 30 minutes.

Icing

2½ cups confectioners' sugar
1 8-ounce package cream cheese
½ stick butter
2 teaspoons vanilla
1 cup finely chopped nuts

Ice in pan and cut into 1½″ squares. This freezes well in pan before cutting. *One small can well-drained crushed pineapple may be added to icing. The food processor makes this recipe child's play.*

Yields 4-5 dozen

Leone Guthrie Reeder

Coconut Bars

1½ cups flour
2 sticks butter
2 tablespoons sugar

Cream together and pat into a 9″ × 13″ pan. Bake at 325° for 20 minutes.

Continued...

Filling

- 2 eggs, beaten
- 1½ cups brown sugar
- 2 tablespoons flour
- 1¼ teaspoons baking powder
- ¼ teaspoon salt
- 1 cup chopped pecans
- ½ cup shortening
- 1 3½-ounce can coconut
- 1 teaspoon vanilla

Mix all ingredients and pour over first mixture. Return to oven at 325° for 20-25 minutes.

Frosting

- 2 cups confectioners' sugar
- 2 tablespoons melted butter
- 1 tablespoon fresh lemon juice
- 2 tablespoons fresh orange juice

Beat well and frost.

Yields 40 bars

Carolyn Lozietz Huff

Baked Apple Pudding with Rum Sauce

- 1 cup flour
- 1 teaspoon baking soda
- 1 teaspoon cinnamon
- ¾ teaspoon nutmeg
- ¼ teaspoon salt
- ½ stick butter
- 1 cup sugar
- 1 egg
- 2 pared apples

Sift together first 5 ingredients. Mix butter with sugar and egg until light and fluffy. Grate apples medium fine; measure 1 cup and add to egg mixture. Stir this into dry ingredients. Bake in 9″ square dish at 400° for 30-40 minutes. Serve with rum sauce below.

- ½ cup butter
- 1 cup sugar
- ½ cup half and half
- Dash nutmeg
- 1 teaspoon vanilla
- 2-3 tablespoons rum

In double boiler mix butter with sugar and cream. Cook stirring 10-15 minutes or until slightly thickened. Add nutmeg, vanilla and rum. Serve warm over apple pudding.

Serves 4-6

Jane Hunter Rudy

Bavarian Apple Tart

Crust

1 stick butter
⅓ cup sugar
¼ teaspoon vanilla
1 cup flour

Cream butter, sugar and vanilla in small bowl. Add flour. Spread dough on bottom of spring form pan and press up one-third of side.

Filling

1 8-ounce package cream cheese
¼ cup sugar
1 egg
1 teaspoon vanilla

Combine cheese and sugar. Add egg and vanilla. Pour into crust.

Topping

⅓ cup sugar
½ teaspoon cinnamon
4 cups sliced and peeled apples (Do not use Delicious apples.)

Combine sugar and cinnamon and toss apples in mixture. Place on cheese mixture in attractive pattern. Bake at 450° for 10 minutes; then reduce heat to 400° for 25 minutes. Let cool; remove side of spring form pan. Serve at room temperature.

Serves 6-8

Helaine Nierman Braunig

Flambé Bananas

- 3 tablespoons butter or margarine
- ¾ cup brown sugar
- ¼ cup dark rum
- 6 medium bananas, sliced lengthwise
- 2 tablespoons brandy
- Vanilla ice cream

Heat butter and sugar in skillet. Add rum. Place bananas in pan and simmer 7 minutes. Heat brandy and ignite. Pour into skillet and stir gently until flame burns out. Serve over vanilla ice cream. *Peaches or other fruit would be just as good.*

Serves 6

Joe B. Boddie

Cherry Cobbler

- ¾ stick butter
- 1 cup flour
- 1 cup sugar
- 2 teaspoons baking powder
- ¼ teaspoon salt
- ¾ cup milk
- 2 16-ounce cans red tart pitted cherries (water pack)
- ½ cup sugar
- ½ teaspoon cinnamon

Melt butter; pour half into 2-quart baking dish. Mix flour, sugar, baking powder, salt and milk. Stir until smooth. Add remaining butter to flour mixture. Spoon batter into baking dish. Drain cherries, reserving juice. Place cherries evenly over batter. Drizzle small amount of cherry juice over all. *Do not stir.* Combine sugar and cinnamon and sprinkle on top. Bake at 350° for 45 minutes or until batter rises on top and is slightly brown. Cool 10-15 minutes before serving.

Serves 8

Lu Ann Alford Browder

Cranberry-Apple Bake

- 2 cups raw cranberries
- 3 cups peeled tart apples, cubed
- ¾ cup sugar
- 1 cup brown sugar
- ⅓ cup flour
- 1 cup nuts
- ⅓ stick melted butter

In a 1½-quart Pyrex dish, make 2 layers of apples and cranberries. Sprinkle ¾ cup sugar on top. Mix next 4 ingredients and place on top of mixture. Bake at 350° for 1 hour. *Any kind of fruit may be substituted.*

Serves 6-8

Rosemary Cherry Futch

Fresh Peach Crisp

- 1 cup flour
- ½ cup sugar
- ½ cup firmly packed light brown sugar
- ¼ teaspoon salt
- ½ teaspoon cinnamon
- ½ cup margarine
- 4 cups sliced fresh peaches
- ¼ teaspoon almond extract
- 2 tablespoons water
- ¼ teaspoon ground nutmeg
- Whipping cream

Combine first 5 ingredients. Cut in margarine with a pastry blender until mixture resembles coarse corn meal. Set aside. Combine peaches, almond extract and water. Spoon into a greased 9″ square baking dish. Sprinkle flour mixture over peaches. Sprinkle nutmeg on top. Bake covered in a 350° oven for 15 minutes. Remove cover and bake 35-45 minutes longer or until the topping is brown. Serve warm with whipped whipping cream.

Serves 6-8

Linda Tharpe Cann

Lemon Sponge

Grated rind 1 lemon
1 cup sugar
3 tablespoons flour
Good pinch salt
1 cup milk
2 egg yolks, well beaten (reserve whites)
Juice 1 lemon
2 tablespoons butter, melted

Mix lemon rind, sugar, flour and salt in a bowl. Then add milk, egg yolks, lemon juice and butter. Beat egg whites until stiff and fold into first mixture. Turn into buttered casserole or individual custard cups. Bake in a pan of water at 325° for 1 hour or in custard cups for 40-45 minutes or until knife inserted comes out clean. When cool, place in refrigerator until chilled, and turn out upside down. Cake will be on bottom and pudding on top.

Serves 6

Rosemary Pate LaFargue

Orange Dessert

2 envelopes unflavored gelatin
¼ cup water
6 large or extra large eggs, separated
1 cup sugar, divided
1 cup orange juice
Juice 1 lemon
2 tablespoons grated orange rind
½ angel food or orange sponge cake, cut in bite-size pieces
½ pint whipping cream, whipped
1 tablespoon sugar

Soften gelatin in water. Put yolks in double boiler and beat. Add ½ cup sugar, orange juice and lemon juice. Cook until thick, stirring constantly. Add softened gelatin and orange rind. Cool. Beat egg whites until stiff, adding remaining ½ cup sugar. Fold beaten yolk mixture and egg whites together. Pour over cake pieces, mixing well. Put in lightly greased tube pan. Refrigerate overnight. When ready to serve, unmold and ice with whipped cream, sweetened with sugar.

Serves 12

Frances Hodges Smitherman

Pineapple-Banana Delight

- 1 12-ounce box vanilla wafers, divided
- 1 stick margarine, melted
- 1 8-ounce package softened cream cheese
- 1 14-ounce can sweetened condensed milk
- 2 tablespoons lemon juice
- 1 15-ounce can crushed pineapple, drained
- 2 medium-size bananas
- 1 13½-ounce container non-dairy whipped topping
- ½ cup chopped pecans
- Maraschino cherries (optional)

Crush about 50 vanilla wafers; pour in margarine and mix well. Press this crust into bottom of 9″×13″ Pyrex dish. Use remaining vanilla wafers in box to go around sides of dish. Mix cream cheese, condensed milk and lemon juice with mixer until smooth. Spread on vanilla wafer crust. Chill 30 minutes. Spread pineapple over filling. Place sliced bananas over this. Cover with non-dairy whipped topping. Decorate with pecans, and dot with cherries if desired. Chill well before serving.

Serves 12

Lynda Bethea Borden

Easy Strudel

Crust

- 2 sticks butter, melted
- 1 tablespoon sugar
- ¾ teaspoon salt
- 1 cup sour cream
- 2¼ cups flour, sifted

Mix all ingredients until they form a ball. Roll in wax paper and refrigerate for 1 hour. Cut into 4 equal parts. Roll out each part on floured wax paper to form a rectangle.

Continued...

Filling

1 6-ounce jar orange marmalade
1 6-ounce jar apricot preserves
½ cup brown sugar
1 tablespoon cinnamon
1 cup chopped pecans
½ cup raisins
Confectioners' sugar

Combine marmalade and preserves and spread on each rectangle of dough. Combine brown sugar, cinnamon, nuts and raisins, and divide into 4 equal parts. Sprinkle on rectangles. Roll up each rectangle like a jelly roll on a greased and floured cookie sheet. Bake at 325° for 1 hour. When cool cut each rectangle into 10 pieces. Sprinkle with confectioners' sugar.

Yields 40

Mary Loeb Fogel

Fresh Strawberry Torte

3 egg whites
1 cup sugar
1 teaspoon vanilla
¼ teaspoon baking powder
⅛ teaspoon salt
⅛ teaspoon soda
1 cup chopped nuts
10 saltines, crushed
1 pint fresh strawberries, sliced
½ pint whipping cream, whipped and sweetened to taste

Beat egg whites until soft peaks form. Add sugar and beat until stiff. Add vanilla, baking powder, salt and soda. Fold in chopped nuts and crushed saltines. Spread in greased 9″ or 10″ pie pan. Bake at 300° for 30 minutes. Let cool. Add strawberries. Cover pie with whipped cream. Refrigerate until serving. *Fresh ripe peaches, blackberries or raspberries may be used.*

Serves 6-8

Betsy Gresham

Strawberries à la Marny

4 tablespoons sour cream
4 tablespoons low-calorie non-dairy whipped topping
2 tablespoons brown sugar
1 tablespoon Grand Marnier
2 tablespoons orange Curaçao
½ tablespoon dark rum
2 pints fresh strawberries

Combine sour cream with low-calorie non-dairy whipped topping. Blend in brown sugar; add Grand Marnier and whip. Add Curaçao and whip. Add rum and whip again. Serve berries in crystal bowl on crushed ice. Serve sauce in individual dishes and dip berries into the sauce.

Serves 4

Melissa LaFleur Simon

Frozen Strawberry Crumb

½ cup butter, softened
¼ cup brown sugar
1 cup flour
½ cup chopped nuts
2 egg whites, beaten
1 10-ounce package frozen strawberries
2 tablespoons lemon juice
⅔ cup sugar
1 13½-ounce container non-dairy whipped topping
1 tablespoon vanilla

Combine first 4 ingredients in a 10″×15″ ×1″ pan. Bake at 350° for 20 minutes stirring occasionally until golden brown. Put two-thirds of this mixture in a buttered 9″×13″ pan. Beat egg whites until stiff. Add strawberries, lemon juice, sugar, non-dairy whipped topping and vanilla. Stir until thoroughly mixed. Pour over crust. Sprinkle with the remaining crust mixture. Freeze until firm.

Serves 16

Cherrie McCrory Iles

Pavlova
(Australian National Dessert)

4 egg whites
Pinch salt
1 cup super-fine granulated sugar, divided
2 scant teaspoons sifted cornstarch
2 scant teaspoons white vinegar
½ teaspoon vanilla
1 pint whipping cream, whipped and slightly sweetened
Fresh fruit

Beat egg whites stiffly with salt. Add ⅓ cup sugar and continue beating. Add remaining sugar 1 tablespoon at a time. Fold in sifted cornstarch, vinegar and vanilla. Use greased pie plate dusted with cornstarch or a ring mold. Flatten meringue in center slightly. Preheat oven to 300°; put meringue in oven; close door and immediately turn oven temperature down to 225°. Bake for 1½ hours. Open oven door and cool. When cool, remove from oven and fill with whipped cream, slightly sweetened, and any fresh fruit. (Passion fruit is very popular in Australia.) *Inside of meringue will have marshmallow texture.*

Serves 6

Marion Smith Hargrove
Houston, Texas

Spicy Melon Bowls

1 cantaloupe half per person
1 teaspoon lime or lemon juice per half
2 scoops orange sherbet per half
1 tablespoon brown sugar per half

Cut melon in half. Remove seeds and drain. Sprinkle lime juice over halves. Refrigerate until ready to serve. When ready to serve, put sherbet in bowl of melon. Sprinkle brown sugar over sherbet and rim of melon. *Use other flavors of sherbet; sprinkle with nuts, coconut or raisins.*

Wesley Lambert Richardson

Butterscotch Toffee Heavenly Delight

1 baked angel food cake

Filling

1½ cups whipping cream
5½ ounces butterscotch sauce topping
½ teaspoon vanilla
¾ pound Heath Bars, crushed

Cut cake in 3 layers. Whip cream until it begins to thicken. Slowly add sauce and vanilla and continue beating until thick and whipped. Spread filling on layers and top generously with Heath Bar crumbs. Spread filling on top and sides of cake and sprinkle with crushed Heath Bars. Refrigerate at least 6 hours.

Megan Barham Richard
Monroe, Louisiana

English Toffee

Crust

½ stick margarine
1½ cups crushed vanilla wafers

Grease 8″ × 8″ pan with margarine. Mix 1¼ cups crumbs with margarine. Mix well and line pan with crumb mixture. Bake in 425° oven for 5 minutes.

Continued...

Filling

- 1 stick margarine
- 1 cup confectioners' sugar
- 3 eggs, divided
- 1½ squares melted semi-sweet chocolate
- ½ teaspoon vanilla
- 1 cup nuts
- ½ pint whipping cream, whipped

Cream margarine and sugar. Add well beaten egg yolks. Add melted chocolate, vanilla and nuts. Beat egg whites until very stiff and add to mixture, folding in gently. Pour into crust and sprinkle with remaining crumbs. Refrigerate. When ready to serve, top with whipped cream. *Good made day ahead.*

Serves 8 — Dean Daniel Drake

Zuppa Inglese

- 1 3-ounce box instant vanilla custard
- 5 tablespoons light rum, divided
- 1 loaf-size (10¾-ounce) pound cake
- 8 ounces whipping cream, whipped
- 1 teaspoon sugar, or 1 tablespoon confectioners' sugar

Prepare custard using directions on box and blend 3 tablespoons of rum into it. Place custard in refrigerator 10-15 minutes to thicken. Split cake evenly, lengthwise, in half. Punch small holes with a fork all over surface of top half of cake. Using basting brush, brush other 2 tablespoons of rum over hole-covered surface. Smooth half of the custard on bottom half of cake. Place in refrigerator to set before adding top. Put top on carefully. Stir sugar into whipped cream and ice cake with whipped cream. Return cake to refrigerator to set. *Remaining rum custard may be used on another cake which can be frozen and then carefully wrapped in foil to pull out when company comes.*

Serves 6-8 — Lucille Long Reed

Fruit and Cheese Filling for Crêpes

- **2 heaping teaspoons cream cheese**
- **2 tablespoons sour cream**
- **2 crêpes***
- **½ cup strawberries, frozen in syrup**
- **1 tablespoon sugar**
- **2-3 tablespoons butter**
- **1½ teaspoons strawberry liqueur**
- **1 tablespoon brandy, heated**

Mix cream cheese and sour cream together in a bowl. Fill each crêpe with half of this mixture and roll up. In a skillet or chafing dish add strawberries, sugar and butter. Heat until light syrup forms. Add strawberry liqueur, heated brandy, and flame. When flame dies, pour over crêpes and serve.

*See Index for recipe.

Yields 2 crêpes — Chef Joe Fertitta

Saturday Sundae

- **1 quart frozen lemon yogurt**
- **1 20-ounce can crushed pineapple, drained**
- **Toasted coconut**

Spoon yogurt into individual dessert dishes. Top with pineapple and sprinkle with toasted coconut according to taste. *Serve with tea cakes or Pepperidge Farm Molasses Cookies.*

Serves 8 — Margaret Hunkin Crow

Floating Island

3 egg yolks
¼ cup sugar
⅛ teaspoon salt
2 tablespoons flour
2 cups scalded milk
1 teaspoon vanilla

Beat egg yolks slightly. Add sugar, salt and flour. Gradually add milk, stirring constantly. Stir in double boiler over hot water until mixture coats spoon. Cool. Add vanilla.

Meringue

3 egg whites
3 tablespoons confectioners' sugar

Beat egg whites until stiff. Add sugar. Drop spoonfuls of egg whites onto cookie sheet and place under broiler for 1 minute or until meringue is slightly browned. Cool. Serve meringue floating on custard either in individual dishes or one large crystal bowl. *For company, add fresh strawberries to custard. Top with extra strawberries and toasted slivered almonds.*

Serves 6

Jan Manning Sample

Lemon Cup Custard

3 eggs
1 14-ounce can condensed milk
1½ cups milk
1 teaspoon salt
1 teaspoon vanilla
½ cup sugar
½ cup fresh lemon juice
½ teaspoon grated lemon peel

Beat eggs. Add condensed milk, milk, salt, vanilla and sugar. Mix. Add lemon juice and peel. Mix well. Pour into buttered custard cups. Bake in pan of water at 350° for 30 minutes until set.

Serves 6

Maggie Gerlicher McElroy

One-Two-Three Cup Custard

Brown sugar
3 eggs
2 cups milk
1 cup sugar
2 teaspoons vanilla

Grease 6-8 custard cups. Cover botom of each cup with a thin layer of brown sugar. As custard cooks, this will form a caramel sauce. In a bowl, beat eggs. Add milk, sugar and vanilla and mix well. Pour mixture gently into custard cups. Don't be alarmed if some sugar floats to the top. It will settle in cooking. Place custard cups in a pan filled with water that comes about 1″ up the side of the cups. Bake at 325° for 1 hour or until a knife inserted in custard comes out clean.

Serves 6-8 Charlotte Donald Walter

Eggs cook better when started out at room temperature. They also get more volume.

Iced Lemon Soufflé with Wine Sauce

Soufflé

1 envelope unflavored gelatin
¼ cup cold water
5 eggs, separated
2 teaspoons lemon rind, grated
¾ cup fresh lemon juice
1½ cups sugar, divided
1 cup whipping cream, whipped

Soften gelatin in cold water. Mix yolks with lemon rind, juice and ¾ cup sugar. Place in double boiler and cook until thickened, about 8 minutes. Remove from heat and stir in gelatin until dissolved. Chill 40 minutes. Beat whites and add remaining sugar gradually until stiff. Fold in whipped cream; then fold into yolk mixture. Pour into 2-quart soufflé dish. Chill.

Continued...

Wine Sauce

½ cup sugar
1 tablespoon cornstarch
½ cup water
3 tablespoons lemon juice
1 teaspoon lemon rind, grated
2 tablespoons butter
½ cup dry white wine

Mix sugar and cornstarch in a saucepan. Add water, lemon juice and rind. Cook until mixture comes to a boil and continue cooking until thickened, stirring constantly. Remove from heat; add butter and wine. Chill and serve over soufflé.

Serves 8-10 Mary Graham Pate

Rum Pudding with Raspberry Sauce

1½ packages gelatin
¼ cup cold water
1½ cups boiling water
3 egg yolks
½ cup sugar
½ cup white rum
1½ cups whipping cream, whipped

Soften gelatin in cold water. Dissolve this mixture in boiling water. Cool this mixture in the refrigerator, stirring occasionally, until mixture becomes thickened. Beat egg yolks with sugar until lemon colored. Gradually stir into the cooled and slightly thickened gelatin mixture. Stir in white rum. Whip cream and fold into mixture. *Spray 8 one-half cup molds with non-stick coating for easy removal.* Pour mixture into molds and chill.

Raspberry Sauce

2 10-ounce packages frozen raspberries
1 cup sugar

Place frozen raspberries in saucepan with sugar. Boil for 5 minutes. Strain, if desired, and chill. Serve over pudding.

Serves 8 Edna Potter Perritt

Soufflé Grand Marnier

Soufflé

3 tablespoons butter, divided
3 tablespoons flour
¾ cup milk
⅓ cup sugar + 1 tablespoon
4 egg yolks
2 teaspoons vanilla
3 tablespoons Grand Marnier liqueur
5 egg whites
Salt

Butter inside of 2-quart soufflé mold with 1 tablespoon butter. Rub butter on the entire surface with wax paper; then coat the buttered surface with a small amount of sugar.

To make the soufflé base, put flour in saucepan with milk. Blend well. Add ⅓ cup sugar and stir over high heat until mixture thickens and boils. Remove from heat and beat to cool for 2 minutes. Drop yolks one at a time into mixture, beating constantly by hand. (Save the egg whites.) Add 2 tablespoons butter to the mixture. Add vanilla and Grand Marnier to soufflé base, mixing well.

Beat 5 room-temperature egg whites with pinch of salt. (These are the egg whites left over from step 2 plus 1 more egg white.) Beat until they form stiff peaks. This is best done by hand with a wire whisk in a copper bowl, but may be done in mixer. You should be able to turn container upside down without having the egg whites fall out. Sprinkle 1 tablespoon sugar on top.

Fold egg whites into soufflé base by adding less than one-fourth of egg whites and beating by hand. Fold rest of egg whites into soufflé base with slicing motion until mixed, but do not destroy the thick, puffy quality of the egg whites.

Pour the mixture into the mold. Place the mold into a 400° oven, and immediately turn the temperature down to 375°. Bake for approximately 16 minutes or until a straw placed into the center of the soufflé comes out clean. This may be served with Crēme Anglaise.

Continued...

Crême Anglaise

½ cup sugar
4 egg yolks
1 teaspoon cornstarch
1¾ cup milk
1 tablespoon vanilla

This sauce may be made before or after the soufflé base is complete. Beat sugar into egg yolks with mixer for about 3 minutes or until pale yellow. Add cornstarch. Beat this mixture while *slowly* adding 1¾ cups boiling milk, being careful not to overheat and scramble the eggs. Pour the mixture into a saucepan and heat slowly, stirring constantly until the sauce thickens enough to coat the spoon. Do not boil. Add vanilla. Pour sauce over individual soufflé servings and serve immediately.

Serves 6

Jack S. Resneck, M.D.

Soufflé Froid au Chocolat

2 1-ounce squares unsweetened chocolate
½ cup confectioners' sugar
1 cup milk
1 envelope unflavored gelatin (softened in 3 tablespoons cold water)
¾ cup sugar
1 teaspoon vanilla extract
¼ teaspoon salt
2 cups whipping cream, whipped

Melt chocolate squares over hot water. When melted, stir in confectioners' sugar and mix well. Heat milk just until a film shows on the surface and stir slowly into melted chocolate. Cook stirring constantly until it reaches the boiling point, but do not boil. Remove from heat and mix in softened gelatin, sugar, vanilla and salt. Place in refrigerator until slightly thickened. Beat mixture until light and airy.

In separate bowl, whip cream until it holds its shape. Then combine the 2 mixtures and pour into a 2-quart soufflé dish. Chill 2-3 hours in refrigerator or until ready to serve.

Serves 8

Nancy Stutsman Lewis

Peach Soufflé

2 pounds fresh peaches
¼ cup lemon juice, divided
1 cup sugar, divided
1 envelope unflavored gelatin
4 eggs, separated
⅛ teaspoon salt
¼ teaspoon almond extract
1 cup whipping cream, whipped

Peel peaches and slice. Sprinkle lemon juice over peaches, reserving 1 tablespoon for filling. Set aside about 10 peach slices for decoration. Add ½ cup sugar to remaining peaches and mash with fork. Let peaches stand at room temperature until syrup forms. Put syrup into fine sieve and let liquid drain into bowl. Pour ¾ cup of syrup into top of double boiler and sprinkle gelatin over it.

Beat egg yolks lightly and stir into gelatin mixture. Place over simmering water until gelatin dissolves, stirring constantly, about 5 minutes. Remove from heat; stir in reserved 1 tablespoon lemon juice, salt and almond extract. Cool and refrigerate until thick as unbeaten egg white, about 30 minutes.

Meanwhile prepare a wax paper collar for a 1-quart soufflé dish. To make a 3″ wide collar, fold wax paper strip in half for double thickness. Make strip long enough so ends overlap. Tape around outside of soufflé dish so that the collar extends above rim.

Press mashed peaches through sieve and combine with remaining syrup. Beat egg whites until they stand in peaks. Beat in ½ cup remaining sugar gradually until whites are stiff and shiny. Beat the whites just before removing gelatin mixture. Beat gelatin mixture until smooth. Add sieved peaches and beat until blended. Fold this mixture into egg whites. Fold whipped cream into fruit mixture.

Decorate soufflé by pressing reserved peach slices around inside of paper collar. The moisture makes them stick. Spoon soufflé mixture into dish, being careful not to dislodge peach slices. Chill 4 hours or overnight. Remove collar before serving.

Serves 10

Flora Fogel Lebowitz

Mousse au Chocolat

- **1 6-ounce package semi-sweet chocolate morsels**
- **2 teaspoons instant coffee, dissolved in 2 tablespoons water**
- **½ cup sugar, divided**
- **½ teaspoon vanilla extract**
- **3 egg yolks**
- **3 egg whites**
- **1 cup whipping cream, whipped and sweetened**

Combine chocolate morsels, dissolved coffee and ¼ cup sugar in double boiler and cook until chocolate is melted and sugar dissolved. Remove from heat and beat with wooden spoon until smooth. Let cool slightly and add vanilla. Beat in egg yolks, one at a time, beating well after each addition.

In another bowl beat egg whites until soft peaks form; add remaining sugar, 1 tablespoon at a time, keeping the soft peaks. Fold the 2 mixtures together and refrigerate at least 1 hour. Garnish with whipped cream. *Can be made the night before and add whipped cream at the last minute. May add 1 extra egg white for a lighter mousse.*

Serves 6-8 — Cynthia George Wood

Pots de Crème

- **¾ cup milk, less 2 tablespoons**
- **1 cup semi-sweet chocolate morsels**
- **1 egg**
- **2 tablespoons sugar**
- **1 tablespoon orange liqueur**
- **Pinch salt**
- **Whipped cream**
- **Orange peel, freshly grated**

Scald milk. Place next 5 ingredients in a blender and give them a whirl. Add hot milk and blend at low speed for about 1 minute. Pour into pot de crème containers or demitasse cups. Cover cups with plastic wrap and chill before serving. Serve with whipped cream topped with freshly grated orange peel. *One teaspoon vanilla may be substituted for liqueur. Flavor whipped cream with orange liqueur.*

Serves 6 — Joan Yarbrough Gresham

Lemon Mousse

- **¾-1 cup sugar**
- **1 envelope unflavored gelatin**
- **1½ teaspoons cornstarch**
- **2 teaspoons finely grated lemon peel**
- **1 cup lemon juice**
- **4 beaten egg yolks**
- **1½ cups whipping cream, whipped**
- **2 tablespoons orange liqueur**
- **8 stiffly beaten egg whites**

In a saucepan combine sugar, gelatin, cornstarch and lemon peel. Stir in lemon juice and egg yolks. Cook and stir until thickened and bubbly. Remove from heat and cover surface with clear plastic wrap. Cool; then chill. Beat whipping cream to soft peaks. Put chilled mixture in blender; add orange liqueur and blend until smooth. Pour into large bowl and fold in cream. Fold in egg whites. Turn into serving bowl. Cover and chill 4-6 hours. Garnish with lemon slices and mint leaves.

Serves 12-16 — Mary Gunn Johnston

To freeze a mousse, freeze in mold covered with foil. Take out of freezer, bring to refrigerator temperature, and place back in refrigerator until serving.

Ice Cream Crunch

- **2 cups Rice Krispies, crushed**
- **1 cup grated coconut**
- **½ cup chopped pecans**
- **½ cup chopped almonds**
- **1 stick butter, melted**
- **1 cup light brown sugar**
- **½ gallon vanilla or coffee ice cream**
- **Caramel or butterscotch sauce**

Mix Krispies, coconut, nuts and butter in a pan and brown in the oven. Remove from oven and add brown sugar. Line 9″×13″ pan or ring mold with wax paper. Halve crunch mixture; layer half of crunch in pan and put ice cream on top. Top with remaining crunch mixture. Cover and freeze. Serve with caramel or butterscotch sauce as topping. *This can be made days in advance.*

Serves 12 — Melanie Harrell Springmeyer

Biscuit Tortoni

1 pint whipping cream
½ cup sugar
4 ounces rum
1 quart vanilla ice cream
4 tablespoons chopped glazed fruit or cherries
1 cup crushed macaroons or nuts
Additional crushed macaroons for topping

Whip cream with sugar; add rum and ice cream which is soft enough to blend easily. Add fruit and macaroons. Fill ramekins almost to overflowing as it will settle. Freeze. When serving, dip top of cups in additional macaroons.

Serves 8

Nancy Stutsman Lewis

Bourbon Parfait

½ gallon vanilla ice cream, softened
2 dozen coconut macaroons
4½ ounces bourbon

Crush cookies and mix with softened ice cream. Add bourbon; stir until well mixed and put into parfait glasses. Keep frozen until ready to serve.

Serves 12

Mary Tullie Wyrick Critcher

Frozen Cappucino

¼ cup milk
⅓ cup brandy
1 quart jamoca almond fudge ice cream, slightly softened
Chocolate curls (optional)

Pour milk and brandy into blender. Add 6 scoops slightly softened ice cream. Whirl until just blended. Pour into serving dishes or stemmed glasses. Top with chocolate curls if desired. Place in freezer for couple of hours.

Serves 4-5

Alice Ann Buchanan Schwendimann

Grasshopper Parfait

20 marshmallows
½ cup milk
1 cup whipping cream, whipped
3 tablespoons crème de cacao
3 tablespoons crème de menthe
Chocolate wafers, crumbled
Non-dairy whipped topping
Mint sprigs

In a double boiler, melt marshmallows in milk. Let cool. Fold in whipping cream and liqueurs. Alternate layers of filling and chocolate wafers in parfait glasses. Top with non-dairy whipped topping, some crumbled wafers, and a sprig of mint. Freeze. *Take out of freezer 5 minutes before serving.*

Serves 4

Virginia Ferguson Chastain

Mint Chocolate Mousse

1 pint rich fudge chocolate and pecan ice cream (from an ice cream shop)
1 pint mint ice cream (from an ice cream shop)
1 1-pound box gingersnaps
½ cup unsalted butter, melted
1 cup whipping cream, divided
1½ cups chopped pecans

Let ice cream soften while you prepare gingersnap crust. Melt butter in a pan; crumble gingersnaps; moisten thoroughly with melted butter. Press into a 9″ freezer-proof pie pan. Whip cream until stiff. Add half to chocolate ice cream and mix well; add other half to mint ice cream and mix well. Spread one layer of ice cream into pie shell; freeze until stiff. Add the other flavor of ice cream making a second layer; smooth over top. Return to freezer until top layer is stiff. Add pecans; cover top. Return to freezer until ready to serve; cover if it will be a long time before serving. Needs no topping, but more whipped cream is great. *Any 2 of your favorite ice creams make a great dessert.*

Serves 6-8

Wesley Lambert Richardson

Praline Parfait

Sauce

2 cups dark corn syrup
1/3 cup sugar
1/3 cup water
2 cups chopped pecans

In a medium saucepan, heat all sauce ingredients. Stir constantly just until it comes to a boil. Remove from heat and allow to cool.

Parfaits

Vanilla ice cream
Whipped cream
Maraschino cherries

In a parfait glass, alternate ice cream and sauce ending with sauce. Top with whipped cream and a maraschino cherry.

Yields 4 cups of sauce

Linda Howard Long

Ice Cream Chocolate Dessert

1 cup vanilla wafer crumbs
2 squares bitter chocolate
2/3 cup butter
2 cups confectioners' sugar, sifted
1 cup chopped pecans
1 teaspoon vanilla
2 tablespoons water
2 egg whites, beaten stiffly
1/2 gallon butter pecan ice cream
1 square milk chocolate, shaved

Spread cookie crumbs on bottom of 9″ × 13″ Pyrex dish. Melt chocolate in butter and cool. Stir in sugar, pecans, vanilla and water. Fold in egg whites. Spread this mixture on top of cookie crumbs. Freeze for 2 hours. Soften ice cream and spread on top. Refreeze. Sprinkle shaved chocolate on top. Cut into squares to serve.

Serves 12

Evelyn Humphreys Quinn

Banana Ice Cream

- 6 eggs
- 1½ cups sugar
- ½ teaspoon salt
- 2 tablespoons vanilla
- 1 teaspoon lemon juice
- 1 14-ounce can sweetened condensed milk
- 1 can water (use milk can)
- 1 13-ounce can evaporated milk
- 3 large bananas, mashed
- Homogenized milk to fill gallon freezer ⅔ full

Beat eggs and sugar together well. Add salt, vanilla, lemon juice, condensed milk, water, evaporated milk and bananas. Stir well and pour into freezer. Then add milk until freezer is ⅔ full. Churn in freezer.

Yields 1 gallon
Serves 8 generously

Laura Stevens Boyd

Chocolate Ice Cream

- 2 cups milk
- 2 cups sugar
- 4 eggs, separated
- 4 1-ounce squares unsweetened chocolate
- ¼ teaspoon salt
- 1 tablespoon vanilla
- 2 cups half and half
- 2 cups whipping cream, whipped

Scald milk and sugar in double boiler and pour over well-beaten egg yolks,beating while pouring. Return to double boiler and cook 5 minutes. Melt chocolate and combine with above mixture. Cool. Add salt, vanilla and half and half. Beat egg whites until stiff and fold into chocolate mixture. Then fold in whipped cream. Turn into 9″×13″ pan and freeze. When partially frozen, remove from pan and put in mixer; beat until smooth. Then freeze again, covered with plastic wrap.

Serves 10-12

Sissy Masters Harper

Fig Ice Cream

2 quarts peeled fresh figs
2½ cups sugar
3 pints half and half
1 cup whipping cream
Juice 1 lemon
1½ teaspoons vanilla
Pinch salt

Purée figs in mixer or blender. Add sugar and lemon juice. Combine other ingredients. Add fig mixture. Freeze in electric ice cream freezer for about 30 minutes.

Yields 4 quarts

Virginia Wise Morgan

Homemade Peach Ice Cream

3 eggs
2½ cups sugar
Juice 3 lemons
2 5.3-ounce cans evaporated milk
10-12 peaches, peeled and mashed
Milk to fill freezer

Beat eggs well; while beating, add sugar slowly, then lemon juice. Stir in evaporated milk and peaches. Place mixture in ice cream freezer. Add milk to fill line and freeze. *May substitute 3 pints strawberries.*

Yields 1 gallon

Sara Hitchcock Lang

Homemade Vanilla Ice Cream

4 eggs
2½ cups sugar
3 tablespoons flour
1 14-ounce can condensed milk
1 13-ounce can evaporated milk
1 tablespoon vanilla
1 pint half and half
1 pint whipping cream
Homogenized milk

Beat eggs. Add sugar and flour. Mix well. Add condensed milk, evaporated milk, vanilla, whipping cream and half and half. Mix. Pour into ice cream freezer. Add milk to fill line on freezer. Churn in freezer.

Yields ½ gallon

Mallie Beard Daniel

Cranberry Ice

1 quart cranberries
1 quart water
2 cups sugar
Juice 3 lemons (can use bottled, reconstituted lemon juice)
½ pint dry sherry

Boil cranberries in water. Strain through a food mill. Add sugar, lemon juice and sherry. Refrigerate until well chilled. Freeze in ice cream freezer. This may be kept in freezer all through the Thanksgiving and Christmas holidays. *Suggest tripling recipe before Thanksgiving and having on hand until New Year's. It is a beautiful shade of red and a very special holiday delicacy.*

Yields 1 quart

Dot Willius Knight

Grapefruit Sorbet

3½ cups grapefruit juice
¾ cup sugar
2 tablespoons kirsch

Squeeze grapefruit juice; strain; add sugar and stir until dissolved. Add kirsch and freeze. If freezing in trays, stir occasionally until solid.

Serves 8

Cookbook Committee

Caramel Sauce

2 cups sugar
¼ stick butter
1 cup dark corn syrup
Pinch salt
1 5.3-ounce can evaporated milk
1 tablespoon vanilla

Mix first 4 ingredients. Bring to a boil. Remove from fire. Add last 2 ingredients. Mix well. May serve hot or cold over ice cream. *This would make a nice gift at Christmas.*

Yields approximately 1 pint

Mary Pearl McClanahan Jarrell
Monroe, Louisiana

Cardinal Sauce

1 10-ounce package frozen raspberries, thawed
2 tablespoons sugar
1 teaspoon fresh lemon juice
¼ cup orange liqueur

Put all ingredients in a blender and blend until smooth. Serve over fresh strawberries, fresh peaches, frozen yogurt, pound cake or any combination of these.

Serves 8

Barbara Horner Burrell
Naples, Flordia

Chocolate Sauce

4 squares bitter chocolate
½ cup boiling water
2 cups sugar
½ stick butter
1 5.3-ounce can evaporated milk
Pinch salt
1 tablespoon vanilla

In top of double boiler, melt chocolate squares and add boiling water to make a paste. Add sugar and butter. Cook until smooth. Add evaporated milk, salt and vanilla. Serve hot or cold.

Yields 1 quart

Mary Pearl McClanahan Jarrell
Monroe, Louisiana

Creamy Hard Sauce

½ stick butter
1 tablespoon flour
½ cup sugar
1 cup hot water
¼ teaspoon vanilla

Melt butter; stir in flour until smooth. Stir in sugar; then add hot water and bring to a boil. Lower heat and continue cooking until desired consistency to spoon over cake. Stir in vanilla. This sauce will thicken a little as it sets. May be refrigerated and reheated.

Serves 6-8

Jan Jones Jenkins

Plum Sauce

1 pound dark red plums, very ripe
1⅓ cups sugar
½ cup water
¼ cup dry kirsch white brandy

Remove pits from unpeeled plums. Make a sugar syrup: combine sugar and water and cook mixture until it reaches 238° on candy thermometer. Add plums to syrup and cook over low heat until they fall apart and mixture is thick. Watch carefully while cooking. Blend sauce in blender and add kirsch. Best made the day before and put in refrigerator.

Yields 2 cups

Mary Virginia Saunders Quinn

Russian Sauce

3 egg yolks
½ cup sugar
⅓-½ cup orange juice
1 tablespoon grated orange rind
1 cup whipping cream, whipped
½ cup toasted nuts, or ½ cup toasted coconut

In top of double boiler, cook the egg yolks, sugar and orange juice, stirring constantly until thick. This takes about 15 minutes. Stir in orange rind. Cool. Fold this mixture into stiffly whipped cream. Fold in nuts of choice or coconut. Serve over sliced sponge or pound cake.

Yields 4 cups

Jeanne Futch Muslow

Crunchy Butterscotch Morsels

4 6-ounce packages butterscotch morsels
1 12-ounce can cocktail peanuts
4 peanut cans corn flakes

Melt butterscotch in double boiler. Do not cook. Add peanuts and mix well. Stir in corn flakes, 1 can at a time. Drop from a spoon on wax paper. Allow to harden.

Yields 4 dozen

Eleanor Gordon
Lake Charles, Louisiana

Bride's Candy

1 3⅛-ounce package vanilla pudding (not instant)
1 cup sugar
½ cup brown sugar
½ cup evaporated milk
1 tablespoon butter
1½ cups chopped pecans

Mix all ingredients except pecans. Cook stirring constantly over medium heat in heavy pot for about 5 minutes or until a few drops of the mixture will form a soft ball in a cup of water, or candy thermometer reads 235°. After it has reached the right temperature, remove from heat. Add pecans and beat about 5 minutes. Drop with teaspoon on buttered cookie sheets. The candy will still be runny as you drop it, but it turns hard when it cools. Work fast. *You may wish to toast pecans before adding.*

Yields 3 dozen

Lynda Bethea Borden

Chocolate Crunch

2 8-ounce Hershey Bars
2 ounces bitter chocolate
6 cups corn flakes

Melt Hershey Bars and bitter chocolate in a double boiler. Slightly crush the corn flakes and add to the chocolate mixture and mix well (leaving over hot water). Drop from spoon onto wax paper. Put in refrigerator to harden.

Yields 5 dozen

Mimi Wile Hussey

Microwave Fudge

- **1 1-pound box confectioners' sugar**
- **½ cup unsweetened cocoa**
- **¼ cup milk**
- **1 stick butter**
- **2 teaspoons vanilla**
- **½ cup chopped nuts**

Lightly grease an 8″ square pan. Place confectioners' sugar and cocoa in a medium-size heat resistant, non-metallic mixing bowl. Stir; add milk and butter to sugar-cocoa mixture. Do not stir. Heat uncovered on full power for 2 minutes. After cooking, stir just to combine ingredients. Add vanilla and nuts. Stir until blended. Pour into greased pan and refrigerate for 1 hour before cutting and serving.

Yields 2-3 dozen

Sharon Jenkinson Boddie

White Fudge

- **2¼ cups sugar**
- **½ cup sour cream**
- **¼ cup milk**
- **2 teaspoons butter**
- **1 teaspoon light corn syrup**
- **¼ teaspoon salt**
- **2 teaspoons vanilla**
- **1 cup coarsely chopped nuts**
- **⅓ cup quartered candied cherries**

Combine first 6 ingredients in a heavy 2-quart boiler. Stir over moderate heat until sugar is dissolved and mixture reaches a boil, or until candy thermometer reaches 238°. Remove from heat and allow to stand until 110°, about 1 hour. Add vanilla and beat a very short time, until candy loses its gloss and begins to hold its shape. Quickly stir in nuts and cherries and turn into greased 8″ x 8″ pan. When cool, cut into squares.

Yields 3 dozen

Frances Carolyn Wood Pavletitch
Jacksonville, Texas

World's Greatest Fudge

- 4½ cups sugar
- ⅛ teaspoon salt
- 4 tablespoons butter
- 1 13-ounce can evaporated milk
- 12 ounces semi-sweet chocolate
- 12 ounces German's sweet chocolate
- 1 pint marshmallow cream
- 2½ cups pecans

Boil first 4 ingredients for 6 minutes, stirring constantly; remove from heat and add last 4 ingredients. Beat until melted. Pour onto wax paper and let set for 3 hours.

Yields 7 dozen 1½″ pieces

Rosemarie Wimer Gerhardt

Meringue Champignons (Mushroom Confections)

- 6 egg whites at room temperature (equal to ¾ cup)
- ⅛ teaspoon salt
- ¼ teaspoon cream of tartar
- 1½ cups sugar
- ¼ teaspoon almond extract
- ¾ teaspoon vanilla
- 2 teaspoons cocoa (unsweetened)
- 6 ounces semi-sweet chocolate

Beat egg whites until foamy. Add salt and cream of tartar. Add sugar gradually. Add almond extract and vanilla. Beat at high speed until stiff (about 7 minutes). Place mixture in a pastry bag without tip. Make stems first by pressing out meringue while lifting bag until stems are about ½″ to ¾″ tall. Press out onto cookie sheets covered with wax paper. Next, press out caps in rounds about 1″ in diameter. Make them high and puffy. If caps have points, press flat with moistened finger. Sprinkle caps with cocoa. Place cookie sheets in 225° oven. Bake for 1 hour without opening door. Turn off heat and allow to cool overnight in oven with door closed. Cut points off stems with serrated knife. Melt chocolate and spread on flat inside of cap. Stick on stem. Allow to cool upside down.

Yields 36

Ellen Daniel Brown

Millionaires

1 14-ounce package Kraft Caramels
2 tablespoons milk
3 cups coarsely chopped nuts
6 1.05-ounce plain Hershey Bars
⅓ block paraffin (¼ pound)

Melt caramels and milk in double boiler. Add nuts and mix well. Drop by spoonful on wax paper. Melt Hershey Bars with paraffin in double boiler. Dip candy into chocolate mixture. Let cool.

Yields 3 dozen

Jan Manning Sample

Orange Walnuts

1½ cups sugar
½ cup orange juice
Grated rind 1 small orange
3 cups walnut halves

Boil sugar and orange juice until candy thermometer reaches 234° or a small quantity of mixture dropped in cold water forms a soft ball. Remove from heat. Add rind and walnut halves. Stir until mixture looks cloudy. When it begins to sugar, drop each walnut on wax paper. Let harden. *Wonderful Christmas recipe.*

Yields 3 cups

Neal Campbell Siskron

Creamy Pralines

2 cups sugar
1 cup brown sugar
1 5.33-ounce can evaporated milk
3 tablespoons light corn syrup
1 tablespoon butter
Dash salt
1 teaspoon vanilla
2 cups or more pecans

Combine first 4 ingredients and cook to soft ball stage. Remove from fire and cool a little. Add butter, salt, vanilla and pecans. Stir. Drop by teaspoon on buttered wax paper. Leave until cool and hard.

Yields 3 dozen

Lola Weir Herndon

Sugary Pralines

1 cup brown sugar
1 cup sugar
1 stick butter
¼ cup hot water
2 cups pecan halves

Mix first 4 ingredients in a heavy pot. After the sugar mixture starts to bubble around the edge, dump the pecans in. After it returns to a boil, cook exactly 8 minutes, stirring occasionally. Be sure to keep on medium heat. Drop on buttered cookie sheet.

Yields 24

Flora Brown Masters

Pecan Divinity

2 egg whites, room temperature
3 cups sugar
½ cup light corn syrup
½ cup water
1 teaspoon vanilla
3-4 cups pecans, chopped

Beat egg whites until stiff. While they are beating, make a syrup of the sugar, syrup and water. Cook this to the soft ball stage. When the egg whites are very stiff, slowly pour half of the syrup into them while still beating. Return other half of syrup to the fire and cook to hard-crack stage. Pour slowly into mixture while beating. Then add vanilla and keep beating until candy loses some of the shine. Add pecans. Then very quickly drop by teaspoonfuls on wax paper. *After mixing, the secret is to work quickly before it hardens.*

Yields 6-8 dozen

Doris Yearwood Elgin

Peanut Brittle

2	cups raw peanuts	⅔	cup light corn syrup
1	cup sugar	1	tablespoon baking soda
¼	teaspoon salt		

In a deep, heavy saucepan bring peanuts, sugar, salt and corn syrup to a rolling boil. When the mixture turns to caramel and the candy thermometer reads 285°, quickly add soda and stir rapidly. When mixture bubbles and expands, pour as soon as possible onto large greased cookie sheet. When hard and completely cool, break into pieces. Store in airtight container.

Michele Armstrong
Qvistgaard-Petersen

Popcorn Snack

6	quarts popped popcorn	1	teaspoon salt
2	sticks butter	½	teaspoon soda
2	cups brown sugar	1	teaspoon vanilla
½	cup light corn syrup		

Bring butter, brown sugar, corn syrup and salt to a boil and stir constantly. Remove from heat and stir in soda and vanilla. Spread popcorn about 1″ thick in several Pyrex dishes and pour syrup on popcorn. (The amount depends on how sweet and thick you desire.) Stir it fast as it hardens quickly. Bake at 250° for 1 hour stirring or tossing every 15 minutes. Let cool completely. This is similar to caramel corn.

Yields 6 quarts

Kathy Folds Walker

Mrs. Stancil's Sugar Candy

2½ cups sugar, divided
Dash salt
½ pint whipping cream or half and half
1 tablespoon corn syrup
2 tablespoons butter
1 teaspoon vanilla
2-3 cups pecans, broken or halves

Pour ½ cup sugar into heavy aluminum or iron skillet and place over low heat. Begin stirring with wooden spoon, and keep sugar moving so it will not scorch at all. It will take about 20 minutes to melt sugar completely, and at no time should it smoke or cook so fast that it turns dark. It should be the color of light brown sugar syrup. Meanwhile, pour the remaining sugar, salt, cream and corn syrup into a heavy kettle and set it over low heat to cook slowly. When sugar in skillet is melted, begin pouring it into the kettle of boiling milk mixture, keeping it on very low heat, stirring constantly. To mix these ingredients, pour a stream no larger than a knitting needle and stir across the bottom of the kettle at all times. Continue cooking and stirring until the mixture forms a soft ball when dropped into cold water, or reaches 236° on a candy thermometer. Remove from heat. Stir in butter, vanilla and nuts. Beat until thick. Pour onto buttered platter or drop from tablespoon on wax paper.

Yields 36 2" pralines

Jean Yauger Laster

INDEX

D

Q

R

S

T

Junior League of Shreveport-Bossier Inc.
520 Olive Street
Shreveport, Louisiana 71104
318-221-6144

Please send me _____ copies of *Revel Cookbook* @ 19.95 ea. = ______________

Shipping and Handling $4.55 for one book = ______________

Add $1.50 for each additional book = ______________

Total = ______________

Name ____

Address ____

City __________________ State __________ Zip ______________

Phone (_____) ______________________________________

Make checks payable to Junior League of Shreveport, Inc.

Charge to: ___ Visa ___ MasterCard Account # ______________________

Valid thru ________________ Signature ______________________

Junior League of Shreveport-Bossier Inc.
520 Olive Street
Shreveport, Louisiana 71104
318-221-6144

Please send me _____ copies of *Revel Cookbook* @ 19.95 ea. = ______________

Shipping and Handling $4.55 for one book = ______________

Add $1.50 for each additional book = ______________

Total = ______________

Name ____

Address ____

City __________________ State __________ Zip ______________

Phone (_____) ______________________________________

Make checks payable to Junior League of Shreveport, Inc.

Charge to: ___ Visa ___ MasterCard Account # ______________________

Valid thru ________________ Signature ______________________

Where did you hear about this cookbook? ______________________________

____

____

What local store would you like to see carry this cookbook?______________

____

____

Store Name ____

Address ____

City ______________________ State __________ Zip ______________

Phone (______) ____

- -

Where did you hear about this cookbook? ______________________________

____

____

What local store would you like to see carry this cookbook?______________

____

____

Store Name ____

Address ____

City ______________________ State __________ Zip ______________

Phone (______) ____